A LINGUISTIC INTRODUCTION TO THE HISTORY AND STRUCTURE OF THE ENGLISH LEXICON

A LINGUISTIC INTRODUCTION TO THE HISTORY AND STRUCTURE OF THE ENGLISH LEXICON

Paul McFetridge

SIMON FRASER UNIVERSITY
PUBLICATIONS

A LINGUISTIC INTRODUCTION TO THE HISTORY AND STRUCTURE
OF THE ENGLISH LEXICON
Copyright © 2008 by SFU Publications

Third Printing, July 2010

All rights reserved. The use of any part of this publication whether reproduced, transmitted in any form or by any means, electronic, mechanical, photocopying, recording, or otherwise stored in a retrieval system, without the prior consent of the publisher, is an infringement of the copyright law.

Copyright of all other material belongs to the respective authors and institutions as acknowledged and no editorial or cited material may be produced wholly or in part without the express permission of the copyright holder. The material from the Merriam-Webster's dictionary, 11th edition has been reproduced with permission, (*Merriam-Webster's Collegiate® Dictionary*, 11th Edition. Springfield Mass., USA: Merriam-Webster Inc., 2007) (www.m-w.com). Resale or further copying of this material by any means is strictly prohibited.

Every effort has been made to trace ownership of copyrighted materials and to secure permission from copyright holders. In the event that questions arise pertaining to the use of these materials, we will be pleased to make the necessary corrections in future printings.

Library and Archives Canada Cataloguing in Publication

McFetridge, Paul
    A linguistic introduction to the history and structure of the English lexicon / Paul McFetridge ; editors: John Whatley, Nancy Earle.

Includes bibliographical references and index.
ISBN 978-0-86491-291-6

    1. English language--Etymology. 2. English language--Semantics. 3. Lexicology. I. Whatley, John, 1944 Aug. 8- II. Earle, Nancy III. Title.

PE1576.M34 2007   422   C2007-903705-4

Printed in Canada by Hignell Book Printing
Cover design by Greg Holoboff
Book Design and Typesetting by Robert D. MacNevin

Simon Fraser University Publications
1300 West Mall Centre
8888 University Drive
Burnaby, British Columbia v5A 1S6
Canada

Contents

Preface	ix
Acknowledgements	xi
Notational Conventions	xii

1 Introduction — 1
- Organization and Presentation — 2
- Representation — 3
- Etymology — 3

2 Linguistic Change and the Structure of Language — 5
- Introduction — 5
- The Structure of Language — 7
  - Orthography — 7
  - Phonetics — 9
  - Morphology — 14
  - The Lexicon — 15
  - Syntax — 16
  - Semantics — 17
- Summary — 19
- Why Languages Change — 20
- Conclusion — 24
- Further Reading — 24

ORIGINS AND HISTORY — 25

3 Origins — 27
- Introduction — 27
- Indo-European — 28
- Germanic Consonant Shift — 36

	Borrowing	38
	Describing the Germanic Consonant Shift	46
	Voiceless Stops	46
	Voiced Stops	48
	Voiced Aspirates	49
	Summary	52
	Patterns of Borrowing	54
	Greek	54
	Latin	57
	Summary	59
	Periods of Latinate Borrowing	60
	The Germanic Period	61
	The Old English Period	64
	The Middle English Period	66
	Contemporary English	68
	Summary	70
	Conclusion	70
	Further Reading	72
4	**The Alphabet**	**73**
	Introduction	73
	History of the Alphabet	76
	Origins	76
	Letter by Letter	79
	The Roman Alphabet	83
	Later Developments	86
	Spelling Rules	91
	Conclusion	97
	Further Reading	99
5	**The Structure of Words**	**101**
	Introduction	101
	The Map Is Not the Territory	102
	Inflection	104
	Relatedness of Words	108
	Terminology	111
	Derivational Rules	114
	Conclusion: On the Notion of Word	118

6	**Integration**	**121**
	Introduction	121
	Structure and Borrowing	121
	Hybrids	125
	Summary	129
	Change and Structure	129
	Summary	135
	Change and Borrowing	135
	A Complete Analysis of the Negative Prefixes	140
	Conclusion	144
	Further Reading	144
7	**Identifying Morphemes**	**145**
	Introduction	145
	Homonyms	146
	Synonyms	147
	English Locative	147
	Greek Locative	148
	Summary	149

THE LATIN PARTITION		**151**
8	**The Latin Verb**	**153**
	Introduction	153
	The Structure of the Verb	154
	Derivation from Latin Verbs	156
	Past Participle Stems	156
	The Phonology of the Past Participle	159
	Exceptions	168
	Present Participle Stems	172
	Assibilation	174
	Productivity	175
	Summary	176
	Structure	177
	Change	177
	Representation	177
	Conclusion	177
9	**Latin Prefixes**	**179**
	Introduction	179
	Prefixes	179

  ad- (to)   180
  dis- (off, away, opposite)   185
   Naturalization and the Age of Words   186
  ex- (out)   187
  abs- (away)   192
  re- (back, again)   193
  prod- (before, forth)   194
  sed- (apart)   195
  sub- (under)   196
  ambi- (both)   198
  trans- (across)   198
 Other Prefixes   200
 Extensions   200
 Further Reading   201

10 Other Operations in Latin   203

 Introduction   203
 The Nasal Increment   203
 Medial Vowel Weakening   212
  Medial Vowel Weakening and the Nasal Increment   217
 Other Alternations   219
  Rhotacising Roots   219
  Alternations between u/v   221
  Vowel Raising   222
 The "s" Increment   223
 Epenthesis   226
 Reduplication   227
 The verb *to be*   228
 Further Reading   229

11 Latin Suffixes   231

 Basic Suffixes   231
  -al (pertaining to)   231
  -ic (pertaining to)   234
  -ity (quality of)   235
  -bil (able to)   236
  -ous (characterized by)   240
 Past Participial Suffixes   241
  -or (Agentive)   241
  -ion (act of)   242

-ure (result of)	243
-ive (nature or quality of)	243
Extensions	244
Diminutive -ul-	244
Adjectival -il-	245
The Inchoative	246
Further Reading	248

THE GREEK PARTITION   249

12 Greek Borrowings   251

Introduction	251
Prefixes	252
syn- (together, with)	252
ana- (up, throughout)	254
dia- (through, across)	255
cata- (down)	256
para- (beside)	256
meta- (after, change)	257
anti- (against)	257
epi- (upon, in addition)	258
endo- (within)	259
apo- (from, off)	259
hypo- (below)	261
eu- (good)	262
hyper- (over)	262
A note on Latin and Greek Cognates	263
ex- (out)	264
exo-, ecto- (outside, external)	264
dys- (bad, difficult)	265
Suffixes	265
-oid (resembling)	266
-tomy (cut)	266
Ablaut	267
Compounding	271
Further Reading	274

THE FRENCH PARTITION   275

13 After the French Invasion   277

Introduction	277
Lenition	280

Vocalization	283
Clusters of Rules	285
Syncope	288
Epenthesis	289
Cluster Simplification	291
Prothesis	292
Assibilation	293
Assibilation of Velars	293
Assibilation of Labials	296
Assibilation of Nasals	298
Contraction	298
Conclusion	298

THE ENGLISH PARTITION — 299

14 Word Formation Processes — 301

Introduction	301
Shortening	301
Acronyms and Abbreviations	301
Backformation	302
Clipping	303
Blends	304
Zero Derivation	305
Brand Names	307
Fusion	309

15 Representation and Sound Change — 311

Introduction	311
The Great Vowel Shift	314
Conclusion	318
Further Reading	319

Index	**321**
Index of Latin Roots	**325**
Index of Latin Words	**329**
Index of Greek Roots	**341**
Index of Greek Words	**344**
Index of French Words	**349**

Preface

This book is an introduction to the history and structure of the English lexicon using linguistic concepts. Alternately, it is an introduction to linguistics through the medium of the English lexicon. Or, it is both.

An intimate knowledge of the history of English and the structure of English words is valuable. If one has a varied intellectual life—and one hopes that undergraduate university students do—then encountering new words or familiar words used in new ways will be a frequent experience. The ability to find familiar forms among the new can provide a sense of confidence. More exciting and subtler is the recognition that a skilled writer is also aware of the history of words and is able to use it to effect. If one is at all interested in literature, this kind of knowledge of English will add more texture to it.

The acquisition of this knowledge isn't really possible without linguistics. Linguistics provides the tools to dissect the lexicon and to explain its structure. Thus, linguistic concepts, methods, and calculus are used throughout this text. While necessary for the study of English, it is hoped that students will see that the study of linguistics is interesting in itself. I have occasionally tried to broaden the scope of the discussion beyond the study of English to suggest larger issues that interested students might pursue.

This book is intended for a first-year undergraduate audience. While it attempts to serve two masters—students of English and students of Linguistics—it is expected that the majority of the students will be looking to improve their knowledge of English. This is not a grammar book and doesn't pretend to teach the grammar of English, although necessarily grammatical concepts will enter the discussion. The focus of the book is the English lexicon, its structure and the structure of its occupants. It is hoped that by laying out the English lexicon, both native and non-native English speakers will gain greater facility with the language and a greater appreciation of language in general.

Paul McFetridge
Vancouver, Canada
Bangkok, Thailand
May, 2007

Acknowledgements

In the early 1980s Professor James Foley created a course at Simon Fraser University for first-year students of linguistics called *The Wonder of Words*. While teaching this course, he published a textbook of the same title. The book is now out of print, and when I surveyed the field I was unable to find another that paid the same kind of attention to linguistics in its presentation of the English lexicon. In the hopes of filling a perceived need, I have followed Professor Foley's lead and used English to illustrate linguistic concepts.

Merriam-Webster's Collegiate® Dictionary (11th edition) is my source of reference for etymologies. There were occasions when I disagreed with its analysis and deliberately departed from this source. Any mistakes are my own.

My sincere thanks to Kasetsart University and the NAiST Laboratory for providing me with a quiet place for escape and work.

I would like to thank and acknowledge Nancy Earle for her rigorous copy editing of the manuscript, Robert MacNevin for wrestling it into aesthetic shape and John Whatley for shepherding this project to its completion.

Finally, I would like to thank several Linguistics 110 classes at Simon Fraser University for their comments and reactions.

Notational Conventions

Much of what we talk about in this book is phonetic and phonological change—that is, change of sounds over time and derivational change. It is usual to represent sounds with a phonetic alphabet. There are occasions when this will be necessary. However, whenever possible change in pronunciation will be illustrated by changes in orthography. This trick serves to eliminate many of the details irrelevant to the task at hand. When an orthographic character is used, it is presented in italics to distinguish it from a phonetic representation.

It is common in linguistics to use the arrow "→" in both structure-building rules in morphology and content-changing rules in phonology. As a consequence, the expression α → β is ambiguous between *α consists of β* and *α changes to β*. I have chosen to disambiguate by retaining "→" for content-changing rules, as found in phonology, and use "⇒" for structure-building rules, as found in morphology.

A LINGUISTIC INTRODUCTION TO THE HISTORY AND STRUCTURE OF THE ENGLISH LEXICON

1 Introduction

We usually use words without thinking. We speak, and, through processes not yet understood, the words we use inspire what we hope are thoughts similar to those we intended in our listeners. We don't think much about words. We often don't realize that words have structure. And since we don't perceive structure, we don't see the poetry of words.

Consider a simple word like *nest*. When we think on this word, it seems quite straightforward: the word *nest* refers first to the place where many animals and insects and the odd marsupial mammal lay their eggs and, by extension, to a place of comfort and safety. But, in fact, this word is not atomic. It consists of two components. The first is *ne*, which was originally *ni* and exists now in English only in this word. It means "down". The second is *st*, which means "sit" and is in fact the word *sit* without the vowel. So, *nest* actually consists of components which together mean "sit down".

There is a poetic beauty to this view of words, that from simple components, words have been and are being created. This book is an examination of this process, the creation and evolution of words in a language. It focuses on the English lexicon, but the general principles can be applied to any language. In fact, as we shall see, because of the history of English, we will be forced to consider other languages as well.

Considerations of aesthetics aside, recognition of structure and etymology is important in other areas. Rather a lot of religious discourse centres on the origins of words. Trying to accurately discern the meaning of a religious text can require contemplation of why certain words were chosen and what nuances were intended. Similarly, poets choose words for their sounds as well as the resonance they have in the culture, and literary criticism consists in part of an examination of the appropriateness and beauty of phrasing.

On a more prosaic and mundane level, the ability to create new words is a skill that is sought after by business. Rather like Adam from the story of Genesis who was given the responsibility for naming all things,[1] a business with a new product (or a research scientist with a new medicine, an engineer with a new technique, a mathematician with a new algorithm) requires a name for it. Not any old name is appropriate. It must first communicate the function of the product either directly or by suggestion. For example, the name of the drug *Viagra* shares sounds with words like *vitality* and *vigorous*, suggesting concepts that the manufacturers want consumers to associate with their product. The second property that a name must have is that it must travel well. The manufacturer hopes that it travels through time so that it is not necessary to change the name of the product very soon. But also, in the age of globalization, the name must travel to other countries. The business world has many stories of inappropriate names. For example, an apocryphal story is that Chevrolet could not sell a car named *Nova* in Latin America. On reflection, the name was likely at least part of the problem because in Spanish *no* means "not" and *va* means "go". Their mistake was rather like naming a car for the English-speaking market *Turtle*.

The study of words, then, both looks backward to explain the structure of the lexicon and how it has been used in history, and forward by isolating the principles by which words are created, in anticipation of the need for new words for new objects and concepts.

Organization and Presentation

As one works through this book, I hope that it becomes clear that there is an arc to it. Chapters 2 through 7 lay a foundation that is exploited in the rest of the book. The first sections of this book introduce the study of Language and describe a bit of the history of English. The goals of these sections are establishing, first, the structure of Language, second, the structure of a word and, third, the structure of the English lexicon. In addition, the problem of representation is introduced.

Once these issues are established, it is then possible to explore the English lexicon in detail. The tone changes in Chapter 8. From this point on, we examine aspects of English using the tools built in the introduction.

The sections on Latin and Greek examine both the material out of which words are constructed and the rules that subsequently perturb them. When different formations are presented, they are illustrated with various roots which are themselves often illustrated with examples from other formations. It is useful to learn the roots so that they can be recognized wherever they occur. Understanding the root of a word is often the first step to unpacking the word's structure and recognizing which rules have applied to it.

---

1 Adam seemed to lack imagination in at least one area. When presented with thousands of similar but distinct species, the best he could do was name each *beetle*.

Representation

A central issue in any study is that of representation. The question is always how the object of study and the processes in which it participates should be represented. In order to discuss a subject, it is necessary to have a system for referring to the various objects and processes that make up that subject. This is a nontrivial problem and occupies all serious investigations.

An inadequate representation system can hinder an investigation more than it helps. The classic example of this is the representation of numbers. The Roman numeral system, which adapted the Roman alphabet to the number system, is adequate for counting and relating the results of a count. However, it is not at all useful for doing even simple arithmetic operations and hopeless for serious mathematics. Notice that there is no easy way to calculate the answer to the multiplication of ix and iii as xxvii. Worse, because the Roman number system did not have a symbol for zero, it is impossible to do any serious arithmetic or mathematics with it. It was not until the Arabic[2] number system was imported into Europe that Europeans were able to do mathematics and, subsequently, sophisticated physics which depends on mathematics as its representation system.

Part of the story of modern linguistics has been the search for an adequate representation for the objects and processes that comprise language. In this book, I have chosen a simple representation scheme for phonological and morphological processes for pedagogical rather than theoretical purposes. However, in recognition of the ultimate importance of getting representation right, I allude where possible to the issue of evaluating potential representations, including these used here.

Etymology

A second lesson from the story of the replacement of the Roman numeral system with that created by the Arabic and Hindu scholars is the footprint that events like this leave in the lexicon of a language. Consider the etymologies that *Merriam-Webster's Collegiate® Dictionary* (11th edition) gives for the first few numbers:

> *one*: [ME *on, an* fr. OE *ān*, akin to OHG *ein* one, L *unus* (OL *oinos*), Skt *eka*][3]

---

2 Although the number system universally used is called the *Arabic number* system, it is more likely that it was developed by Hindu mathematicians, borrowed by Arabs and introduced to Europe by them.

3 p. 866.

two: [ME *twa, two* fr. OE *twā*, (fem. & neut.); akin to OE *twēgen* two (masc.) *tū* (neut.), OHG *zwēne*, L *duo*, Gk *dyo*][4]

three: [ME, fr. *three*, adj., fr. OE *thrīe* (masc.) *thrēo*, (fem. & neut.); akin to OHG *drī*, L *tres*, GK *treis*][5]

four: [ME, fr. four adj., fr. OE *fēower*, akin to OHG *fior* four, L *quattuor*, Gk. *tessares, tettares*][6]

five: [ME fr. *five*, adj. fr. OE *fīf*; akin OHG *finf* five, L *quinque*, Gr *pente*][7]

Notice that in each case, it is possible to trace the history of the word back to its form in Old English (OE), the earliest form of English. It is also often possible to find similar words in Old High German (OHG), Latin (L), Greek (Gr) and Sanskrit (Skt), languages that are related to English. That the etymologies for numbers include words from these ancient languages indicates that these are very old words in English, as would be expected, given they are words that would be necessary in any culture and would be expected to be in common use.

Consider now the etymology of *zero*:

[F or It; F *zéro* fr. It *zero* fr. ML *zephirum*, fr. Ar *ṣifr*][8]

This states that the word was borrowed from French (F), which in turn borrowed it from Italian (It), which in turn borrowed it from Medieval Latin (L), which in turn borrowed it from Arabic (Ar). Not only is this a very different history from the other numbers, but Arabic is from a language family unrelated to the language family that includes English, Latin and Greek (or, at least, very, very distantly related).

It is clear just from comparing the histories of the words for various numbers that the number 0 zero has a recent history in English. The etymologies of numbers mirror the history of mathematics.

Often, the results from historical linguistics can provide this kind of confirming evidence for histories that have been created from other sources.

---

4 p. 1353.
5 p. 1302.
6 p. 495.
7 p. 473.
8 p. 1456.

2 Linguistic Change and the Structure of Language

Introduction

Consider the following phrase:

> þās gelǣhte se dēma and gelǣdde hī tō þām dēofolgyldum and cwæð
> mid ōlecunge þæt hī æþele cempan wǣron

There are few people who can understand this or even identify the language.

In fact, the language is Old English, the form of English that was spoken in England from approximately 450 CE until 1100 CE.[1] The phrase was written by Ælfric, the Abbot of Eynsham and a famous English preacher and grammarian, who lived about the time of the first millennium.

To see the relationship between Old English and Contemporary English, we can first examine a word-by-word translation:

> þās   gelǣhte se   dēma   and galǣdde hī   tō   þām dēofolgyldum
> *those   seized   the judge   and led   them to   the idols*
>
> and cwæð mid   ōlecunge þæt   hī   æþele cempan   wǣron
> *and said with flattery that they noble soldiers were*

This helps a bit, but can be misleading. For example, a naive reading of the first clause

> þās   gelǣhte se   dēma
> *those   seized   the judge*

---

[1] CE abbreviates *Contemporary Era*. It is now used instead of AD (*Anno Domini* "The Year of Our Lord") which was introduced by Christians to distinguish eras in that religion. The calendar developed by the Western Christian culture has been adopted by many other cultures, but the annotation AD is not relevant to non-Christian cultures. The annotation CE acknowledges both the original calendar and its multicultural use.

may suggest that some people have seized a judge. In fact, an Old English speaker would recognize immediately that the judge seized the soldiers, because the word we have translated as "judge" ends with -a. This ending is the nominative case marker and indicates that the word is in a phrase that functions as the subject. If we wanted to say that someone had seized the judge, we would inflect that word as *dēman*.

A better translation would be:

The judge seized them (the soldiers) *and led them to the idols and flattered them by saying that they were noble soldiers.*

What has happened? How is it that the ancient language of England is no longer recognizable by people who think of themselves as English speakers?

The fact is that English has changed over time. It is not unique in this; every language changes in response to the social conditions in which it is used. The contrast between Old English and Contemporary English is striking because a period of more than 900 years separates them, enough time for the language to have changed in dramatic ways. We can fill in that space a bit by examining Middle English, as exemplified by Chaucer, who wrote in the 15th century, about halfway between Ælfric and us:

> *Soune ys noght but eyre ybroken*
> *And every spech that ys yspoken,*
> *Lowde or pryvee, foule or faire,*
> *In his substaunce ys but aire*

This is much better: although the spelling is a bit off. If we read this poem aloud we can immediately recognize it as English:

> *Sound is nought but air broken*
> *And every speech that is spoken,*
> *Loud and pryvee (private), foul or fair,*
> *In its substance is but air*[2]

Two questions arise when we ponder this situation: Why do languages change? And what is changing? We will postpone the first question to the end of this chapter. The second forces us to examine how languages are constructed.

---

2 Notice that Chaucer spells *air* two different ways: *eyre* and *aire*. The concept of a fixed (and correct) way of spelling a word is a recent one. At the time of Chaucer, spelling could be used for effect. Here he spells it *aire* to emphasize the rhyme with *faire* and as *eyre* to tie it to the other words containing *y*.

The Structure of Language

We will approach the structure of language by noting differences among Ælfric, Chaucer, and the form of English that we now use. That is, by noting what has changed from Old to Middle to Contemporary English, we will discover facts about how languages are constructed. We are so accustomed to our everyday language that we are unaware of its structure. By watching it change, we can ask questions about what is changing and, consequently, see how language is constructed.

Orthography

Perhaps the first thing that we noticed when we first examined the Old English text was that it used characters that Contemporary English does not use. Three of these are ash (æ/Æ), thorn (Þ/þ), and edh (Ð/ð). These characters together with those that are more familiar, comprise the orthography[3] that was used to represent Old English. Thus, we might say that Old English and Contemporary English differ in their respective orthographies.

We must be careful here. An orthography is used to represent a language; it is not the language itself. Many different orthographies exist in the world. English uses one adapted from the Roman alphabet,[4] which was adapted from the Greek alphabet, which was adapted from a Phoenician syllabary,[5] which was adapted from Egyptian hieroglyphics. Other orthographies that you may have seen include the Japanese katakana and hiragana (both syllabaries), the Chinese kanji, the Arabic syllabary, and the Thai and Korean alphabets. This is by no means an exhaustive list.

Often, an orthographic system will have characteristics designed for some feature of the original language. For example, the Japanese katakana is a syllabary wherein each symbol represents a possible syllable of Japanese. It happens that Japanese has tight constraints on syllable structure so that there is a relatively small number of possible syllables in Japanese. In contrast, English permits a much greater range of syllable types. For example, hasp and haps are both legitimate English syllables, but neither is legitimate in Japanese (because Japanese is very selective about what can appear at the end of the syllable). So, the katakana does not represent either of these perfectly fine English syllables.

Thus, the katakana would not be a good choice for representing English. But, this is a fact about the katakana, not about Japanese or English. There is nothing to stop us from creating an orthography that is equally good at representing

---

3 *Orthography*: from the Greek *ortho*, "straight or correct", and *graphos*, "writing". *Ortho* is also found in *orthodontist*, "a specialist who corrects teeth". *Graph* is found in *graphology*, *telegraph*, and so on.
4 *Alphabet*: from the first two letters of the Greek alphabet: α *alpha* and β *beta*.
5 A syllabary is an orthographic system in which symbols represent syllables. Contrast this with an alphabet in which symbols should represent individual sounds.

English and Japanese. We could, for example, add more symbols to the katakana so that it represented all the English syllables as well as Japanese syllables.

In fact, linguists have attempted to create a representation that will work for all languages. By examining languages from around the world, linguists have catalogued the sounds that are found in every human language, or at least are close to completing this task. Part of this cataloguing process is assigning a symbol to each sound. The result is a phonetic alphabet, in which each symbol is unambiguously assigned to one sound and each sound is unambiguously assigned one symbol.

It is instructive to consider whether the English orthography would be a useful phonetic alphabet. We want each symbol to be assigned to one and only one sound. Immediately, we note that the character *c* does not meet this criterion: in the word *city*, it is homophonous with the *s* of site, and, in the word *clock*, it is homophonous with the *k* of *kick*. We also want each sound to have a single symbol associated with it. Again, we note that for the English orthography of *fails*: the first sound of *fail* is represented with an *f* but with *ph* in *phone*. It is easy enough to think of other examples that preclude English orthography from consideration as a phonetic alphabet.

There are two phonetic alphabets used by the majority of linguists: the International Phonetic Alphabet (IPA) and the North American Phonetic Alphabet (APA). There are many deviations from these two alphabets: some traditions, such as Germanic philology, developed character sets before linguists proposed the IPA and North American standards and continue to use them. We will use the IPA set when we need to refer to sounds for which the English character set is inadequate.

Why does Contemporary English no longer use the same character set that Old English used? Largely for social reasons. The French-speaking Normans invaded England in 1066. As the French language supplanted English in importance, the printers reverted to the characters necessary for French. These did not include the peculiar Old English characters and so those characters were dropped. The loss of these characters had nothing to do with changes in language itself but in the social circumstances in which the language was spoken. In fact, the sounds that those characters represented are still used in the English used today.

It should now be apparent that we are not noting anything remarkable about language when we observe that there are differences in the orthographies used by Old and Contemporary English. To insist that the difference between Old and Contemporary English was the orthography is analogous to studying the human body by studying fashions in clothing over the ages. Fashions change without any effect on the human body plan. Similarly, orthographies can be applied to any language without necessary changes to the language itself and, importantly, the language can change without concomitant changes in the orthography.

Phonetics[6]

What does the orthography tell us? In the case of an alphabet as it was used for representing Old English, it tells us how words were pronounced. It happens that the Old English orthography was very good at representing the pronunciation of Old English words.

When we compare how Old English was pronounced to how Contemporary English is pronounced, we can see that there has been considerable change. In order to talk about this, we will have to introduce some phonetic symbols.

When learning to spell in the English orthographic system, we all are exposed to a bit of linguistics. For example, in grammar school, we are told that the letters represent two types of sounds: consonants and vowels. Like so much that we learn in school this isn't quite right, but it will do for now. The vowel characters, we were told, are *a, e, i, o, u*, and sometimes *y*. Unfortunately, these five (and sometimes six) symbols are not enough to represent all the vowels of English. Table II.1 is a very much simplified description of the vowels of English. Even this simplified description isolates 11 different vowels, or about twice as many vowels as there are characters. Even worse, these symbols are not used consistently (and we want to build a system in which each symbol is used consistently and unambiguously): for example, the *i* in *pin* is pronounced much differently from that in *pine*.

The way linguists begin defining a phonetic alphabet is to describe the sounds that each symbol will represent. In the case of vowels, we can start by describing each vowel on three dimensions: whether it is produced in the front, middle, or back of the oral cavity (the mouth); whether the tongue is in a high, mid or low position; and whether the tongue itself is tense or lax.[7] There are other dimensions that colour the sound and serve as part of its description (such as, *inter alia*, whether the lips are round or spread, whether there is air flow through the nose, and the status of the pharyngeal muscles), but these three will serve us for now.

We will use the vowel chart in Table II.1 to assign symbols to descriptions of vowels. Each of the symbols represents a vowel sound from English and is paired with a key word illustrating the sound being described. The chart provides a description that includes each of the three dimensions for each vowel. For example, the vowel [i] is a high tense front vowel and the vowel [ɔ] is a mid lax back vowel.[8]

---

6 *Phonetics*: from the Greek *phone*, "sound", found in words like *telephone*.
7 The tongue is a muscle and, like any other muscle, can be flexed. Typically, for vowels, it has two positions flexed or unflexed, or, more technically, tense or lax.
8 Note that when we wish to use the symbols of the phonetic alphabet we enclose them in square brackets. This is to distinguish this use as special characters representing human speech sounds from their ordinary use in the orthographic representation of English.

Table II.1: Vowel Chart

		Front		Middle		Back	
High	Tense	i	beet			u	boot
	Lax	I	bit			ʊ	book
Mid	Tense	e	bait	ə	about	o	boat
	Lax	ɛ	bet			ɔ	board
Low		æ	bat			a	bought

There are three other English sounds that are often naively classed as vowels. These are found in *boy, buy,* and *bow* (the verb as in *I bow to your superior intellect*). In fact, these are not single sounds but two sounds bound together (see Table II.2). They are called *diphthongs*.[9] If you say them slowly and carefully, you can feel that there is more than one sound.

Table II.2: Diphthongs

	Front		Middle	Back	
High					
Mid				oy	boy
Low	ay	buy		aw	bow

It is important to emphasize two points. First, providing a key word illustrating the sound associated with each symbol works only if you speak a dialect in which these words actually do have the appropriate sound. For native English speakers, this should not be a problem, but non-native English speakers may not make the distinctions required for English and consequently may not match the sound that they produce to the appropriate symbol. For example, Brazilian Portuguese speakers do not distinguish between [i] and [I] and, consequently, pronounce *beat* and *bit* identically and may wonder why we are insisting on having two different symbols for the vowel sounds of *beat* and *bit*. For many speakers of English, native and non-native alike, the key word *bought* may not be appropriate for the low back vowel [a]. Some may not hear a difference between the vowels in *board* and *bought*. The low and back region is an area of considerable variation in the vowels of English dialects.

---

9 *Diphthong*, from Greek *di-*, "two" and, *phthong*, "sound". A diphthong is two sounds together.

The second point to keep in mind is that we are using what is called a *broad transcription*. In fact, it is very broad. By this we mean that we are omitting many details that practicing linguists would consider important in the representation of these vowel sounds.

For the purposes of this book we are more interested in the concept of phonetics than the details. It is important to understand that these symbols represent individual and unique speech sounds, that each sound has a unique description—a recipe, if you like, that describes how to create that sound—and to be able to associate a description to a symbol.

To experience the vowel chart kinesthetically, repeat the front and then back key words from high to low (e.g., *beat, bit, bait, bet, bat*). Regardless of your dialect of English, you should feel your tongue and perhaps jaw drop as you proceed through the list.

A final detail is necessary before we return to the evolution of Old English into Contemporary English. We are taught in school that the difference between the vowels in *keep* and *kept* is length, that the vowel of *keep* is long, while that of *kept* is short. Again, we find that what we are taught in school is not always correct, although here the mistake is more egregious. When one pronounces these words (and here it is important that you actually say these words aloud), one observes that while there may be some difference in the length of the vowel, the important difference is that *the vowels in these words are completely different sounds.*

If we try to locate these sounds on our vowel chart, we note that the vowel in *kept* is [ɛ], that is, the same vowel as in *bet*. The vowel in *keep* is [i], the same as in *beat*. When we write these sounds out in our phonetic alphabet as [ɛ] and [i], it is evident that they are different, that the difference is not one of length but of quality. These are simply different vowels.

Many languages do distinguish vowel sounds by length. Old English was one of these languages; it had long and short versions of each vowel. To be clear, we mean by this that the same vowel was produced but that long vowels had a longer duration than short.

Sometimes, the length of the vowel was important in determining which word was intended. That is, the same string of sounds could be different words depending on whether the vowel is long or short. In modern transliterations of Old English, the macron[10] is used to indicate a long vowel. Thus *dēma* contains two vowels: a long version of [e] and a short version of [a].

With this background, we can now examine the change in the pronunciation of words.

Old English orthography was quite good at representing pronunciation. In particular, the vowel symbols it used correspond reasonably to the vowel

---

10 *Macron*: from the Greek *macros*, "long". A macron is a short straight line placed over a vowel to indicate that it is long.

chart in Table II.1, so we can determine how the words were pronounced with accuracy.

The first word to examine using this knowledge is *dēma*, "judge". Using the vowel chart, we know that the first vowel is like that in *bait* but longer. That is, the Old English spelling system used the symbol *e* to represent the vowel [e]. The noun *dēma* no longer exists in English, but we do have a verb that is formed from the same root: *deem*, meaning "to judge". There are two things to notice about the word *deem*. First, the spelling reflects another way in which long vowels were once represented: by doubling the character (as *ee*). Unlike the macron which has been lost from English orthography, this spelling convention is frozen in the language. For example, the vowel of *beet* must have once been long because it is represented with two vowels, while that of *bet* must have been short.

The second thing to note is that when we locate the vowel in *deem* on the chart, we see that it no longer corresponds to that in bait, but instead it corresponds to the vowel in beet, that is, that represented as [i].

When we examine other Old English words with [ē], we observe that they follow the same pattern. Table II.3 gives examples of Old English words with their Contemporary English forms. Comparing these, we find that Old English *ē* is often represented in Contemporary English orthography as *ee* and pronounced [i].

Table II.3

Old English [ē]	Contemporary English [i]
bēte	beet
sēcan	to seek
mētan	to meet
cēpan	to keep

We can propose the following rule describing this aspect of the evolution of English:

$$\bar{e} \to i$$

Here, we introduce another bit of representation: The arrow "→" is read as "changed/changes to", so that this rule reads as "a long [e] changed to [i]". We will refer to this as a phonological rule.

The change described by this rule is not random. If we refer to the vowel chart, we see that this is a shift in height, from a mid vowel to a high vowel. We might wonder how general this change is. For example, this change affected front mid vowels and both [e] and [i] are front vowels. What of back mid vowels? One way to check this is to find Old English words with long back mid vowels, compare them to their Contemporary English equivalents, and observe the pronunciation.

Table II.4 illustrates Old English words containing [ō] (the back mid long vowel), along with their Contemporary English forms. Note that the Contemporary English words have vowels that correspond to the symbol [u] in the vowel chart.

Table II.4

Old English [ō]	Contemporary English [u]
rōt	root
hrōf	roof
mōd	mood

Thus the rule seems to be:

ō → u

This, too, is a shift from a long mid vowel to a high vowel.

Given these two rules, we can hypothesize a general rule:

Part of the change from Old English into Contemporary English was a shift of long mid vowels to high vowels.

There is certainly more to say about this and we will say more in subsequent chapters. However, for the moment, we have discussed enough to realize that if we are to understand a language, one of the things that we must understand is its phonetic structure.

Each oral language[11] uses a set of speech sounds, out of which meaningful units, such as words, are constructed. Different languages do not necessarily use the same set of sounds. In fact, one of the reasons that we often have an accent when we learn a new language is that we must learn to produce new sounds, sounds that are not in our native language. For many, learning these new sounds is an imperfect process.

---

11 The restriction to "oral languages" is necessary because the sign languages of the deaf are true languages, but use manual configurations and movements, rather than sound, to convey meaning.

Morphology[12]

As we examine the words in Chaucer and ignore the unusual spelling conventions, we note that even when we recognize a word, it sometimes has extra material attached to it. For example, we can query the function of the *y* in *ybroken* and *yspoken*. Contemporary English gets along fine without this *y*. Why does Chaucer need it?

When we move farther back in time to Old English, we note a similar problem: *gelǣdde* is the earlier form of led. It is possible to unpack *gelǣdde*: it has a prefix *ge* and a base *lǣd* (compare this with the modern led), to which *ge* has been added. In fact, the *ge* of Old English is an earlier form of the *y* from Middle English.

But what is this prefix *ge/y*? To determine what function it has, we need to review the forms that the English verb can take. Table II.5 lists the inflectional[13] paradigm for the English verb *break*. Inflection is the process by which the form of a word is changed to express a grammatical concept such as tense (e.g., broke is inflected for the past tense) or subject/verb agreement (e.g., breaks is inflected to agree with a 3rd singular subject).

Table II.5: The English Verbal Inflectional Paradigm

infinitive	to break
3rd singular present tense	breaks
non3^{rd} singular present tense	break
past tense	broke
present participle	breaking
past participle	broken

English has a rather impoverished inflectional system. In the present tense of verbs, it distinguishes only between 3rd and non3^{rd} singular subjects. Many languages distinguish among 1st, 2nd, and 3rd singular and plural subjects. Aside from the present tense, the only other tense that English inflects for is the past. Many languages will inflect for other tenses, moods, and aspects. English does not inflect for these, but instead forms them paraphrastically (e.g., English expresses the future with the auxiliary will, among other ways).

---

12 *Morphology*: from the Greek *morphe*, "shape" and *logos*, "science". Morphology is literally the science of shapes. When used in linguistics, it refers to the shapes of words.

13 *Inflection*: from the Latin *flectere*, "to bend", and *in-*, "in". The root is also found in the word *flex*.

When we examine the inflectional paradigm in Table II.5, we note that the Old and Middle English forms we are interested in (*gelǣdde* and *ybroken*) are past participles and are formed, in part, by adding *ge* and *y* at the front of the word. The relevant difference between Old and Middle English, on the one hand and Contemporary English, on the other, is that Contemporary English no longer forms the past participle with this prefix.[14] This is an example of morphological change, a change in the ways in which words are created.

There is a fossil in Contemporary English that still exhibits the Middle English method of forming the past participle: *yclept*, "named". This is the participle of the verb *clypian*, "to call". Interestingly, the verb itself has been lost; only the participle remains and it is very infrequent. German, a sister language to English, still shows the older method for forming the past participle: compare *denken*, "to think", with the participle *gedachte*, "thought".

This kind of change highlights one of the important components of Language: all languages have word-building functions. As language users, we are aware of these word building functions to varying degrees. It should be obvious that *antibacterial* has internal structure and that we can work out the meaning of the word from its components. At the very least, we can discern *anti* and *bacterial*. Slightly more obscure is a word like *understand*; it clearly has internal structure (*under* + *stand*) but it is not immediately obvious how it gains its meaning from the meanings of its parts. Most obscure is a word like *nest*. It appears to be atomic, without internal structure or component parts. But, as noted previously, it was created from a prefix *ni-*, "down", now lost, and a root *st*, from which the English word *sit* developed.

The Lexicon[15]

We have noted already that *dēma*, "judge", is no longer present in English. It is unlikely that anyone would recognize *dēofolgyldum*, "idol". These illustrate that the list of words that comprise a language, its vocabulary or lexicon, will change over time. A little thought demonstrates why this is so.

We would be surprised if someone from the Old English period understood words like *thermonuclear, computational,* or *motorcycle*. Words like this did not exist during that period because the concepts and objects that they denote did not exist. The lexicon of a language is sensitive to the environment in which the language is used. When the environment changes through invention of new artifacts, contact with other cultures, and creation of new ideas, then

---

14 *Prefix*: from the Latin *pre-*, "before" and *figere*, "to attach". The root is also found in words like *figment* and *fix*. A prefix is literally something that is attached in front.
15 *Lexicon*: from the Greek *logos*, "word".

the vocabulary of the language will be augmented so that speakers will have words to use to talk about these new ideas and artifacts. Thus, *thermonuclear*, *computational*, and *motorcycle* are all relatively new words in English, words of recent invention.

As we have noted, words (e.g., *dēma*) can be lost as well. One reason for the loss of a word is underuse because the concept or object that it denotes is no longer used in the culture. For example, *weregeld*[16] denotes the practice of paying money to a family for the wrongful death of one its members. The practice dates to a time before the English had a well-established system of law that would punish the person responsible, and it served to forestall family feuds. *Weregeld* is no longer practiced and consequently, the word is no longer used.

Why would *dēma* die out in favour of *he* seemingly synonymous *judge*? Because during the period after 1066 CE, the period of the Norman conquest of English, the language of the judicial system was French. Judge was borrowed from French during this period and replaced the local word *dēma*. During this period, French was a more prestigious language than English, particularly in areas of government and law, so French words were used in place of English words.

Words and descriptive phrases can become stigmatized and, as a consequence, fall out of use. When a word becomes stigmatized it acquires such negative characteristics that it is felt impolite or even offensive to use it. What is sometimes characterized as "politically correct" language is a result of the recognition that some terms are felt to be offensive or otherwise inhibiting and should be replaced with neutral terms. For example, in Canada the term *Indians* has been replaced with *First Nations* people when referring to the first inhabitants of North America. Much of the language that presupposes that the referent must be male has been replaced with more inclusive terms. So *chairman* has been replaced with *chair* or *chairperson*, *policeman* with *officer*, and *mailman* with *postal carrier*.

Syntax[17]
We previously noted that without knowledge of the inflectional morphology of Old English nouns, we will misunderstand the phrase *þās gelǣhte se dēma*. To understand this phrase, we need to recognize that *se dēma* is inflected for nominative case and that it is, therefore, the subject of the sentence.

The fact that Old English nouns inflected in ways that expressed their function provided speakers with greater opportunity for variation in the order of words. In Contemporary English, the primary method for expressing function is word order. In the sentence,

---

16 *Weregeld*: Old English *were*, "man" (see *werewolf*), and *geld*, "gold".
17 *Syntax*: from the Greek *syn-*, "together", and *tassein*, "arrange". Syntax is literally the arrangement of words together.

> The judge seized them

we know that the judge is the subject because it appears before the verb. If we reverse the order to,

> They seized the judge

the phrase the judge is marked no differently but is nonetheless interpreted as the object because it appears after the verb.

In Old English, word order was much less important for expressing function and could be used for effect instead. So a possible translation of *þās gelǣhte se dēma* is *It was them that the judge seized*, because the object *þās*/them appears at the front of the sentence and is thereby highlighted. The word order emphasizes them (the soldiers) and talks of an action that happened to them. If we reversed the order to *se dēma gelǣhte þās*, we could translate it as the judge seized them.

A second example of a difference in syntax is the phrase

hī	æþele	cempan	wron
they	*noble*	*soldiers*	*were*

In contemporary English, we might accept this as an example of poetry, where we allow the writer to violate the ordinary rules of grammar for effect. But, we would not produce this in ordinary conversation or accept it. In Contemporary English, we could also accept as poetic

> *noble soldiers were they*

But more likely is

> *they were noble soldiers*

Neither of these is the word order of the Old English word phrase where the verb is at the end of the sentence, a normal position in a Germanic language.

Semantics[18]
Ferdinand de Saussure once compared linguistic units, such as words and phrases, to coins. Just as a coin has two sides (heads and tails), a word or phrase is composed of two elements: a sequence of sounds we utter and a meaning we

---

18 *Semantics*: from the Greek *semainein*, "to signify".

intend to convey. We have seen that the first can change over time. The same is true of the latter: words can change meaning.

Corn is a word that has existed in the English from its beginning. It can be found in Old English and in many other related languages, indicating that it was probably present in the parent language (see Chapter 3). Interestingly, the word now signifies a New World grain. Since English speakers have only lived in North America for approximately 500 years, this word could not have had the meaning it currently has in Old English and related languages. Indeed, the evidence shows that it once mean "grain" in general and only recently narrowed to its contemporary meaning.

A word may also generalize its meaning. The word *tail* once applied only to hairy appendages; on this meaning, cats had tails but alligators did not. Its meaning has generalized by removing the stipulation that the appendage be hairy.

Figure II.1

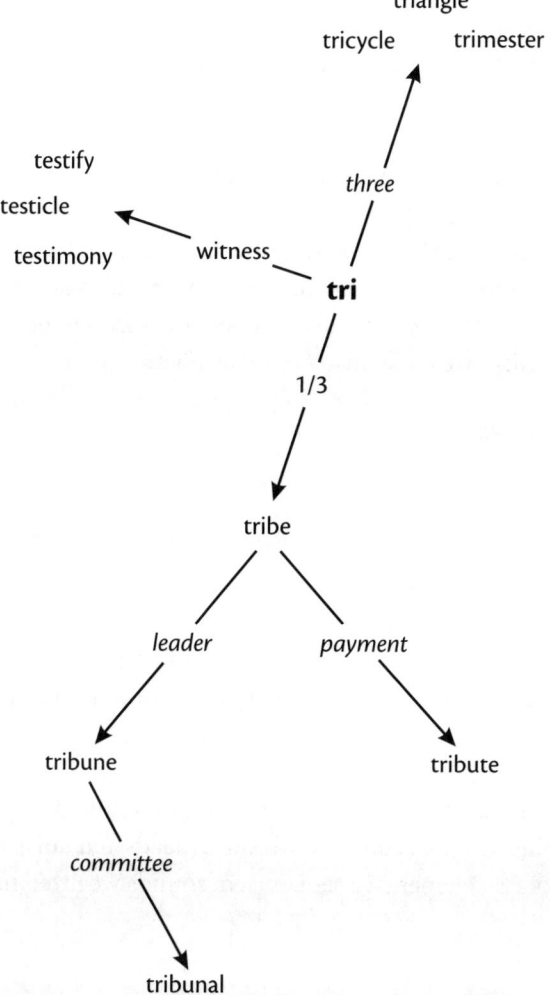

Words can take on nuances of meaning because of their association with other activities. For example, the Latin root *tri-* means "three".[19] It can be found with this meaning in words like *tricycle, trimester,* and *triangle.* The Roman nation was originally conceived as composed of three parts, each of which was called a tribe. The word *tribe* no longer carries the basic meaning of "three" but instead refers to a community of people. Each tribe requires a chief. In Roman times, the chief was called a *tribune* and the council that he headed was a *tribunal.* The tax that citizens paid to the tribune was called a *tribute.* Eventually, *tribute* came to mean any kind of forced payment and, finally, any gift that showed praise or gratitude.

Another notion is that the third person in an incident is the witness of that incident. The Latin language combined *tri-* with the root *sta-*, meaning "stand", to create the base form *test*; the *r* of *tri-* has deleted, and the *i* of *tri-* has changed to *e*. From the base test, meaning "witness", are created words such as *testify, testimonial,* and even *testicle.* Figure II.1 illustrates how the meaning of *tri-* has changed due to on the circumstances in which it was used.

Summary

From our observations of the ways in which English has changed over the previous millennium, we have uncovered the components of language, which are summarized in Table II.6.

Table II.6: The Components of Language

Phonetics	The sounds that comprise a language (to this we can add phonology, the way in which these sounds interact)
Morphology	The method for constructing new words
Lexicon	The list of words (with their properties) in a language
Syntax	The method for constructing phrases and sentences from words
Semantics	The meanings of words, phrases, and sentences

Our primary concern throughout this book is with the first three of these components. We will be studying the English lexicon, the store of words that comprise the English language. Many of these words have structure, even at times, a poetic quality. We can structure the English lexicon along the dimensions of age and source: whether of old or recent creation and whether native to English or borrowed from languages such as Latin or Greek. As we have seen, words come and go in response to cultural changes. Some words have recent origin but some are ancient. The structure of the recent words is often transparent, while that of ancient words has been obscured by the changes in

---

[19] In fact, it is cognate with the English word *three*.

pronunciation. The English lexicon is also stratified by borrowings from other languages. English contains large numbers of words of Greek, Latin, and French origin. To this day, when we create new words, we often look to those languages for the building blocks rather than to English.

Why Languages Change

The situation that we have observed for English is the same for all languages the world over. None are static. Each has changed and is changing. Geographically, the effect of change is the creation of dialects in different places. Eventually, these changes accumulate until the dialects are mutually incomprehensible. At some point, this process intersects with political differences, and there is agreement that two dialects are now different languages.

An excellent example is Latin. The Roman Empire extended over much of Europe, and Latin-speaking peoples spread into the empire. Local people found that being able to speak Latin was an advantage. As changes entered into the language in different parts of the empire, different dialects arose and became increasingly different from each other. Eventually, the empire collapsed, but the dialects remained and became identified with the countries that were subsequently created. Thus, while today no one speaks Latin natively, its "children" persist in the form of French, Spanish, Portuguese, Italian, Romanian, Sardinian, Catalan, and many other less well known dialects.

A similar process can be observed for English. When we scan the various dialects of English that are spoken around the world, we are struck by the considerable variation. An obvious source of variation is the lexicon where we find the same objects named differently: *lorry* or *truck*, *bonnet* or *hood*, *chesterfield* or *davenport* or *sofa*.

We can also often locate people's origins from their accents. The southern dialects of the United States, the Bronx dialect, Australian and Indian English, and the dialects of England are all distinctive.[20] In some cases, the differences are so dramatic that some dialects are mutually incomprehensible. For example, when the makers of Mad Max, an Australian film starring a young Mel Gibson, prepared the film for international distribution, they dubbed it into a less distinctive dialect because they were concerned that audiences in other countries would not understand the Australian dialect. In the 1990s, films from Scotland and Wales became internationally popular. Often, these films or bits of them are subtitled because the dialects of the characters are dramatically different from those spoken by the rest of the English-speaking world.

These examples demonstrate how difficult it is to determine if different dialects are actually different languages. Although there are many varieties of English, some of which diverge so far from each other as to be unintelligible

---

20 The British have a saying to describe this phenomenon: *branded by the tongue*.

to speakers of other English dialects, we nonetheless think of all of them as English. This is because they historically descend from the same language, and there are political and economic advantages to maintaining affinity among the English-speaking countries.

In contrast to the English example—where very different dialects are considered the same language—there are also instances of very similar dialects which we unquestioningly consider to be different languages. For example, the dialects of Dutch and German spoken along the border between the Netherlands and Germany are mutually intelligible; speakers can easily understand each other. However, we think of these dialeccts as instances of Dutch and German, depending on which side of the border the speakers live, largely for political reasons. Dialects of Spanish and Portuguese are another example of closely related languages that have mutually intelligible dialects.

To return to the original question, why should there be different dialects at all? It would seem that a single language, a single dialect, would be sufficient for the human race. What is more, the steady accumulation of changes and subsequent creation of different languages, in the sense of mutually unintelligible dialects, inhibits communication. This process seems to be a bad idea.

Increasingly, linguists, sociologists, and evolutionary psychologists look to the human need to establish and maintain community for the answer to this question. We each of us live in a network of friends, family, co-workers, and associates. It is important to us to maintain this network because we rely on it for emotional support, help with our jobs, studies, and life's problems, and even for financial assistance.

The importance of the network lies in the calculations we do when we consider when to help others, when we consider whether to spend our resources on someone else. Generally, we are more likely to rank family higher than friends, and friends higher than strangers. We may be happy to help family with their problems, and are perhaps willing to help friends, but we think long before helping strangers.

But we can also distinguish among strangers and find potential friends among strangers who would rank higher than other strangers. Anyone who has travelled in other countries is familiar with the welcome feeling of meeting someone from one's own country. Stranger or not, they are not as strange as the truly foreign people one has been meeting. They have similar values, similar interests, and similar histories, and they speak the same language.

Given that it is important that we know who is a member of our family or our neighbourhood or some important group with which we affiliate, we need methods of signalling group membership. For example, gang members such as those in the Hell's Angels signal membership by wearing their colours; colours consist of appropriate clothing and, especially, insignia imprinted on the clothing.

One problem that gangs have is that it is easy to fake membership: we only need to buy the appropriate clothing to pretend we are members. That is why gang members react so extremely when they discover someone wearing their colours who is not a legitimate member of the gang.

A more intimate method of "showing our colours" is the dialect that we use. For most of us, this is the dialect that we learned as children. Our dialect signals immediately to whomever we speak where we were raised as children. Our psychology will initially accept someone who speaks our dialect as someone who shares the same values and as someone who is more like us than it will accept someone who does not speak the same dialect. Thus, the importance of dialects is that they signal group membership and they do so in a way that is difficult to copy. Not many of us can convincingly copy another dialect and convince speakers of that dialect that we are one of them, the way we might be able to if we wear a group's colours. Dialect is an effective way of eliminating fakes from the group.

A couple of points need to be acknowledged. First, most of us control several versions of our dialect and use different versions depending on the social situation. For example, we use a different style of language when applying for a job than when joking with friends. Nonetheless, there is commonality among all versions, so much so that we can identify people's geographic origins by the dialect they use. Second, some people, most commonly actors, are able to acquire new dialects. That this is necessary underscores the importance we unconsciously give dialects. It is disconcerting when an actor doesn't get a dialect right or when actors play characters who are family members with different dialects. Sean Connery played an impressive Agamemnon, the king of Mycenae, in Terry Gilliam's Time Bandits, except that he played the Greek king with a Scottish accent. Similarly, in The Hunt for Red October, he played a Russian submarine captain with the same Scottish accent.

Sometimes, when people move to a location where a different dialect of their language is spoken, they lose identifying characteristics and may acquire aspects of the local dialect. This is particularly easy to do if identifying characteristics of their dialect are considered to be signals of unwanted personality characteristics, such as low intelligence.

A rather dramatic example of the role of dialect in eliminating fakes is found in the book of Judges (chapter 12, verses 1–15) from the Hebrew Tanakh and Christian Old Testament. The story relates the battle between the Gileadites and the Ephraimites. After the Gileadites had defeated the Ephraimites, they barricaded escape routes from the battlefield in order to capture the Ephraimites. But how to distinguish escaping Ephraimites from Gileadites leaving the battlefield, since no one wore uniforms? The Ephraimites spoke the same language as the Gileadites and would not want to admit to being Ephraimite lest they be killed. The solution to the Gileadites' problem was that although the two groups spoke the same language, they spoke different dialects. In particular, the Gileadites spoke a dialect that had the sh sound (like <u>sh</u>eep) but the Ephraimites did not and could not pronounce <u>sh</u>. So the solution was:

> when those Ephraimites which were escaped said, Let me go over; that the men of Gilead said unto him, art thou an Ephraimite? If he say Nay; Then said they unto him, Say now Shibboleth: and he said Sibboleth: for he could not frame to pronounce it right. Then they took him, and slew him at the passages of Jordan: and there fell at that time of the Ephraimites forty and two thousand.[21]

But the observation that dialect is a true demonstration of group membership takes us back to the original question. Why do dialects change? If they are effective signals of group membership, shouldn't they remain static? That is, shouldn't we strive to hold our dialect stable so that others recognize us?

Many answers have been proposed, including the observation that change is a fact of existence, so it should be no surprise that dialects change as well. To my mind, there are two additional compelling and compatible explanations.

The first explanation concentrates on the need to detect and eliminate fakes from the group. In our Pleistocene history, this was important because we had limited resources to share among the members of the group. Supporting freeloaders who were not members of the group was wasteful. A dialect that remained static is like a password on a computer account that is never changed, or a secret code among spies who never change the key. Eventually, someone breaks the code, discovers the password, or learns the identifying characteristics of the dialect. Once the outsider learns the dialect, it is easier for them to pass as a member of the group. Thus, there is good reason for a dialect to slowly change over the generations. Each generation has a version that works well for it, but the next generation should introduce small changes to protect it from outsiders.

The second explanation concentrates on the importance of group membership and provides the mechanism for the process of change that the first explanation suggests. No sufficiently large group is homogenous; there are subgroups internally who will also want to distinguish themselves from other subgroups inside the main body. In society as a whole, an obvious schism is that between teenagers and young adults, on the one hand, and older adults, on the other. One of the important periods of life is adolescence, during which we begin to affiliate more with our peers than with our families. One of the obvious linguistic manifestations of this reconfiguration of our affiliations is the development of a specialized vocabulary often called teenage slang. This

---

21 Judges 12: 5–6.

vocabulary is used only within a particular age group. It sounds faintly ridiculous, if not pathetic, when an adult uses the slang of teenagers. The invention of this slang gives each generation a start at distinguishing itself from the older generation.

More subtly, investigations in high schools have found that this process is also found in the pronunciation that teenagers will affect. Teens adopt slight changes in the sounds that they use that distinguish them from their parents and even from other students in the same high school. These studies have found what every high-school student knows: that the schools are stratified into different groups who claim territory in the school and who do not interact with each other and who may express animosity towards each other. Careful examination of the linguistic sounds that the teens from different groups use shows that they are changing their style of speech to identify themselves as members of a particular group and to distinguish themselves from members of other groups.

In conclusion, the reason that languages change is the very human need to establish, maintain and advertise group membership. The subtle and not so subtle differences in the dialects that we speak tell others how close or far we are in kinship.

Conclusion

This chapter has introduced two of three principle themes of this book. First is **change**. We have seen that languages will change over time. Second, in order to talk about change, it has been necessary to create a **representation**. In particular, to understand phonetic change we need a representation of linguistic sounds and a representation of how those sounds change. Representation is a common thread that runs throughout our consideration of the English lexicon. We will introduce another theme—**structure**—in Chapter 5. The two ideas that a language has structure and that structure will change over time and, more subtly, will create the opportunity for change will be explored further as we examine English vocabulary.

Further Reading

Dunbar, Robin. *Grooming, Gossip and the Evolution of Language*. Cambridge, Mass.: Harvard University Press, 1996.

Eckert, Penelope. "Social Polarization and the Choice of Linguistic Variants." In *New Ways of Analyzing Sound Change*, edited by Penelope Eckert. San Diego: Academic Press, 1991. 213–232.

Freeborn, Dennis. *From Old English to Standard English: A Course Book in Language Variation across Time*. Ottawa: University of Ottawa Press, 1998.

Origins and History

*Therefore is the name of it called Babel;
Because the Lord did there confound
the language of all the earth.*
Genesis 11:9

Nothing endures but change.
Heraclitus

High thoughts must have high language.
Aristophanes

3 Origins

Introduction

In the late 18th century, a British official named Sir William Jones arrived in India to serve as a judge. In order to better understand the legal code of India, Sir Jones studied Sanskrit. Like Latin in Europe, Sanskrit was no longer spoken in India as a native language but it still served as the language in which learned matters were conducted. In particular, the law codes were written in Sanskrit.

As a learned man, Sir Jones was also familiar with Latin and Ancient Greek. As he studied Sanskrit, he was struck by the many similarities among these languages. He correctly realized that this was a phenomenon that couldn't be explained by coincidence. There are simply too many common words and patterns among these languages. Table III.1 contains some of the words that Sir Jones noticed in his studies.

Table III.1

Latin	Greek	Sanskrit	Gloss
pater	patēr	pitar	father
mater	mētēr	matar	mother
frater		bhrātar	brother
soror		svasar	sister
pēs/pedis	podos	pad	foot
cornū	keras	crnga	horn
dēns/dentis	odous	danti	tooth
penna	pteron	parna	feather

Latin	Greek	Sanskrit	Gloss
mūs	mus	mūs	mouse
musca	muia	maksa	fly
ruber	eruthros	rudhira (*bloody*)	red
ignis		agni	fire
stēlla	estēr	star	star
trēs	treis	traya	three
novus	neos	nava	new
mel	meli	madhu	honey

In 1786, Sir Jones presented the results of his study of the similarity among Latin, Ancient Greek, and Sanskrit to the Asiatick Society. He ended with the conclusion that there was a strong resemblance among the three,

> [stronger] than could possibly have been produced by accident; so strong, indeed, that no philologer could examine them all three, without believing them to have sprung from some common source, which, perhaps, no longer exists.[1]

Indo-European

Sir Jones's presentation initiated a research program into the history of languages. This program had two branches. One was the search for the Ur-language, the original language. At first, there was considerable sympathy for the view that Sanskrit was the original language from which Latin and Ancient Greek had evolved. This sympathy arose less from any linguistic grounds than from prejudices about languages and change. There was a belief, still noted today, that language change is degeneration and that the Ur-language must have been almost, if not, perfect. Although the notion of "perfection" cannot be defined for language, at that time it was felt that languages with large numbers of inflecting categories were closer to perfection than were those like English which had very few.[2] Since Sanskrit had more inflecting categories than Latin

---

1 Garland Cannon, "Jones 'Sprung from Some Common Source': 1786–1986" in *Sprung from Some Common Source: Investigations into the Prehistoy of Language*, eds. S.M. Lamb and E.D. Mitchell (Stanford Calif.: Stanford University Press 1991) 31.
2 Recall, that English inflects verbs, nouns and adjectives. There are only two inflections for nouns, three for adjectives and six for verbs.

Figure III.1: Partial Diagram of the Indo-European Language Family

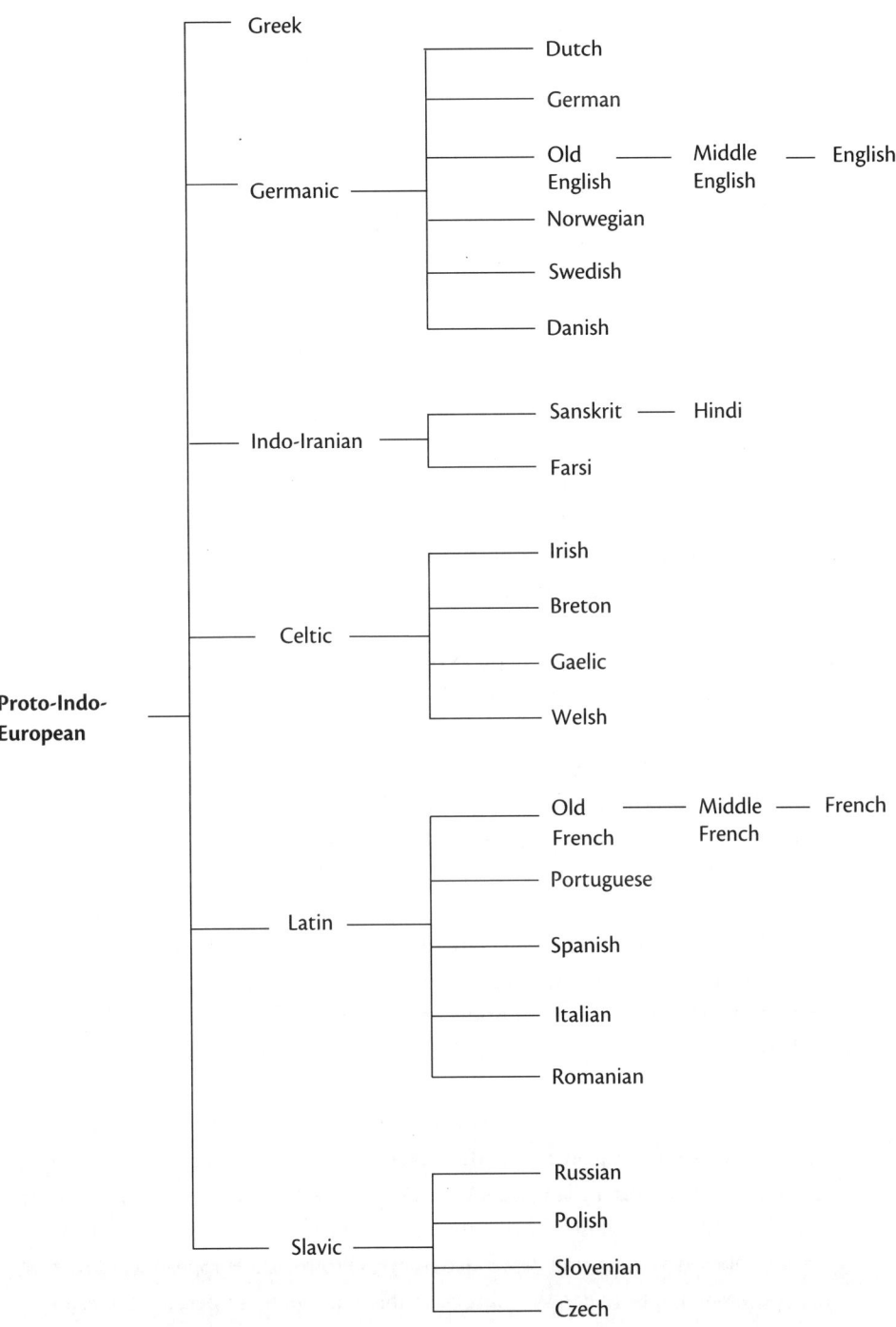

and Ancient Greek, the reasoning went, it must be closer to perfection. Since it was closer to perfection, it must be older.

Eventually, it was demonstrated linguistically that Sanskrit could not possibly be the ancestor of Latin and Greek. Jones's original view was the correct one: the three languages had descended from a common ancestor. This common ancestor is called *Proto-Indo-European* (PIE). There are no written records of this language, but many of its properties can be reconstructed by comparing its daughter languages. Much research was devoted to reconstructing the original language and the history of its speakers.

The second branch of investigation examined other languages to determine if they were also related to Latin, Greek, and Sanskrit. It was eventually determined that most of the languages of Europe, as well as those of Northern India and what is now Iran, could be arrayed in a tree of familial relationships.

This language family is now called Indo-European. The Indo-European language family can itself be divided into subfamilies. Figure III.1 presents a simplified and incomplete tree demonstrating relationships among the Indo-European languages. The tree is read left to right. It is rooted at the parent language *Proto-Indo-European*.

One of the hypotheses about the origin of Indo-European places the original people in the Russian Steppes about the 5,000 years ago. After the domestication of the horse, these people spread west throughout Europe and south into what is now India and Iran in successive waves, conquering the indigenous peoples and replacing them. This explanation rests primarily on linguistic evidence: common words in most Indo-European languages for snow, plants, and animals point to an origin in the temperate area of Europe.

A second hypothesis places them in the area that is now Turkey. It has been proposed that the development of agriculture in this area provided a technology that permitted and even forced people to spread to new areas.

Whatever the origin of the Indo-European people, the dialects of Proto-Indo-European gradually changed, probably for the reasons discussed in Chapter 2. In the north of Europe, the Germanic language family developed. At the beginning of the first millennium CE, Germanic speaking people invaded the island now known as England. The combination of the various dialects spoken by these people became the language we have identified as Old English.

Each row in Table III.1 provides words from Latin, Ancient Greek, and Sanskrit that are related. The explanation of this relatedness is that they descend from the same word in the parent language. We can illustrate this with a tree, as in Figure III.2. This diagram illustrates that the Latin, Ancient Greek, and Sanskrit words that we glossed as *mother* all descended from an Proto-Indo-European word that is hypothesized to be *māter*. We must claim this as a hypothesis because there are no records of Proto-Indo-European. Instead, it has been reconstructed, much as paleontologists reconstruct extinct animals from the fossils left behind, making inferences about the structure of the body/language from the available evidence and knowledge about how bodies/languages work.

Figure III.2

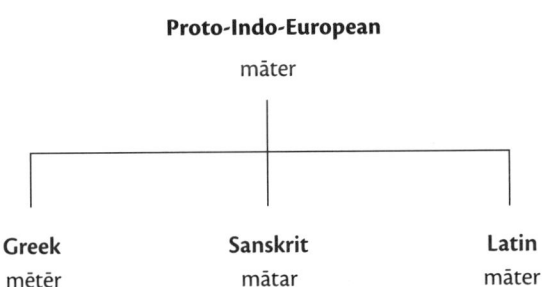

Words that stand in this relationship—words in different languages that are descended from the same word in the parent language—are called *cognates*.[3] The original word is called an *etymon*,[4] the words that evolved from the etymon are its *reflexes*.[5]

For example, in Figure III.2 the proposed Proto-Indo-European form *māter* is the etymon, the Greek, Sanskrit and Latin forms are its reflexes and are cognate with each other. The English form is *mother*.

If English is a language related to Greek, Sanskrit, and Latin, then it should be possible to discover English words that are cognate with some of those in Table III.1. In fact, this is relatively easy to do, once one can spot the regular changes that have occurred in English. Table III.2 replicates Table III.1 with English cognates instead of glosses. Note that most of the words given as glosses in Table III.1 are in fact cognates.

Table III.2

Latin	Greek	Sanskrit	English
pater	patēr	pitar	father
mater	mētēr	matar	mother

---

3 Cognate: from the Latin *co-*, "together", and *gnatus*, "born". Cognates are words that were born together.
4 Etymon: from the Greek *etymos*, "true". The etymon is, in a sense, the true form, the form before any changes have occurred.
5 Reflex: from the Latin *re-*, "back", and *flect*, "bend". Related to *reflect* and *reflection*, a reflex is an image, a reflection, of the etymon.

Latin	Greek	Sanskrit	English
frater		bhrātar	brother
soror		svasar	sister
pēs/pedis	podos	pad	foot
cornū	keras	crnga	horn
dēns/dentis	odous	danti	tooth
penna	pteron	parna	feather
mūs	mus	mūs	mouse
ruber	eruthros	rudhira (*bloody*)	red
stēlla	estēr	star	star
trēs	treis	traya	three
novus	neos	nava	new

What happened to produce English? If we scan the first three sets of words, we note that whenever a word from a classical language contains a *t*, the corresponding English cognate contains a *th* [θ]. We might hypothesize a phonological rule

$$t \rightarrow \theta$$

as responsible for part of the change from Proto-Indo-European to English.

Is this rule correct? When we scan down the list of words, we find that it is true of *tooth*, cognate with Latin *dentis*, and of *three*, cognate with Latin *trēs*, but not of *star*, cognate with Latin *stēlla*.

Another example of the failure of this rule to apply when we think that it should is *guest*, which is cognate with Latin *hostis*. The words where the rule fails have a common property: the *t* is preceded by *s*. For some reason, which doesn't concern us here, a preceding *s* will block the rule.

We note a similar change when comparing *foot* with *pedis* and *pad*, or *father* with *pater*. Here, we have a rule

$$p \rightarrow f$$

Once aware of this correspondence, one can note other cognates: e.g. *fish* and Latin *piscis*, *fire* and Greek *pyre*. The correspondence that includes *feather* is an example of both of the two rules we have seen. Note that the Greek *pteron* has the root *pter*. When we apply these rules and insert a vowel, we arrive at the English word.

Finally, we note that when the classical languages had a [k] (which is sometimes represented with the letter *c*), English has an *h*. Note, Latin *cornū* and English *horn*, Latin *canis* and English *hound*, and Latin *cor/cordis* and English *heart*. Thus, it appears that there is also a rule:

k → h

Recall that in our discussion of the change from Old English to Contemporary English, we noted that the rules seemed to be organized into more general patterns. There we noted that the rules:

ē → i

ō → u

could be summarized as a more general rule:

Long mid vowels raise to high vowels

Can the same be said of these rules?

In order to understand how each of the above rules is an instance of the same general rule, we must review the phonetics of consonants, just as we have previously reviewed the phonetics of vowels.

Consonants can analyzed on three dimensions: where in the vocal tract they are articulated; how they are articulated; and whether or not the glottis is vibrating. Let us take these one at a time.

We can distinguish consonants by the way in which they are articulated. For example, if we close our lips, stop the air from flowing out of the mouth and then release the air in a little explosion, we will have produced a [p] or [b].[6] However, if we do exactly the same but allow the air to flow out the nose, we will produce [m]. Go ahead and try it. Correspondingly, we call sounds like [p] and [b] *stops* and sounds like [m] *nasals*.[7] If we continue to make a sound like [p], but open the lips a bit so that air passes out of the mouth and rest the lower lip against the upper teeth, we will produce [f] or [v]. These sounds are called *fricatives* because they produce friction. We can combine stops and fricatives to produce *affricates*. These

---

6 Recall that we enclose characters inside square brackets to indicate that we are using a phonetic alphabet.
7 *Nasal*: From the Latin *narus*, "nose".

are sounds like the first in *chap* which start as a stop, but release as an fricative instead of the explosion characteristic of usual stops. Sounds like [w] and [y] are called *glides* because the tongue changes position as they are produced; in effect, it glides in the mouth. Finally, [r] and [l] are called *liquids*; they produce no friction at all, much like vowels.

Consonants can be produced in various points in the articulatory tract. We have already seen that they can be produced with the lips or with the lips and teeth. These are *labial* and *labio-dental* sounds. Sounds such as the first consonants of *thing* and *that* are *interdentals*, so-called because the tongue is placed between the teeth. [t] and [d] are produced by placing the tongue against the bony ridge behind the teeth and stopping the air. This bony ridge is called the alveolar ridge. The first sound in <u>shine</u> [ʃ] is *palatal*; it is produced by moving the blade of the tongue to the palate. Is [ʃ] a stop or fricative? The sounds [k] and [g] are produced by moving the back of the tongue to the velum and stopping the air. The velum is the tissue behind the palate. When the velum is lowered, air can pass through the nose. When the velum is raised, air can pass only through the mouth. Finally, [h] is produced in the glottis. The glottis is the opening between the vocal cords in the larynx.

Finally, we can distinguish consonants by whether or not the vocal cords are vibrating. The difference between [s] in *sip* and [z] in *zip* is just the state of the vocal cords. They are made in the same way and at the same place, but when we produce [s] the vocal cords are not vibrating and when we produce [z] they are. You can verify this by place your fingers on your larynx (or stick your fingers in your ears) and contrasting [sssss] with [zzzzz]. You should be able to feel a buzz when producing the latter but not the former. We say that a sound like [z] is *voiced* and a sound like [s] is *voiceless*.

Usually, nasals, liquids, and glides are voiced. For our purposes, we will assume that they always are. However, stops and fricatives come in voiced and voiceless pairs.

Let us summarize this with a table (Table III.3) that categorizes each consonant and provides a key to illustrate how that consonant is produced. The table is based on the fact that consonants can be described on three parameters: place of articulation (the row on top), manner of articulation (the left hand column) and whether it is voiced or voiceless. You will note some unfamiliar symbols and perhaps some contrasts of which you were unaware. For example, many people are unaware that the initial sounds of *thing* and *that* are different. They are almost the same, but they differ in voicing.

Something else worth noting is that there are many gaps in the chart, many possible descriptions for which there is no corresponding symbol. In a few cases, this is because there is no possible corresponding sound. For example, it is not possible to produce a glottal nasal consonant. However, in most cases, the gap indicates only that there is no corresponding sound in English. If we investigate other languages

Table III.3: Consonant Chart

		Labial	Labiodental	Interdental	Dental	Palatal	Velar	Glottal
Stops	Voiceless	p *pride*			t *trip*		k *crime*	ʔ La_tin_
	Voiced	b *bride*			d *drip*		g *grime*	
Fricatives	Voiceless		f *few*	θ *thing*	s *sip*	ʃ *shine*		h *hot*
	Voiced		v *view*	ð *that*	z *zip*	ʒ *measure*		
Affricates	Voiceless					tʃ *church*		
	Voiced					dʒ *judge*		
Nasals	Voiced	m *met*			n *net*		ŋ *sing*	
Liquids	Voiced				l *late* r *rate*			
Glides	Voiced	w *wet*				y *yet*		

we will have to fill in these gaps, because those languages will contain these sounds. For example, German has both labiodental affricates (e.g., *Pfeffer*, "pepper") and dental affricates (e.g., *Zimmer*, "room", pronounced [tsɪmər]).

Having categorized the sounds that we are concerned with, we repeat our rules using phonetic orthography:

$$t \rightarrow \theta$$

$$p \rightarrow f$$

$$k \rightarrow h$$

When we compare [p], [t], and [k], we see that they are all voiceless stops. Similarly, when we compare [θ], [f], and [h], we note that they are all voiceless fricatives.

The general rule is:

voiceless stop → voiceless fricative (except after [s])

Table III.4 (next page) further illustrates that these three changes are the result of a single general rule.

Germanic Consonant Shift

The rule that we have isolated is, in fact, part of an even more general set of changes. This set is known as the Germanic Consonant Shift because it distinguishes the Germanic languages from the others in the Indo-European family. It was first proposed by Jacob Grimm in the 19th century and was known then as Grimm's Law. Jacob Grimm, with his brother Wilhelm, collected folk tales as part of their interest in German traditions and history.[8] They also researched the history of the German language as part of the general interest in Indo-European mentioned previously. Jacob Grimm discovered a series of changes that could be perceived as a single trend. This discovery was one of the foundations that established linguistics as science. Until then, the changes that languages undergo were perceived as random and haphazard. That Grimm was able to postulate a "Law" that described a major development in the history

---

8 The folk tales collected by the Grimm brothers are popularly known as *Grimm's Fairy Tales*. Many of them have entered popular culture. Familiar titles include *Snow White*, *Hansel and Gretel*, *Rapunzel*, *Cinderella*, and *The Golden Goose*, among many others. *National Geographic* presents some of the texts of these tales with audio at http://www.nationalgeographic.com/grimm/. The complete texts are available from http://www.familymanagement.com/literacy/grimms/grimms-toc.html, 1999.

Table III.4: Germanic Consonant Shift (Part I)

		Labial	Labiodental	Interdental	Dental	Palatal	Velar	Glottal
Stops	Voiceless	p *pride*			t *trip*		k *crime*	ʔ *La<u>t</u>in*
	Voiced	b *bride*			d *drip*		g *grime*	
Fricatives	Voiceless		f *few*	θ *thing*	s *sip*	ʃ *<u>sh</u>ine*		h *hot*
	Voiced		v *view*	ð *that*	z *zip*	ʒ *mea<u>s</u>ure*		
Affricates	Voiceless					tʃ *<u>church</u>*		
	Voiced					dʒ *ju<u>dg</u>e*		
Nasals	Voiced	m *met*			n *net*		ŋ *si<u>ng</u>*	
Liquids	Voiced				l *late* r *rate*			
Glides	Voiced	w *wet*				y *yet*		

of the Germanic languages suggested that there were underlying principles governing language change.

In this section, we will describe Germanic Consonant Shift—or, more romantically, Grimm's Law—and its reflection in the English lexicon. To do so, we will compare English with the classical languages Latin, Ancient Greek, and Sanskrit. Not many people understand much of the classical languages, so we won't use words directly from those languages. Instead, we will use words borrowed from them as they appear in English.

Borrowing

But that means that before examining Grimm's Law, we first need to establish the concept of *borrowing* and examine its effects in the English lexicon.

We have previously noted that every language must have mechanisms adding new words to the lexicon in the face of cultural and technological change. One of the mechanisms is derivational morphology, which permits us to create new lexemes. Another mechanism is *borrowing*, incorporating words from another language into our own lexicon. Examples of borrowing abound in English. Once we understand that English incorporates words from the languages of the cultures with which it has come in contact, it is easy to see borrowings. Table III.5 gives a very small sample of some borrowings from various languages. It should be evident in each case that these are not native English words, but words that have been taken from other languages.

Table III.5: A Sample of Borrowings

	sushi
Japanese	*origami*
	kimono
	algebra
Arabic	*algorithm*
	alcohol
	zero
	pizza
Italian	*spaghetti*
	casino
Malay	*orangutan*

Russian	*borscht*
	vodka
German	*blitzkrieg*
	schnitzel
Persian	*pajamas*
	checkmate
	brassiere
French	*detente*
	menu
Nahuatl	*chocolate*
	chili

Yiddish	schmaltz
	schmuck
	mensch

Irish	leprechaun
Spanish	taco
	salsa
Turkish	yogurt

In a sense, borrowing saves us the trouble of making up a new word. When a new word is required, we can just borrow from a language that already has the word that we need.

But, some also view borrowing as the erosion of the language. For example, the invasion of the computer into our economic, educational, and personal lives has made us familiar with numerous aspects of computer technology. In almost every language in the world, the words used to describe computer technology are borrowed from English. The dilemma faced by cultures that don't use English was humorously noted by the *Bangkok Post*:

> Russian MPs do not talk (*parlare*[9]) in parliament like most, they think (*dumat*, in Russian) in the Duma; last week the thinkers thought they should order the Academy of Sciences to find a new Russian equivalent for that darned *foreign* word 'computer', [the] thinkers thought the best replacement would be 'elektronno-vytchislitelnaya mashina', literally *electronic calculating machine*; no one thought to point out to the thinkers that two of the three words are foreign.[10]

Two of the languages from which English has frequently borrowed are Latin and Greek. The tradition began when Germanic tribes were warring with the Romans, and it continued with the influence of the Christian church on European culture. Latin and Greek were the principle languages in which the Christian religion was conducted until the 16th century, when the Bible was translated into local languages. Formal education was conducted in Latin and Greek in Europe, and, consequently, it was natural to extend its use to science and medicine as these disciplines matured.

The consequence of this history for English and other European languages is that whenever a term is required by science, religion, technology, or medicine, it is natural to look to Latin or Greek because there is already a history of coining words from those languages for concepts in these disciplines. In English and many other languages, the practice has extended further to include other sorts of activities, such as cuisine, diplomacy, fashion, etc.

---

9 Compare the French *parler* "to speak". The national governing institution in Canada is the Parliament.
10 *Bangkok Post Database Technology Section*, 11 November, 1998.

The observation by the *Bangkok Post* cited above illustrates that while we may notice that some words seem unusual, if not foreign, we are not always aware of borrowed words. One of the reasons we are not aware of borrowings is that they have become naturalized: over time, a word changes so that it aligns itself with the ways other words in the language are pronounced. Each language has strict rules on allowable sequences of sounds. If a word is borrowed with a sound sequence that is not permitted, that sequence will eventually be changed. For example, the spellings of *psychiatrist* and *pneumonia* represent how the words were pronounced in Greek. But English speakers do not tolerate the sequences *ps* and *pn* at the beginnings of words and so the pronunciation, though not the spelling, has become naturalized.

One can see naturalization at work when a word is borrowed twice from the same language at different periods. This situation has occured often with borrowings from French (for reasons that will be elucidated later).

The Germanic languages are distinguished by word initial stress. That is, under most circumstances, the first syllable in the word received the main stress. Since English is a Germanic language, native English words will show word initial stress. French, on the other hand, prefers word final stress. When English borrows a French word, it borrows the stress pattern as well. Thus, when a French word is first borrowed it will show French stress. However, if it is naturalized it will come to show the English word initial stress.

Table III.6 compares words that have been borrowed into English from French twice. Notice that the naturalized forms, the forms that have been in English longer, show stress on the first syllable (indicated by the accent of the vowel) while forms that are not naturalized show stress over the last syllable.

Table III.6: French Borrowings

Naturalized French Borrowing	French Borrowing
húman	humáne
úrban	urbáne
mínute (noun)	minúte (adjective)
sécond (noun)	secónd (verb)
pérsonal	personnél

As mentioned, there are some who believe that borrowing words is inappropriate. In some cultures, academies have been established to provide the appropriate word in the local language whenever there is a perceived need; occasionally, there are even legal mechanisms in place to ban borrowings from advertisements and business names. In English letters, George Orwell is famous for deriding the custom of using borrowings in English:

> Except for the useful abbreviations *i.e.*, *e.g.*, and *etc.*, there is no real need for any of the hundreds of foreign phrases now current in the English language. Bad writers, and especially scientific, political, and sociological writers, are nearly always haunted by the notion that Latin or Greek words are grander than Saxon ones, and unnecessary words like *expedite, ameliorate, predict, extraneous, deracinated, clandestine, subaqueous*, and hundreds of others constantly gain ground from their Anglo-Saxon numbers.... [T]he normal way of coining a new word is to use Latin or Greek root with the appropriate affix and, where necessary, the size formation. It is often easier to make up words of this kind (*deregionalize, impermissible, extramarital, non-fragmentary* and so forth) than to think up the English words that will cover one's meaning. The result, in general, is an increase in slovenliness and vagueness.[11]

Although many examples of bad writing may turn out to include large numbers of Latin and Greek words, these words are nonetheless explicitly defined and are often necessary. For example, *underwater* and *subaqueous* have parallel structures: a root meaning "water" and a prefix meaning "under". However, they do not mean the same thing. *Underwater* refers to a location while *subaqueous* was coined to refer to the condition of living underwater. This is a useful distinction and requires different words to make it.

On a recent occasion, the native English word has been judged by many to be completely inappropriate. Following the terrorist attacks on September 11, 2001 the Bush administration established a Department of Homeland Security. Many felt uneasy about the use of the word *Homeland*, preferring, among other possibilities, *Domestic*. This is a case where the borrowing is preferred over the native word. Mickey Kraus, writing in the on-line journal *Slate*,[12] identified three problems with the term *Homeland Security*:

1. It is un-American in at least two senses. First, it is not a word that Americans use and is "uncomfortably Teutonic-sounding". Second, it identifies the land as needing security rather than Americans generally or the abstract principle of freedom which most Americans feel is the foundation of their culture.

---

[11] George Orwell, "Politics and the English Language", in *A Collection of Essays* (Garden City, NY: Double Day, 1954) 162–177.

[12] Mickey Kaus, "The Trouble With 'Homeland'," *Slate* 14 June 2002 <http://www.slate.com/?id=2066978>.

2. It is too new. After the terrorist attacks, Americans needed reminders of familiar virtues rather than something that seems like a public relations maneuver.
3. It is creepy. Attempts by what will be a police force to hide behind a soft and cuddly name are frightening.

Orwell is right that Latin and Greek words often sound "grander", but that is one of the reasons that they are used. For example, the original term for the study of geology was *earth lore*, a term that doesn't carry quite the prestige of *geology*. There is a general feeling that a science deserves a name of appropriate status.

To return to the study of Grimm's Law, the fact that English has borrowed so heavily provides us with a mechanism for illustrating Grimm's Law without leaving the English language. We will compare English words with their cognates from the classical languages that have been borrowed into English. For example, the rule $p \rightarrow f$ is illustrated by the words *helicopter, pen*, and *feather*. The first is borrowed from Greek; it is composed of *helico-* (found in the word *helical*) and *-pter* (as in *pterodactyl*). The second originated in Latin and developed into a French word (see the family tree in Figure III.1) that was borrowed into English. Finally, the last is a native English word. Notice that the Greek and Latin words begin with p and that this p has developed into f in English; that the Greek root follows with t, which has developed into th [θ] in English (this t is obscured in Latin because it has become n), and that both the Greek and English forms refer to aspects of flight. The semantic relationship of the Latin borrowing *pen* may not be obvious until it is remembered that the original pens were quills made from feathers.

It is useful to have a notation to illustrate the relationships among cognates in English in order to distinguish those that are native to English from those that were borrowed from other languages and to chart the various histories of these words. How does one discover this information? A good dictionary will provide etymological[13] information about words.

For example, the *Merriam-Webster's Collegiate® Dictionary*, 11th Edition, gives the etymology of feather as:

> [ME *fether*, fr. OE; akin to OHG *federa* wing, L *petere* to go to, seek, Gk *petesthai* to fly, *piptein* to fall, *pteron* wing][14]

---

13 *Etymology*: from the Greek *etymon*, "true form" and *-ology* "science of". Etymology is the study of the original forms of words.
14 *Merriam-Webster's Collegiate® Dictionary*, 11th Edition. Springfield Mass., USA: Merriam-Webster Inc., 2003, p. 458. Unless otherwise specified, all further references to *Merriam-Webster's* are to this edition.

It is important to understand how information is represented in dictionary entries. The string *fr.* abbreviates *from*. Thus, the entry above states that *feather* developed from Middle English (ME) *fether*, which itself developed from Old English (OE). The word is cognate with—*akin to*—Old High German (OHG) *federa*, as well as Latin (L) *petere* and Greek (Gk) *pteron*. In fact, all of these are believed to have developed from the Indo-European base **pet*. Using this information, we can construct a partial tree (Figure III.3) showing the native development from Indo-European *pet* to English *feather*.

Figure III.3: *feather*

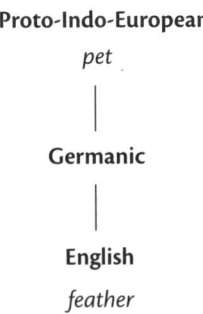

Proto-Indo-European
pet

Germanic

English
feather

We have ignored some of the details in Figure III.3, but have conveyed the central idea, that *feather* is directly descended from the Indo-European root *pet*. Not all dictionaries will give the Indo-European form. The actual form is not very important for our purposes: knowing Indo-European roots is not a valuable skill these days. But, recognizing the difference between native and borrowed words is a useful skill. And recognizing cognates can provide a comfortable English word to associate with less familiar Latin and Greek words.

The rest of the entry after the Indo-European root illustrates some of the developments in other Indo-European languages: for example, that the original root developed into Greek *pteron*.

We next examine the entry for *pen* from *Merriam-Webster's*:

> [ME *penne* fr. AF feather, pen fr. L *penna, pinna*, a feather; akin to Gk *pteron* wing—more at FEATHER][15]

We note first that *pen* developed from Middle English (ME) *penne*, which in turn comes from French (in this case Anglo-French (AF), the form of French spoken by the invading Normans). Our first question is whether this is a native word or a borrowing. If we consult the family tree in Figure III.1, we note that it cannot be a native word because English is not a daughter language of

---

15 p. 915.

Middle French. Instead, it must be a borrowing. Finally, we note that *pen*, as was *feather*, is cognate with—akin to—Greek *pteron*. This is the proof that *feather* and *pen* are cognates: they descend from the same word in the parent language. When we add this to our diagram, we require a notation that will distinguish native words from borrowings. We will adopt the convention of using solid lines to indicate native development and dashed lines to indicate borrowings. See Figure III.4.

Figure III.4: *feather* **and pen**

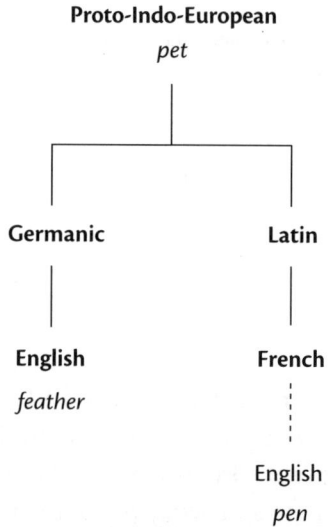

This example highlights the fact that many dictionaries do not distinguish borrowing from the evolution of word in its language. In other words, the word "from" is ambiguous and it is necessary to determine which of its two possible meanings are intended. To determine if a word is borrowed, it is necessary to refer to the family tree of languages. If the two languages in question are sisters, the word is borrowed. If they are in a mother/daughter relationship, the word developed natively.

Finally, the *pter* of *helicopter, pterodactyl,* and *dipterous* is borrowed from Greek. The vowel from the Indo-European base *pet* has been lost in Greek. This information is incorporated into the final diagram in Figure III.5.

Somewhat more subtle are words such as *legal*. The etymology given in *Merriam-Webster's* is:

> [AF, *legal* fr. L *legalis*, fr. *leg-*, *lex* law][16]

---

16 p. 710.

Figure III.5: *feather, pen,* and *helicopter*

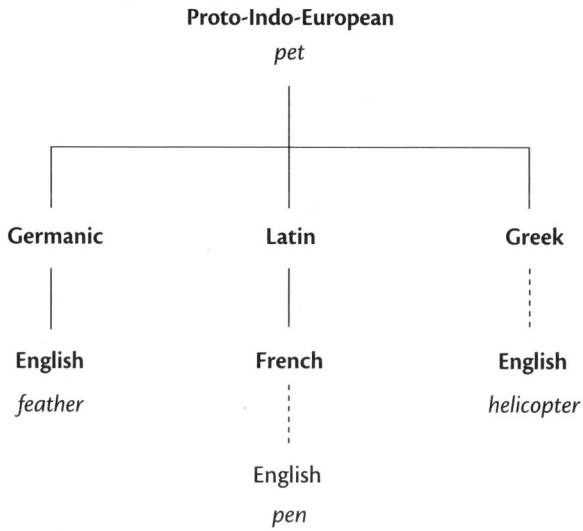

If we ask from where English inherited this word, the answer initially seems to be French, because the word was borrowed from French (again, from Anglo-French). However, if we follow its history we note that the word entered French from Latin. Tellingly, it did not develop from Latin into Old French. A check with Figure III.1 demonstrates that the evolution from Latin to Old French to Middle French is the natural development. Instead, *legal* skipped Old French and was borrowed into French from Latin. In this case, we will say that *legal* is Latin, despite its brief period in French.

Why make this subtle distinction? Because, when a word develops natively in a language, it is subject to the rules of that language. When it is borrowed, it is usually exempt from the majority of the rules of the new language and, for at least the period following its introduction into the new language, continues to behave as though it was in the original language, not in the new language. For example, the native development of Latin *legal* into French is *loyal*. Here we see a couple of common French rules in action: the change of *g* to *y* and the change of *ey* to *oy*. Compare also Latin *regal* and French *royal*. Although *legal* appeared in Middle French, the fact that it was borrowed and did not develop natively explains why it does not have the true French *oy*. Thus, we don't want to consider it as a French word, but as a Latin word.

Eventually, a word may become naturalized but in the intertwined histories of English and French this process did not occur in the class of words that have this kind of history.

In summary, if a word has developed natively from language X to language Y and is then borrowed into English, we will say it is a word of language Y, because it is subject to the rules of language Y. However, if a word is borrowed from language X to language Y and then is borrowed into English, we will say that it is a word of language X, because it is subject to the rules of language X.

A final example will further illustrate. The etymology of *lasagna* from *Merriam-Webster's* is:

> [It *lasagne* fr. VL **lasania*, cooking pot, its contents fr. L *lasanum*, chamber pot, fr. Gr *lasanon*][17]

If we follow its history to its origin, it first appears that this is a Greek word. It was borrowed from Greek into Latin. However, the development from Latin to Vulgar Latin (VL) to Italian is a native development (see Figure III.1), and so the word has undergone specifically Italian changes. As a consequence, we will say that it is an Italian word, not a Greek word, although it originated in Greek. As an Italian word, we expect it to follow the rules of Italian, not Greek. For example, the characters *gn* are used in Italian to represent the sound [ñ][18], a sound that did not exist in Greek.

Describing the Germanic Consonant Shift

With a firm understanding of the difference between a native development and borrowings, we can use borrowings in English to help illustrate Grimm's Law or the First Germanic Consonant Shift. In particular, we can use the borrowings from Latin and Greek and compare them with their true English cognates. In addition to studying this important event in the history of English, we should also be learning to distinguish native English words from borrowings, so that those who agree with Orwell can stop using them (and use the purely English word *whirlybird* to replace *helicopter*).

In the following, we will take the classical languages Latin and Greek as representative of the original sound that we are investigating. This works only because, for many of the sounds in which we will be interested, either Latin or Greek or both were unaffected, and we can use them to represent the original. This will work until we come to the last section on Grimm's Law where none of these languages retains the original sound.

Voiceless Stops

We have already examined the behaviour of the voiceless stops [p], [t], and [k] but it is useful to review. The general rule is:

> Voiceless stops became corresponding voiceless fricatives.

---

17 p. 701.
18 This is a palatal nasal.

Examples of these are:

Table III.7: p → f

Latin	Greek	English
pedestrian	podiatry	foot
paternal	patriarch	father
	pyre	fire
piscine		fish
lupus		wolf
plenty	plethora	full
paucity		few

Table III.8: t → θ

Latin	Greek	English
tertiary	tripod	three
tumescent		thumb
maternal	metropolis	mother
dentist	orthodontics	tooth
astonish	stentorian	thunder
pen	pterodactyl	feather

Table III.9: k → h

Latin	Greek	English
cordial	cardiac	heart
cornucopia	rhinoceros	horn
	cannabis	hemp
quality		who (< hwo)
century		hundred
canine		hound

Voiced Stops

Just as the voiceless stops behaved in concert, the voiced stops also underwent the shift together.

> Voiced stops became voiceless stops.

The voiced stops are [b], [d], and [g]. Each of these became its corresponding voiceless counterpart. Examples are given below.

Table III.10: b → p

Latin	English
vibrate	whip
labial	lip
cannabis	hemp

Table III.11: d → t

Latin	Greek	English
dental	masto<u>don</u>	tooth
edible		eat
domestic		tame
duo	<u>d</u>ilemma	two
deity		<u>T</u>uesday
pedal	tri<u>pod</u>	foot
persuade	he<u>d</u>onism	sweet

Table III.12: g → k

Latin	Greek	Sanskrit	English
<u>g</u>enuflect	poly<u>g</u>on		<u>k</u>nee
co<u>g</u>nition	dia<u>g</u>nosis		<u>k</u>now
margin			mark
sub<u>j</u>ugate	<u>z</u>ygote	yoga	yoke

Latin	Greek	Sanskrit	English
	gynecology		queen
fragile			break
	erg		work
gelatin			cool
vigilant			wake

Voiced Aspirates

It has been argued that Indo-European contained another series of stops in addition to the voiced and voiceless series. These stops were voiced aspirates, represented as [bh], [dh], and [gh]. They are just like the voiced stops, but accompanied by a puff of air, represented by the [h]. This series had a regular development in Germanic, but quite varied developments in Latin and Greek. Consequently, when we use Latin and Greek as our comparison set, we must first be prepared to "undo" the changes that affected them.

The changes affecting Greek are quite easy to state:

Voiced aspirates became voiceless aspirates.

That is, the following subrules applied in Greek:

bh → ph

dh → th

gh → kh

The changes affecting Latin are more varied and will be identified for each sound.

The shift of the aspirates in Germanic is as coherent as the non-aspirates:

Voiced aspirates became voiced non-aspirates.

That is, the aspirates lost their aspiration in Germanic. This general rule summarizes the following specific rules:

bh → b
dh → d

gh → g

Typically, the labial aspirate in Latin became [f]. Thus, in the following table, a Latin *f* or Greek *ph* represents an Indo-European [bh].

Table III.13: bh → b

Latin	Greek	English
f<u>rater</u>nity		brother
f<u>rag</u>ile		break
Lucif<u>er</u>	phos<u>phor</u>ous	bear (carry)
flagrant	phlegm	black
floral	chloro<u>phyll</u>	blossom
fundamental		bottom
	graphic	crab

The correspondences among Latin, Greek and English are not immediately obvious, even when explained a few times, so it is worth reviewing what these correspondences signify.

When we compared words like *paternal*, *patriarch*, and *father* to illustrate the rule *p* → *f*, we assumed the relationship illustrated in Figure III.6. Notice that both Latin and Greek retain the original sound [p]. It has only changed in English.

Figure III.6

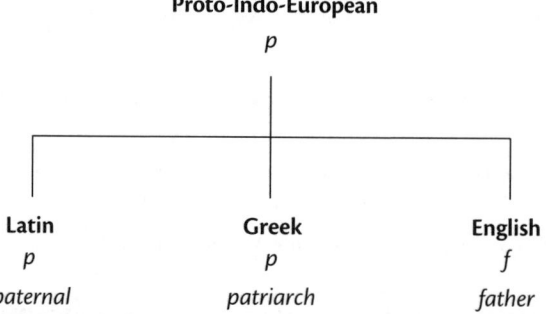

The situation is different when we consider the aspirates. These have undergone changes in Latin, Greek, and English. Consequently, when we compare cognates from each language, the Latin and Greek forms do not directly represent the original form. Instead, the relationships among the languages and to the original Indo-European form is that illustrated in Figure III.7

Figure III.7: The relationships among Latin [f], Greek [ph], and English [b]

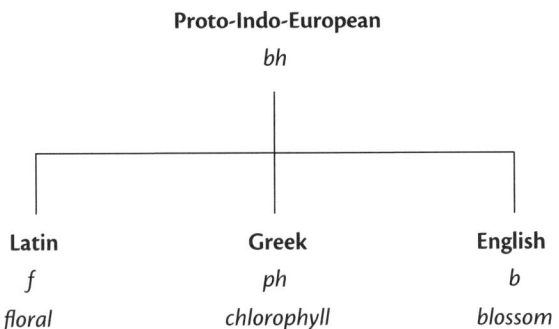

Notice that in this case, none of the languages represent the original. Instead, the original sound [bh] changed into [f] in Latin, [ph] in Greek, and [b] in English.

The development of [dh] is a bit more complicated in Latin. When it occurred at the beginning of a word it, like [bh], shifted to [f] (so that both English [d] and [b] can correspond to a Latin *f*). However, internal to the word, [dh] would shift to [b] if it was preceded by [r] or [u]. Thus, the first two examples below contain Latin words with the letter *b* which developed from an original [dh], while the rest contain Latin words with the letter *f* at the beginning of the word.

Table III.14: dh → d

Latin	Greek	English
ru<u>b</u>y	ery<u>th</u>ocyte	red
bar<u>b</u>er		beard
<u>f</u>orum	<u>th</u>yroid	door
<u>f</u>act	<u>th</u>esis	do
<u>f</u>igment		dike
	a<u>me</u>thyst	mead
<u>f</u>ume	<u>th</u>anatophobia	dull
in<u>f</u>erior		under
<u>f</u>uneral		die

Once again, the Latin and Greek forms do not directly represent the Indo-European form. Instead, it is necessary to recall that changes have applied to them as well. The relationship among Latin, Greek, and English is illustrated in Figure III.8.

Figure III.8: The relationships among Latin [f] and [b], Greek [th] ,and English [d]

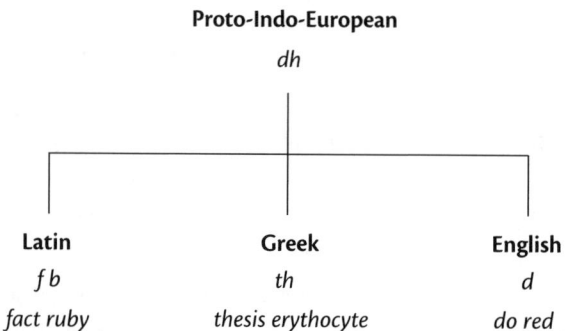

Finally, in Latin the velar aspirate [gh] lost the stop and became simply [h], and so the Latin examples in the following table represent an original [gh]. In the development of English, the [g] that developed from [gh] would often further develop to [y]. Note that this latter change (i.e., [g] → [y]) is a change in English, it is not part of the Germanic Consonant Shift.

Table III.15: gh → g (→ y)

Latin	Greek	English
host		guest
habit		give
horticulture		yard
	chlorine	yellow
vehicle		way

Summary

One of the immediately appealing characteristics of the Germanic Consonant Shift is its coherency. There seems to be a chain of related events. First, as we have seen, the individual rules cluster into more general rules (Table III.16).

Table III.16: The Germanic Consonant Shift

p → f	
t → θ	voiceless stops became voiceless fricatives
k → h	
b → p	
d → t	voiced stops became voiceless stops
g → k	
bh → b	
h → d	voiced aspirates became voiced stops
h → g	

Second, the shift itself seems to be organized as a chain pictured in Figure III.9. Each of the rules that comprise the Germanic Consonant Shift is connected with the others: the output of one is the input to another. This suggests that there might be a single rule responsible for all the changes.

Figure III.9: Germanic Consonant Shift

voiceless aspirates ← voiceless stops ← voiced stops ← voiced aspirates

The discovery of the Germanic Consonant Shift was one of the first descriptions of language change as a coherent rule-governed phenomenon and helped establish linguistics as a science in Europe.

Because the Germanic Consonant Shift played such a large role in the split of the Germanic language family, it is important to recognize its effects. And because English has borrowed so heavily from Latin and Greek, it can be used to recognize words from these languages and to determine their English cognates.

Because the focus of this text is on the English language, any discussion of history will necessarily include a discussion of the Indo-European language family, to the exclusion of other languages and language families.

The same work that has been done on Indo-European can be and has been done on other languages and language groups. This research has isolated several other major families, including the languages of North and South-East Asia, those of North and South America, of Africa and of the South Pacific.

Occasionally, this research uncovers some surprises. For example, Basque, the language of the mountainous region between Spain and France, is unrelated to any known language. Finno-Ugric, a language family which, if not unrelated to Indo-European, is exceedingly distant from it, includes both Finnish and Hungarian which are geographically separated by Indo-European languages.

There have been recent attempts to push the view of languages even farther back in history and to reconstruct a proto-language that includes as many of the major language families as possible. This reconstructed language is called *Nostratic*. Even this putative language does not yet extend to all existing languages. One of the major groups missing is the Sino-Tibetan group, which includes languages such as Cantonese, Mandarin, and Thai, among many others centered in Asia.

There has also been research tying language families to the genetic histories of their speakers in an attempt to map out the migrations of humans across the planet. There is, apparently, a good correlation between the patterning of languages around the world and the patterning of genes among their speakers.

Patterns of Borrowing

Although English borrows from virtually any language with which it comes in contact, the history of Europe and England has created definite conduits through which words flow into English. It is through these conduits that the bulk of English vocabulary is constructed. It is worth spending a moment to review them.

Greek

An important source of ideas in Western civilization is the culture of classical Greece. This culture created philosophy. Much of modern science is rooted in Greek thought, and Western medicine begins with Greek investigations. The Christian religion was first proselytized in Greece, and the books of the Christian bible were first written in Greek. Corresponding to this explosion of ideas was a similar explosion of new Greek words to name these ideas. Eventually, these words were imported into the languages of Europe as those cultures absorbed these new ideas. English is no exception. Throughout its history, English has been using Greek vocabulary in scientific, religious, medical, and philosophical discourse (Figure III.10).[19]

For example, *criterion* is borrowed directly from Greek. Its etymology is

[Gr *kritērion*, fr. *krinein* to judge, decide—more at CERTAIN][20]

---

19 Notice that the English branch of the family is abbreviated. In this section, we do not care particularly when a word entered English. Instead, we are concentrating on the history of the word before it entered the language.
20 *Merriam-Webster's* p. 296.

Figure III.10: Greek Borrowing I

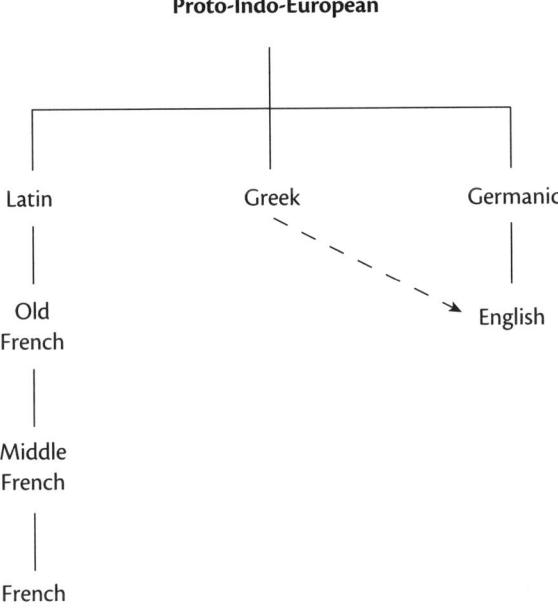

English is not the only language that borrows from Greek. As mentioned, Greek thought exploded out of that country into Europe. In the classical era, the Romans absorbed Greek thought, and, as a consequence, Greek words entered Latin vocabulary. When English borrows from Latin, it does not distinguish whether the words it borrows are native Latin words or Greek borrowings. As a consequence, Greek words enter English from Latin as well (Figure III.11).

Figure III.11: Greek Borrowing II

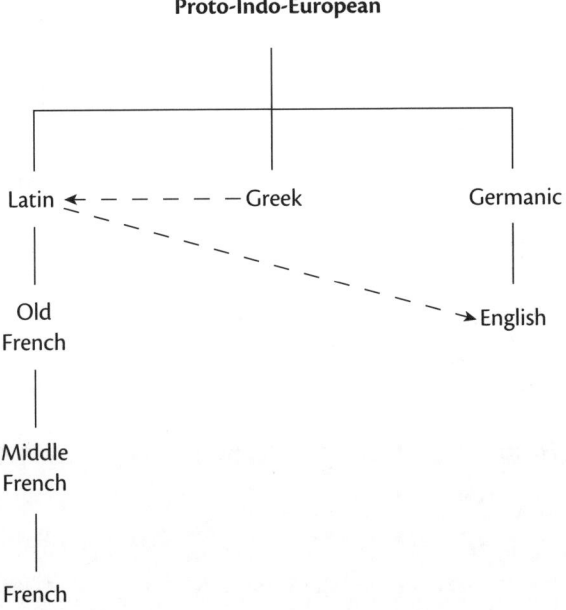

Chameleon is an example of a word that has been borrowed from Greek into English with a stopover in Latin. The etymology given by *Merriam-Webster's* is

[ME *camelion*, fr. MF, L *chamaeleon*, fr. Gk *chamaileōn*, fr. *chamai* on the ground + *leōn*, lion—more at HUMBLE][21]

Notice that although there are small changes in spelling, the word has not changed much. In fact, the Contemporary English spelling has changed from the Middle English so that it more closely resembles the original Greek. Contrast this with the example discussed previously in which Greek *lasanon* was borrowed into Latin but then developed into Italian to become *lasagna*. In that case, not only did the spelling change, but the pronunciation of the word itself changed. We want to say that *lasagna* has become an Italian word, but *chameleon* is still a Greek word.

In the Renaissance period, the influence of Greek continued. Latin and Greek were important languages of the Christian religion, of the growing scientific endeavor, and of medicine. As a consequence, Greek words appear in languages throughout Europe. One of these languages is French. Because the Norman French invaded and conquered England, English has borrowed large amounts of French vocabulary (see Chapter 13). Along with the French words, English accepted the Greek words that French had borrowed as well.

Figure III.12: Greek Borrowing III

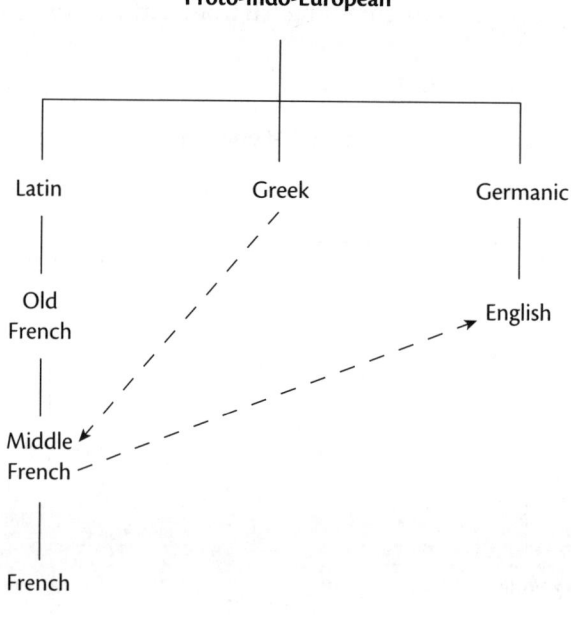

---

21 p. 205.

An example of a word with this sort of history is *odometer*. Its etymology is given by *Merriam-Webster's* as

> [F *odomètre*, fr. Gk *hodometron*, fr. *hodos* way, road + *metron* measure—more at MEASURE][22]

Again, we note that not much has changed about the form of the word. And so, we still consider the word to be a Greek word.

Latin

Greek was exported to the languages of Europe because Greek culture was so intellectually vibrant. Latin was similarly influential, perhaps more so. Whatever the merit of Roman intellectual life, however, Latin penetrated because the Romans militarily conquered Europe, and Latin either became the working language of the local area (as in those areas that eventually became France, Spain, Portugal, and so forth) or it was so influential in education, religion, law, that a culture such as that in England absorbed the words along with the concepts that it needed.

The influence that Latin has had on English vocabulary is documented in detail later. For the moment, we are satisfied with broad strokes. The first stroke is the observation made earlier that English borrows directly from Latin (Figure III.13). An example of a pure Latin borrowing is *restrict*.

Figure III.13: Latin Borrowing

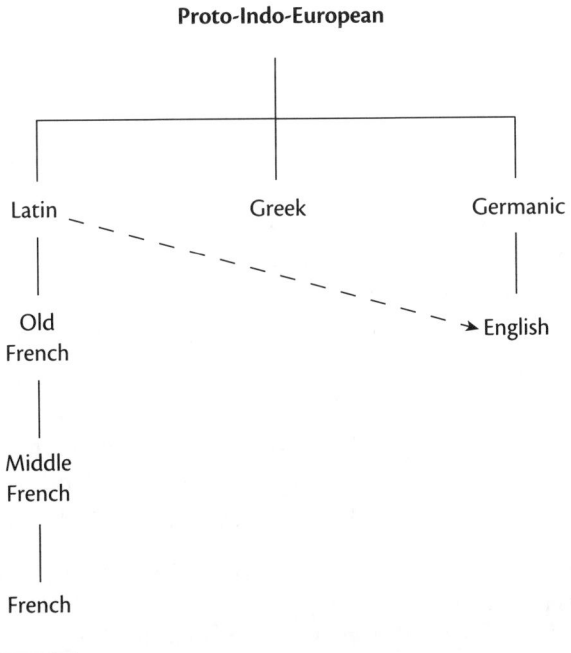

---

22 p. 860.

[L *restrictus*, pp. of *restringere*][23]

As Latin developed into French, English continued to borrow and so inherited French words. As noted below, the period in which Old French had contact with English was a particularly prolific period of borrowing of French words into English (see Figure III.16). An example of a French borrowing is *loyal*:

[Middle French, from Old French *leial, leel*, from Latin *legalis* legal][24]

Figure III.14: French borrowing I

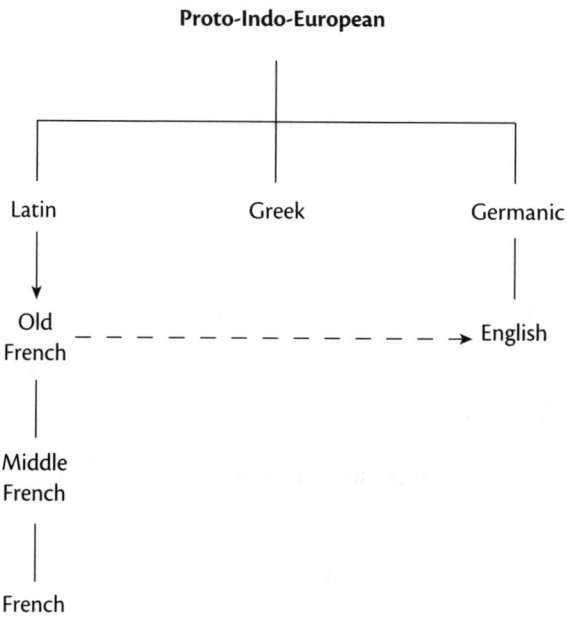

Notice that in this case, the word has developed from Latin into French and that part of this development is the conversion of [k] (*c*) to *i*, represented in English as *y*. We want to say that this is a French word because French imposed its rules on it. It now looks like a French word and not a Latin word.

As mentioned previously, Latin was the language in which science, education, and religion were conducted in Europe, and, consequently, Latin words appear throughout the languages of Europe. French is no exception; it, too, borrowed extensively from Latin. Consequently, we find that not only does English borrow words from French that have developed natively from Latin, it

---

23 *Merriam-Webster's* p. 1063.
24 "loyal." *Merriam-Webster's Online Dictionary*. 2005. <www.merriam-webster.com>.

also borrows words from French that French borrowed from Latin (much like Figure III.11 where English borrows Greek words from Latin, and Figure III.12 where English borrows Greek words from French). Figure III.15 fills in the last piece of the pattern: there is a conduit from Latin to French to English that is a simple chain of borrowings. In this case, we want to say that the word is a Latin word because it has not been naturalized by French. We have previously seen an example of this in the word *legal* (*legal*). Another example is *regal*

[ME, fr. AF or L; AF, fr. L regalis — more at ROYAL][25]

Figure III.15: Latinate Borrowing II

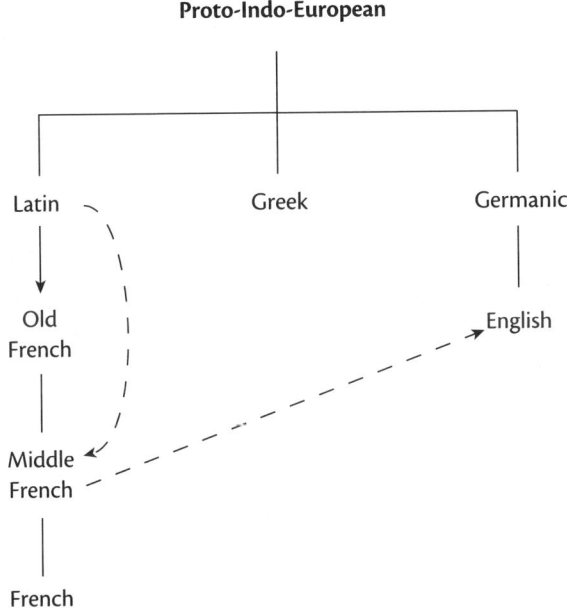

Notice that there is no indication that the word developed through Old French; instead it was borrowed by French from Latin. Notice again that, compared with *royal*, the French form, there has been little change in *regal*. The explanation for this is that because the word was borrowed into French from Latin, rather than developing natively, French rules had little effect on it and so it remains a Latin word.

Summary
In conclusion, there are three languages from which English has borrowed extensively: Greek, Latin, and French. Given the history of European thought, words from Greek and Latin have not always been borrowed directly into Eng-

---
25 *Merriam-Webster's* p. 1047.

lish, but we will, nonetheless, think of them as Greek and Latin words even though they may have had brief stops elsewhere. This is not typically troublesome because a word which originates in Greek, is borrowed into Latin, and then into English is recognizably Greek and the origin can be verified by comparing the Indo-European language family tree. Greek and Latin are sisters and so the conduit from Greek to Latin is borrowing and not the evolution of a Greek word into a Latin word.

However, the concept is sometimes fuzzy when one worries about whether a word is French or Latin because French is a daughter of Latin and so it is possible for a word to evolve from a Latin word into a French one or to be borrowed without change from Latin. As a rule of thumb, we will say that if a word can be shown to have developed from Latin into Old French (as did *pray*) then it will be considered to have evolved into a French word. On the other hand, if it appears in French without having developed into Old French from Latin, then it will not be considered as a French word. Instead, we will say that it was borrowed from Latin into French and is a Latin word. This heuristic parallels the one used previously to determine whether a word is English: when it can be determined that a word developed into Old English and from there into Contemporary English, then we consider it to be an English word.

It is worth emphasizing that this is a heuristic that does not always get at the notion of *associated language* that is important to our study. That is because the dictionary is tracing the history of a word from language to language without documenting the effect of its evolution, much as one could give one's biography without commenting on the effect that incidents in one's life had. Such a biography would not be enlightening to the reader because it would have no explanatory value; it would not indicate how character is built from one's experiences.

The effect that we are interested in is the set of rules that a word obeys. That set might seem to be obviously English since all the words discussed here are part of the English language, but since many words in English are borrowed from different languages, they each can potentially obey either the rules of the language in which they originated or the rules of English or even some combination of both.

Periods of Latinate Borrowing

Throughout its history, English has had contact with Latin. Even before English existed, the Germanic tribes borrowed from Latin and English still contains some of these words. This pattern of borrowing, established in the Germanic period, continued when English was established and continues into the modern period. Coincident with the evolution of English was the evolution of Latin into the Romance languages (see Figure III.1). One of these, which had an important influence on English, was French. English began to borrow significantly from

Old French and continues to borrow from French in the present era. The network of relations between Latin and English is illustrated in Figure III.16. The task of this section is to tease apart this network and illustrate each period.

Figure III.16: Periods of Latinate Borrowing

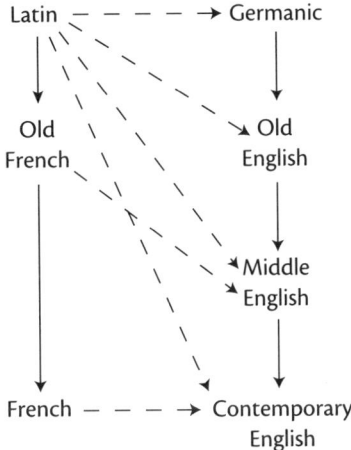

The Germanic Period

Table III.17 gives examples of words that were borrowed from Latin into the Germanic languages, that is, borrowed before the 5th century. These words have persisted into Contemporary English. The forms cited as the Germanic Borrowing are given in their Contemporary English forms. When they were borrowed into the Germanic languages, they resembled the Latin form. Thus, the Contemporary English form shows the changes that have occurred since the word was borrowed. In some cases, an English Borrowing is also cited. In these cases, English has borrowed the same Latin form at a later period. The relationship that we are interested in is indicated by the dotted lines in Figure III.17.

Figure III.17: The Germanic Period

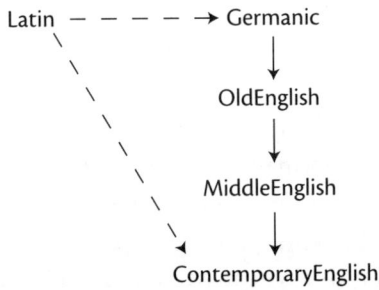

Note that in many cases the same word has entered English on two separate occasions. The column labelled **Germanic Borrowing** contains words that were borrowed in the Germanic period. The column labelled **English Borrowing** contains words that were borrowed more recently.

Table III.17

Latin	Germanic Borrowing	English Borrowing
balteus	belt	
episcopus	bishop	Episcopalian
butyrum	butter	butylene
cupa	cup	cupola
discus	dish	disk
furca	fork	bifurcate
cucina	kitchen	
piper	pepper	piperine
moneta	money	monetary
catillus	kettle	
vinum	wine	vinegar

Two general comments can be made about borrowings from this period. First, like archeologists, we can discern something about the culture of the Germanic peoples by the words they found it necessary to borrow. Notice that many are concerned with food, its preparation and the utensils used to eat it. Rome was much more sophisticated in its cuisine than the warrior Germanic tribes and the Germans adopted many aspects of Roman food and culture. The fact that the Germans did not have words for implements like forks and dishes says something about their eating habits.

We see also bits of Roman society entering the German lexicon. Words like *money* indicate that the Germans were moving away from a barter economy. Importantly, a word like *bishop* shows the beginning of the penetration of religious terms.

A second comment is that we can perceive sound changes that created Contemporary English by comparing the words borrowed during the Germanic period with those borrowed in the modern era. When these words were originally borrowed, they resembled the Latin. As English changed, they changed as well reflecting the new rules in the language. For example, comparing *discus* with *dish*, and *episcopus* with *bishop*, we can see the rule:

sk → ʃ

We can also find this rule in English *fish*, which is cognate with Latin *piscis*.[26]

We can date this change relative to the Viking raids along the coast of England, which began in the late 8th and continued for at least a century. The Vikings (or Norse) originated in northern Europe. After the period of raids, the Viking settled in Northern England. Because of the contact between the English and the Norse, English borrowed words from Norse (Table III.18). Interestingly, the words borrowed from Norse do not show the shift *sk* → ʃ. This indicates that the rule had died by the time of the Viking raids.

Table III.18: Norse Borrowings

Norse Borrowing [sk][2]	Native English [ʃ]
skirt	shirt
skiff	ship
skoff	shove
scab	shave
scall	shell
scar	shear
scrod	shred

This is an important notion: a rule will enter a language and, once it has worked its way through the lexicon, die out. In this sense, a rule is a bit like a virus which propagates itself throughout the organism just as the rule propagates through the lexicon. In the linguistic case, the Norse borrowings show that the rule died out before the encounter with the Norse. The English words show *sk* → ʃ, but the Norse words do not.

---

26 Recall first that these rules apply to sounds, not letters. The sequence *sc* in Latin represented the sound sequence [sk]. The symbol [ʃ] represents the first sound of <u>sheep</u>.

Words like *dish* also provide an opportunity to revisit the notion that a word can be associated with a particular language. The etymology given by *Merriam-Webster's* is:

> [ME, fr. OE *disc* plate, fr. L *discus* quoit, disk, dish, fr. Gk *diskos*, fr. *dikein* to throw][27]

If we add the detail that this word was not borrowed directly into Old English but rather into Proto-Germanic, this etymology gives in text the sequence of events illustrated in Figure III.17. Germanic (*PGmc*) borrowed the word from Latin. It subsequently developed into Old English and then into Middle English. Is it then a Latin word or an English word? It originated in Latin so the dictionary etymology indicates that it is a Latin word. But, this etymology would not explain why it is not pronounced like a Latin word. Specifically, why is it *dish* and not *disc* or *disk*? The heuristic that if a word developed from Old English through to Modern English then it is English would identify it as English.

Which rules does *dish* obey? We have seen previously that the rule $sk \rightarrow \int$ is an English rule, so, in this regard at least, it is obeying English rules. The heuristic gets the identification right.

The Old English Period

The charts of the Indo-European family, such as that provided at the beginning of this chapter, suggest that it is possible to follow a natural evolution from Proto-Indo-European through a Germanic mother language to the languages of today. While it may in principle be possible to chart such an evolution for a language such as German or French—and some would argue that it is not, because of the many social and linguistic influences of other cultures—the origin of English is much less tidy. In fact, Old English is less the daughter of a Germanic mother language than a hybrid of various Germanic dialects.

Prior to the development of Old English, the languages of what is now the island of England were Celtic. Julius Caesar invaded the island of England in 55 BCE and named it *Britannia*, whence came the name *Britain*. The Romans occupied Britain until the early 5th century. During this period, the Celtic languages persisted, although the language of the conquerors was Latin.

The conquest of England by the Germanic tribes began in the mid 5th century. The Roman troops had by this time withdrawn to defend Rome against the Huns and Goths, also Germanic tribes. The German invaders of England, largely composed of the Saxons, Angles (*England = land of the Angles*), Jutes, and Frisians found the country largely undefended except by the remaining Britons, who were by this time exhausted from the long occupation by the

---

[27] p. 359.

Romans and wars with other Celtic tribes. The Picts and Scots, also Celtic tribes, had been regularly and successfully warring with the Britons. The Britons petitioned what were then the three most prominent German nations:[28] the Jutes, Angles, and Saxons for help. The Germans came and fought beside the Britons. After defeating the Picts and Scots, the invading Germans turned their attention to the Britons and defeated them as well. For the next century, there was a constant migration from Continental Europe to England of speakers of the various Germanic dialects enticed by the opportunities in a conquered land. Inevitably, the Britons were completely displaced and either fled to other countries or were assimilated.

The conquest of the Celts took approximately two centuries to complete, although one could argue that it continues to this day. It was during this period that the legend of King Arthur and Camelot arose. He was supposedly a Welsh king who led several successful campaigns against the invading Germans.

The language we call Old English was established during this period as the Angles and the Saxons coalesced (hence the term *Anglo-Saxon*), although there was still considerable dialectal variation throughout England, if only because speakers of different Germanic dialects had landed in different parts of the country. One of the seminal periods was during the northern invasion by the Vikings. King Alfred the Great raised an army to combat the Vikings and push them north. Eventually, a treaty was struck and the Vikings settled into the north. In an effort to both improve the education system, which had been damaged during the Viking wars, and to unite the country under a common language, Alfred had a number of important works translated into Anglo-Saxon, the dialect spoken in the south, as a way of promoting that language.

Old English continued the practice of borrowing terms from Latin. The reasons for borrowing from Latin during this period was that Latin was the language in which the Christian Bible was presented and so was the language of religion for that area at that time Latin had also been established in Europe as the language of education and scholarship. These are intellectual areas that generate new ideas, it was appropriate that the language in which they were conducted contributed the words for these new ideas. This period is illustrated in Figure III.18. Examples are given in Table III.19.

Figure III.18

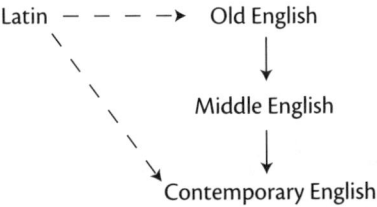

---

28 According to the Venerable Bede, whose *Ecclesiastical History of the English Nation*, completed around 730 CE, is the standard reference.

Table III.19: Latin Borrowings into Old English

Latin	Old English Borrowing	English Borrowing
ancora	anchor	
candela	candle	candelabra
cocus	cook	
credo	creed	credible
discipulus	disciple	
febris	fever	febrile
martyr	martyr	
monasterium	minister	monastery
nonna	nun	
schola	school	scholar
presbyter	priest	Presbyterian
sericus	silk	sericulture
soccus	sock	

A quick scan of Table III.19 reveals four important semantic domains of borrowing: religion, food, clothing, and education. There were other areas of borrowing as well, but these establish a basic pattern that will continue throughout the relationship between English and Latin, and daughter, French.

The Middle English Period

The Middle English period begins with the invasion of English by the Norman French in 1066 and ends with the re-establishment of English as the language of government in the 15th century and eventually the establishment of the London dialect as the prestige dialect. This period is characterized by the continuing borrowing from Latin and the introduction of massive numbers of French words (Figure III.19).

Figure III.19

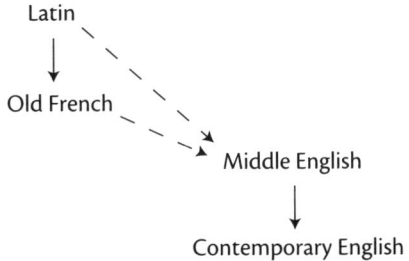

Table III.20 illustrates a few borrowings from Latin into Middle English. It is useful to note that they have not changed much since they were borrowed into the language in contrast to those that were borrowed during the Germanic and Old English periods. The general principle illustrated here is that the longer a word has been in a language, the more it will diverge from its etymon and the more it will resemble words in the new language because more rules will have applied to it than to a more recently borrowed word. Recall that this process is called *naturalization*.

Table III.20: Latin Borrowings into Middle English

Latin	Middle English Borrowing
submittere	submit
scriba	scribe
minor	minor
solitarius	solitary
reprehendere	reprehend
scriptura	scripture

The Middle English period is marked by the influence of French. French words penetrate almost all semantic domains, indicating that French was used in most social circumstances (Table III.21).

Table III.21: Old French Borrowings into Middle English

Old French	Middle English Borrowing
blasme	blame
art	art
sergent	sergeant
digneté	dignity
lettre	letter
chapitre	chapter
trinite	trinity
traitre	traitor
cape	cape
medecien	medicine

Again, we note that the words borrowed into Middle English from French are little changed from the original French.

Contemporary English

In the contemporary period, the practice of using Latin forms to name new objects and ideas is pervasive (Table III.22). Because Latin was the language of science throughout Europe, much scientific terminology derives from Latin. Most of biological nomenclature is Latin. Consider some of the modern borrowings.

Table III.22: Latin Borrowings into Contemporary English

nucleus	stamen
larva	tuber
serum	inertia
insomnia	auditorium
maximum	rabies
lens	tedious

It is useful to notice that these don't look like regular English words. Some of them end with *a* or *ia* which is not typical English, nor are the *um* and *ium* endings. The sequence of *eu* in *nucleus* is also unusual. Observations such as these help to locate the language from which the word is borrowed.

The trend to borrow from French continues to the modern era. As before, French borrowings penetrate every aspect of social life. In particular, French terms for fashion, cuisine, and politics dominate.

Table III.23: French Borrowings into Contemporary English

décolletage	menu
chaffeur	foyer
café	limousine
fiancé(e)	elite
lingerie	coupon
laissez faire	détente
restaurant	cliché

George Orwell didn't like it, but the French terms have a cachet that the corresponding English words do not. *Lingerie* is more attractive than *underwear*, a *chauffeur* has higher status than a *driver*, and a *laissez faire* policy doesn't sound as apathetic as *let them do as they please*.

The modern period is characterized in Figure III.20.

Figure III.20

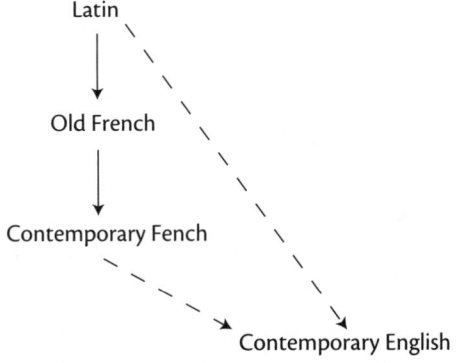

Summary

This brief examination of the relationship between English and Latin shows that English has relied on Latin for parts of its vocabulary since before English existed. And even after Latin ceased to exist as a living language, English continued to borrow from it. The invasion of English by the French extended the borrowing from Latin to borrowing from its daughter as well.

Conclusion

The process of borrowing is an important mechanism by which the vocabulary of a language can be enriched. It is probable that no culture that is in contact with others does not borrow words. When we scan the words from the preceding sections, we note that they are perfectly good words and serve valuable functions. Sometimes their existence provides nuances of meaning that would not be possible if they did not exist. Compare, for example, the difference between *fragile* and *breakable*. The former suggests a delicacy that the latter does not.

New ideas, inventions, and the opportunity to express nuances of meaning are not the only reasons a language will borrow words. Borrowed words can be used to circumvent *taboo*[29] words, words that can no longer be used in polite discourse. These words place speakers in a difficult position if they find themselves in a situation where they must talk about the subjects to which the taboo words refer. The taboo against the words removes the very vocabulary that are needed to discuss the subject.

In English, words referring to male and female genitalia have become taboo. Nonetheless, we have reason to discuss them on occasion, if only with our doctors. Yet, even with a doctor, we do not use the native English words. The problem has been circumvented by words borrowed from another language—Latin, in this case—and designated as the polite forms. Thus, words like *penis*, *testicle*, and *vagina* are suitable for polite discourse, where their English synonyms are not. This is a common solution to the problem of taboo words and highlights an important function of borrowed words. Although Orwell thought that the "grander" sound of borrowings from Greek and Latin leads writers to use them inappropriately, it is this very property that protects these words from becoming taboo, as the English words unfortunately did.

This chapter has introduced one of the ways in which the English lexicon can be divided: by language of origin. In addition to Greek and Latin, English has also borrowed heavily from French. There are, thus, four major divisions in the lexicon. What is the effect of this? There are many effects, but, for the moment, consider spelling rules. Anyone who has studied English spelling has learned the following rule:

---

29 *Taboo*: from Polynesian. A taboo is a social prohibition against certain actions, people, things, or words.

> *i* before *e* except after *c*

The rule is intended to help writers to remember how to spell words like *piece* and *deceive*. Unfortunately, there are numerous exceptions: for example, *height, sleigh, weigh, eight, heifer, neighbour,* and *weird*. The property that these latter words share is that they are all English words. The words that obey the rule are French words (although not all French words follow the rule: see *beige, surfeit* and *seize*). Greek words don't follow the rule either: see *seismic*. The point, then, is that if we want to correctly apply a spelling rule we must start by correctly identifying the language from which the word originates.

We can turn spelling rules around and use them to identify the language from which a word originates. For example, asking someone to spell words like *amethyst, erythocyte,* and *metropolis* may make them uncomfortable because these don't look like common English words. In fact, we know now that they are Greek words. How can we identify them as such?

The first two demonstrate a spelling convention used for Greek transliteration: the use of *y* to represent a vowel internally. Normally, contemporary English spelling conventions use *y* only at the ends of words to represent [i] as in *lively*.[30] Greek transliteration uses *y* internally, where English never would, and so can be used to recognize Greek borrowings.

> If the word contains y internally (and it is not a compound like *copycat*), then it is likely a Greek borrowing.[31]

Notice that English spelling conventions will usually use an *i* internally when the same form has a *y* otherwise; compare *happy* and *happiness*.

The word *metropolis* illustrates another clue to look for: unusual letter combinations. English words do not end in *is*. If we were to naively assume that *metropolis* is a plural noun (and the *-s* normally represents the plural) then the singular would be *metropoli*. This is not a possible ending for an English word.

Finally, the division of the lexicon into Latin, Greek, French, and English units can also be viewed as divisions in time. Just as a geologist can stand in a river valley and see the different deposits as different layers in time, we can examine the English lexicon and see different stages of parts of the Indo-European language family.

---

30 Older English spelling rules did use *y* in other environments than the end of a word to represent vowels, but this practice has been dropped. It has a residue in the infrequently used, and consequently stubborn, *yclept* and in British spellings such as *tyre*, as opposed to the North American *tire*.

31 There are a few borrowings from French which have an internal *y*: e.g., *royal* and *loyal*. In French, these were spelled with *i* (*roial* and *loial*), and the *y* was substituted when they were borrowed into English.

Further Reading

Baly, Joseph. *Eur-Aryan Roots: With their English Derivatives and the Corresponding Words in the Cognate Languages Compared and Systematically Arranged.* London: K. Paul, Trench, Trubner, 1897.

Buck, Carl Darling. *A Dictionary of Selected Synonyms in the Principal Indo-European Languages: A Contribution to the History of Ideas.* Chicago: University of Chicago Press, 1949.

Cavalli-Sforza, L. L. *Genes, Peoples, and Languages.* New York: North Point Press, 2000.

Davies, Peter. *Roots: Family Histories of Familiar Words.* New York: McGraw-Hill, 1981.

Diamond, Jared. *The Third Chimpanzee.* New York: Harper Collins Publishers, 1992.

Dolgopolskii, A. *The Nostratic Macrofamily and Linguistic Palaeontology.* Cambridge: McDonald Institute for Archaeological Research, 1998.

Dunbar, Robin. *Grooming, Gossip and the Evolution of Language.* Cambridge, Mass.: Harvard University Press, 1996.

Freeborn, Dennis. *From Old English to Standard English: A Course Book in Language Variation across Time.* Ottawa: University of Ottawa Press, 1998.

Pyles, Thomas. *The Origins and Development of the English Language.* 4th ed. New York: Harcourt Brace Javonovich, 1993.

Renfrew, Colin. "The Origins of Indo-European Languages." in *The Emergence of Language: Development and Evolution*, edited by . S-Y. Wang, 46–58. New York: W. H. Freeman and Co., 1991.

4 The Alphabet

Introduction

One of the most important inventions in human history is writing, the ability to record our thoughts. A system of writing confers two advantages. First, it extends the range of our communication both in time and geography. A writing system allows us to communicate with others outside of shouting range. Once something is written down, it can be sent as far as anyone can travel. We can also send messages to those who are not yet born, thereby providing a powerful mechanism for cultural transmission. Thus, a writing system allows us to transmit ideas and culture over long distances and down through the generations. The ability to write releases us from the prison of the moment: we are no longer limited to just those in our immediate presence when we communicate. This is a tremendous advantage.

The second advantage is the extension to our memory that a writing system offers. There is a kind of cultural memory that important texts encode and transmit to each succeeding generation. But, a writing system provides a personal memory upgrade as well. We can write important things down and, as long as we don't lose the record, never worry about forgetting them, because even if the memory trace in our brain vanishes the physical record is always there to remind us.

We can distinguish among a number of different kinds of writing systems based on what the symbols represent. The earliest form of writing was a *pictographic* system. In this system, the symbols are actual pictures of the objects that they represent. For example, a tree would be represented as a picture of a tree. There are some obvious disadvantages to a purely pictographic system. First, not everyone is an adequate artist. Those of us who have no artistic skill may have difficulty communicating with others because our "art" is indecipherable. If our dog looks like a cat, and our horses and cows are indistinguishable from each other and from our dogs and cats, people trying to read our messages will be very confused.

A second disadvantage to a purely pictographic system is that some concepts are not obviously pictured. How does one draw *beauty* or *evil* or *mind*? Abstract concepts like these do not have obvious physical representation. How does one draw *son*? A picture of a boy doesn't convey the concept *son* because it is indistinguishable from the concept *boy*.

One way to work around the representation of an abstract concept is to borrow the symbol for a concrete object whose name is a homophone[1] for that of the abstract concept. For example, if we were doing this in English we might represent the concept *son* with the symbol that we are already using for *sun*. We do this quite often with letters and numbers when we are write *b4* instead of *before* or *k9* instead of *canine*. This trick is called a *rebus*[2] and plays an important role in the history of writing systems because it begins the process of associating symbols with sounds in the language, instead of pictures or concepts.

Because of the difficulty of representing abstract concepts, a natural progression of a pictographic writing system is to an *ideographic* system. In such a system, a symbol represents a concept, abstract or concrete. A system like this has certain advantages. It has greater expressiveness than a pictographic system. And, unlike a writing system in which symbols represent sounds, an ideographic system is understandable by speakers of different languages. Thus, although two people may not understand each other when they talk, they could write in a shared ideographic system and crudely communicate. Furthermore, unless the ideographs change over time, it is possible to read literature written in an ideographic system even if the language itself has changed significantly. As we saw in Chapter 2, this is not so easy in systems where the orthography roughly represents how words are pronounced, as it does in the English system.

The move to a writing system in which the symbols represent sounds, rather than concepts, significantly reduces the number of symbols required. After all, an ideographic system requires a separate symbol for each noncompositional concept. It might be possible to represent *mother* and *father* as composed of the concept *parent* and the concepts *female* and *male* respectively, but a vast number of symbols will nonetheless be required. The number of sounds in a language is vastly less than the number of concepts that a language must potentially represent.

A writing system in which symbols represent syllables is a *syllabary*. For example, we could have separate symbols for the syllables *ki, ka, ko, ku*. A language with considerable constraints on syllable structure could have a manageable number of possible syllables and consequently require a relatively small number of symbols for its writing system. Japanese is such a language. The preferred

---

1 *Homophone*: from the Greek *homo*, "same", and *phone*, "sound". Homophones are words that sound identical. For example, *to, too,* and *two* are homophones.
2 *Rebus*: from the Latin *res*, "thing". *Rebus* is the ablative plural of *res* and could be glossed as "(meaning is signified) by the things".

syllable structure is CV; that is, a consonant followed by a vowel. Japanese does not permit a syllable to end in any other consonant but *n*. As it turns out, Japanese uses two syllabaries, the *katakana* and *hiragana*.

An *alphabet* is a writing system in which each symbol ideally represents a single sound. We must qualify this definition for a couple of reasons. First, although a writing system might meet the ideal when first applied to a language, the language changes faster than does the writing system and so the relationship between them becomes distorted. The English spelling system is a good example of this. What is the purpose of *k* in *knee*, *knight*, and *know*? At the time the spelling system was set, the character *k* was necessary to represent the first sound of these words, the same sound as the first consonant in *kick*. Over the course of time, this sound was dropped in *knee*, *knight*, and *know*, but the spelling of these words was not changed to reflect this.

The second reason for hedging the definition a bit is that we usually don't want to represent every possible sound in a language, we only want to represent those that are distinctive.[3] For example, those whose first language is English will pronounce the first consonant of a word like *pit* with an accompanying puff of air, as though it was followed by an *h*.[4] We probably don't want English orthography to represent this because English speakers are unaware of it; it makes no difference if the puff of air is present or not; English speakers still understand the word, although it sounds a bit odd if it is not there. For most Canadian speakers, the vowels of *ride* and *write* are different. This difference is part of what constitutes the Canadian dialect. Although the difference in these vowels is demonstrable, it would not be sensible to develop a Canadian spelling of these words, first because it would separate Canadian texts from others of the English speaking world, and second, and most importantly, because Canadian speakers themselves are largely unaware of the difference. They recognize speakers who do not make the difference as non-Canadians but likely could not say why.

A final reason for the hedge is that sometimes we don't want the orthographic system to accurately represent the sounds at all. For example, it should be clear that *native* and *nation*, or *create* and *creation*, are related words (in some sense that we need to make clear). However, the *t* of *native* and the *t* of *nation* do not represent the same sound. If we represented them the way they are pronounced, we might spell them as *native* and *nashon*. We don't spell them this way because it is useful to use the orthography to signal relationships among words, rather than how they are pronounced.

---

3 However, in a truly phonetic alphabet used by linguists, we do want to represent everything. See Chapter 2.
4 A native speaker of English can feel this puff of air by holding one's hand in front of one's mouth while saying the word *pit*. Contrast this with the word *spit*, where there is no puff.

In order to develop a syllabary or alphabet, it is necessary to do a deeper analysis of the sounds and words of language than is required for a simple pictographic system. It is necessary to understand what the distinctive sounds of the language are. Again this is not as obvious as it seems. As noted above, the English spelling *pit* doesn't represent all the sounds in that word because the aspiration on the consonant represented by *p* is not significant. Moreover, we use the same symbol in *spit* although if we performed acoustic measurements, we would discover that the separate uses of *p* represent different sounds and in a different language (like Thai) those differences would be significant. It is useful to use the same symbol for these different sounds because they are related and English speakers do not hear the difference. In fact, English speakers would simply be confused if it was insisted that these are different sounds and deserve different symbols.

These considerations are indicative of the kind of linguistic work that must be done in a culture before it can become literate. Another bit of work that must be done is the recognition of the notion of *word*; it must become possible for everyone to agree about how a written sentence can be divided up into words. This is also not self-evident. For example, is *hothouse* one word or two? English orthographic conventions usually require that we place a space between words, so it seems that it is one word. But quite clearly, it is composed of two words.

History of the Alphabet

Although we speak of *the* alphabet, there is some debate over how many times this trick has been invented. Most of the alphabets that are currently in use descend from the same source: the Greek alphabet. Others, such as that used for Thai, from the Devanagari. There are others such as the Korean *hangul* which do not seem to be descended from either. However, there is debate about whether they were invented *de novo* or were created after exposure to one of the original alphabets and influenced by that exposure.

We will concentrate on the development of the alphabet used for representing English, keeping in mind that similar processes were likely at work in the development of others.

Origins

The earliest writing systems were not originally based on sounds; they were instead pictographic systems. In fact, the earliest was not originally a system of writing but of images molded from clay. Like so much of human activity, it was born of a need to keep records of business transactions.

Imagine that you are in business in ancient Mesopotamia. You trade with farmers for cows and sheep, and move the cows and sheep to another town to barter for finished goods like amphorae and blankets. If you don't have anything to give the farmers to begin with, you can promise to return with goods that you will give to the farmer in exchange for the cows and sheep that he gave you to trade. However, now you need a method to represent how many cows and sheep you owe the farmer so that both of you have a record.

The first method that was devised to keep records of business transactions and debts was molding clay images of the objects that were part of the trade. If you owe the farmer five cows, you could each keep five little sculptures of cows to remind you.

However, if you are not an honest trader, you might "lose" one of the sculptures and claim later that the original deal was for only four cows. Or, the farmer might mold a sixth image and claim that you owe him goods for six not five cows. To keep everyone honest, people began to put the images in clay envelopes and fired them in an oven into a kind of pottery. Now, both partners could keep their envelopes until the trader returned, at which time they would smash them open and verify how many cows and sheep were owed. If one of the partners broke their envelope prematurely, then the other could take some sort of legal action against him.

Now, suppose that you are a successful trader and instead of trading with one farmer, you trade with several before herding the animals to the next town. As you are planning how you are going to trade with each when you return, you discover that you cannot remember the details of each transaction. Do you owe Seth for three cows and Ham for four, or the other way around? It could be important because Ham isn't very good at bartering and you always get a better deal with him than Seth. You can't break open the clay envelope and count the images, because that would void the deal. You need some method of reminding yourself of what is inside the envelope.

The solution that they happened on was to mark the outside of the envelope before firing it. The marks would indicate how many images were inside the envelope and what they signified. Thus, if you owed someone five cows, you might draw a stylized figure representing a cow with five lines next to it.

The final step in this record keeping system was the recognition that once everyone agrees on the meanings of the marks on the outside of the envelopes, there is no reason to put anything inside the envelopes. The marks are sufficient in themselves. Clay tablets were developed that could be scratched with special tools and fired so that they could not be changed later. There is significant evidence that this innovation was in place before 3000 BCE.[5] Clay tokens have been found from the city of Susa dating from this period. Clay shards found in the same area bear images strikingly similar to the tokens, indicating that these people had used tokens and then switched to a system of writing to record their business transactions.

---

5 That is, 5,000 years ago.

From these beginnings in economics, the system of writing was applied to other areas of life, and, as a consequence, new signs for other concepts were created. Over time, the principles by which signs were interpreted were augmented. In particular, existing signs could be used for their sounds, as well as for their original meaning. As mentioned previously, *4* can be used to refer to the digit, but can also be used for the sound of the digit's name in *b4*, "before". This principle is called *rebus* and it is the principle by which symbols began to represent sounds. The Egyptians began to reinterpret the hieroglyphics[6] using the rebus principle. This gave many symbols a double function. Sometimes, a symbol was used for its original meaning and sometimes for the sound of the word, the rebus. Because symbols were now ambiguous, a second set of symbols, *determinatives*, was used to indicate whether the first should be interpreted as a symbol for an idea or as a symbol for a sound. At the end of its life, the hieroglyphic system consisted of a large set of symbols for ideas and objects, for sounds and determinatives and, significantly, 22–24 symbols for consonants.

The next significant steps in the development of the alphabet were taken by the Semites around 1700 BCE. They first borrowed the symbols for the consonants (ignoring the rest), organized them into an order, and named them. This system is not yet an alphabet, because it did not contain symbols for vowels, but it is a system that represents only sounds. By ordering the symbols and naming them, the Semites created a system that was easier to learn that the jumble of symbols used in the Egyptian and Sumerian systems. The names of the letters were words for the objects that the symbols originally represented. These names should look vaguely familiar to those aware of the Greek system: *alef* "ox", *beth* "house", *gimel* "camel", *daleth* "door", and so on.[7]

A system that represents only consonants may not seem particularly efficient at first. For example, in such a system the previous sentence would be written as *sstm tht rprsnts nl cnsnnts m nt sm prtclrl ffcnt t frst*. This is not very perspicuous. However, the Semitic languages, exemplified in modern times by Hebrew and the various dialects of Arabic, are particularly suited to this representation. A word in each of these languages can be characterized as consisting of a consonantal root that bears the primary meaning (typically three consonants), a set of vowels that signals grammatical notions like part of speech, tense, number, and so on and possible prefixes and suffixes.

To see how this works, consider the words in Table IV.1. In this table, various forms of the roots *ktb* and *gls* are illustrated. Notice that the past tense could be characterized as _a_a_ where the blanks are filled with the consonants of the root.

---

6 *Hieroglyphic*: from the Greek *hiero*, "sacred", and *glyph*, "carve".
7 The Greek system starts as *alpha, beta, gamma, delta*.

Table IV.1: Egyptian Arabic

kitaùb	book		
maktab	office	maglas	council
makaùtib	offices	magaùlis	councils
katab	he wrote	galas	he sat
kaùtib	writing	gaùlis	sitting
yektub	he is writing	yeglus	he is sitting

In a writing system like this, representing vowels is useful but not essential. A skilled scribe reading the sequence *ktb* would immediately recognize that something about writing is intended and interpret whether the word was a noun or a verb from the context. A famous root is *slm* meaning "peace". It is found in *Islam, Muslim,* and *Salaam.*

The Phoenicians used this writing system to establish a trading network that eventually extended to Greece. About 1000 BCE, the Greeks used the Phoenician system as a model to represent their language. Significantly, Greek is not built on the principles illustrated in Table IV.1. Greek is an Indo-European language and operates on principles of word-building similar to those in English. As a consequence, a system that represents only consonants is no more useful for Greek than it is for English.

The Greeks did something interesting. They analyzed the sounds of the Greek language and determined how they could map the Phoenician symbols onto the sounds of Greek. One of the things that they noticed was that while the Semitic languages didn't necessarily need symbols for vowels, it was essential that the representation of Greek had vowel symbols. Coincidentally, they noticed that the Phoenician system had symbols for consonants that did not exist in Greek. Opportunistically, the Greeks used the unneeded consonant symbols for vowels.

Letter by Letter

To see the process in action, we will examine the history of a few letters.

The first character in the Semitic system was *alef,* "ox". Originally, it was an actual picture of an ox. Later, it became stylized by three strokes as in Figure IV.1.

Figure IV.1

By the time that the Phoenicians adopted the system, it had rotated onto its side (Figure IV.2). This character represented a consonant that was produced in the pharynx. We have not discussed the possibility that a sound could be produced there, because it is not present in the English sound system.

Figure IV.2

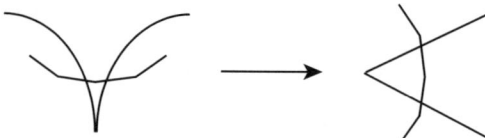

Since Greek did not use this sound either, *alef* was not needed for representing that sound. Instead, it was used to represent a vowel. This move marks the creation of the first true alphabet in which both consonants and vowels are represented. The Greeks gave the symbol another rotation to create the modern character *A* (Figure IV.3) and Hellenized its name as *alpha*.

Figure IV.3

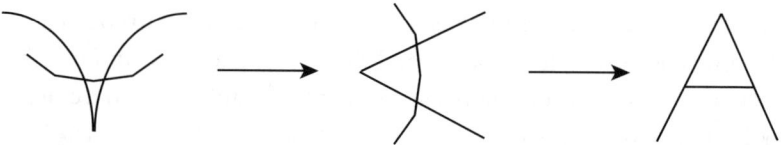

Ouaknin (1999) asks the interesting question of why *alef* was ordered first in the original Semitic syllabary and why it was retained as first in all subsequent alphabets. The answer he gives to his question is that in ancient cultures, both East and West, the ox represents strength and energy. Since it represents power over agriculture, it also represents reproductive energy and economic power. Thus, *alef* or *alpha* represents the elemental energy that drives life and takes a deserved place at the beginning.

The next letter *beth* was a stylized representation of a house (Figure IV.4). From there, it is a short step to the current character *B beta*.

Figure IV.4: *beth*

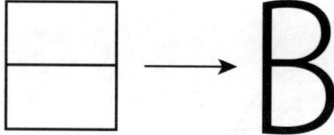

Many of the characters have a history that can be similarly traced to a pictograph. *Daleth* was the image of a door and became Greek *Δ delta* and eventually the Roman character *D*. *Lamed* represented the shepherd's crook and became Greek *Λ lambda* and finally the Roman character *L*. *Minyan* represented water and was used by the Greeks to represent [m] by the character *M* (lower case *μ*) *mu*. This character was borrowed for the same purpose as Roman *M*.

The character *kappa* illustrates another step in the evolution of the alphabet that is used in English. This character originally represented the hand, the fingers represented as lines radiating from a central point, and was oriented in the original Greek in the direction opposite to that used now (Figure IV.5). The early Greeks wrote left to right until the end of the line was reached, at which point they switched directions. Not only did they then switch the progression of letters to right to left, but they also switched the orientation of the letters as well. This style of writing was called *boustrophedon*, literally "as the ox ploughs". Thus, kappa was written in the orientation in Figure IV.5 when writing left to right, but in the orientation that we are accustomed to when writing right to left. When the left to right direction of writing was fixed, the current orientation of kappa was also fixed.

Figure IV.5: *kappa*

Table IV.2 presents the alphabet that the Greeks used in classical times. There are several pertinent observations to make. First, although many of the characters are familiar, some have not survived into English and those that did changed their shape. Some of the characters, such as *psi* Ψ represent sound sequences that do not exist in English as syllable initial sequences. Consider, for example how a word like *psychology* is pronounced in English. The initial *p* is not pronounced because *ps* is not a possible sequence at the beginning of a word in English (although English speakers don't mind it at the end of a word). This sequence was so common in Greek that they used the symbol Ψ to represent it.

Finally, there are some curious sequences in the ordering of the letters. For example, the letter *zeta* Z is clearly the historical antecedent of the character used in the English system. But instead of being the last letter in the ordering, it is sixth in the Greek system.

Table IV.2: The Greek Alphabet

Form	Name	Form	Name
Αα	alpha	Νν	nu
Ββ	beta	Ξξ	xi
Γγ	gamma	Οο	omicron
Δδ	delta	Ππ	pi
Εε	epsilon	Ρρ	rho
Ζζ	zeta	Σσ	sigma
Ηη	eta	Ττ	tau
Θθ	theta	Υυ	upsilon
Ιι	iota	Φφ	phi
Κκ	kappa	Χχ	chi
Λλ	lambda	Ψψ	psi
Μμ	mu	Ωω	omega

The Book of Revelation in the Christian Bible uses the Greek alphabet as a metaphor for God in several places. For example:

> I am Alpha and Omega, the beginning and the ending, saith the Lord, which is and which was, and which is to come, the Almighty.
> (Revelation 1:8)

> I am Alpha and Omega, the beginning and the end, the first and the last.
> (Revelation 22:13)[8]

Examining the order of the characters—α (alpha) at the beginning and ω (omega) at the end—reveals the origin of the metaphor and also the language in which this section of the Christian Bible was written.

---

8 *The Bible*, Authorized (King James) Version. London: Collins, 1953.

The Roman Alphabet

The Romans often looked east to Greece for ideas on religion, government, education and culture. The alphabet was one of the many things that the Romans borrowed, although not directly. The Etruscan civilization was also centred in what is now Italy and served as a filter for many things Greek.

The Romans and Etruscans faced the same problems with the alphabet that the Greeks did when they borrowed symbols from the Phoenicians: many of the symbols were unnecessary and not all of the sounds of their languages were represented. For example, the Etruscans did not need the character *gamma* because their language did not have the sound signified by that letter. This symbol was removed from the Etruscan alphabet. However, when the Romans borrowed the alphabet from the Etruscans, they needed a symbol for the voiced velar stop. The Etruscan alphabet no longer had an appropriate symbol. However, it did have the symbol *zeta*, which the Romans did not need because Latin does not have the corresponding sound. So the Romans converted *zeta* into what is now G. The evolution appears to be as in Figure IV.6. So, although there is no phonetic relationship between the sounds originally represented by G and Z, the characters are nonetheless intimately related.

Figure IV.6

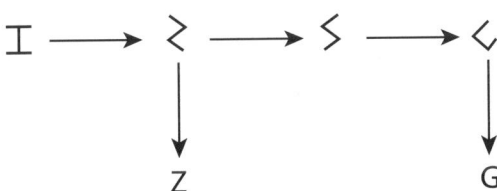

Latin had had versions of the sound [k]. One was much like the one that English uses. This was represented with the character *c*. The other was produced with lip rounding. The Greek system did not make the distinction, so the Romans used the character Q to represent it. This character, called *koppa*, had been dropped from the classical Greek system, though not before the Etruscans borrowed the alphabet. The lip rounding was often emphasized by following this character with a *u* (thus explaining why *q* only appears in English if followed by *u*).

The early Roman alphabet (Table IV.3) consisted primarily of letters from the Greek, some of which represent the same sounds as in the Greek system, some adapted to new sounds, and some changed in shape to create new letters.

Table IV.3: The Early Roman Alphabet

A	M
B	N
C	O
D	P
E	Q
F	R
H	S
I	T
K	U
L	X

Although the character *gamma* Γ was not used in its Greek form in the Latin system, it was adapted to create the letter *C* by rotating it counterclockwise. The phonetic similarity between its function in Greek and its function in Latin should be clear. In the Greek system it represented [g], in the Latin system [k]. Referring back to the description of consonants in Table III.4, we note that the difference between [g] and [k] is voicing. The former is voiced, the latter is voiceless.

So, the Greek symbol for a voiced velar stop Γ was transformed into the Latin symbol for the voiceless velar stop *C*. And Latin added a new symbol for voiced velar stop, *G*.

Other examples of adapting a character to a new sound are the character *eta* H which originally represented a vowel in the Greek system but was adapted to the sound [h] and the character *xi* Ξ which morphed into *X* and was used to represent the sequence [ks]. The sequence [ks] was so common in Latin that a distinct character was felt necessary. One of the many reasons that it was common was that for a large class of nouns, the nominative singular was marked with *-s*. When the root of one of these nouns ended in [k], the nominative appeared with *x*.

For example, the root √*duc* "leader" never appeared by itself. It had to be inflected to indicate its function in the sentence. Table IV.4 shows a bit of the declension of √*duc*, contrasted with that of √*urb* "city".[9]

---

[9] Recall that the nominative case normally marks the subject of a verb; the accusative normally marks the object of a verb; and the genitive normally indicates possession.

Table IV.4: Latin Nominal Inflection

nominative	dux	urbs
accusative	ducem	urbem
genitive	ducis	urbis

Notice that when we compare the various forms of √urb plus its inflectional endings, we arrive at the analysis in Table IV.5.

Table IV.5: Inflection of *urb*

nominative	urb + s
accusative	urb + em
genitive	urb +-is

This analysis predicts that all nouns that inflect the same way as √urb use the same inflectional morphemes as in TableIV.6.

Table IV.6: Latin Nominal Inflectional Morphemes

nominative	ROOT + s
accusative	ROOT + em
genitive	ROOT +-is

If we apply this analysis to the various forms of the root √duc, the accusative and genitive are obvious, but the nominative is not (Table IV.7).

Table IV.7: Inflection of √*duc*

nominative	dux	?
accusative	ducem	duc + em
genitive	ducis	duc + is

Where *urbs* clearly shows that the nominative is *urb + s*, the same cannot immediately be said of *dux*. It first appears that there is some kind of substitution in the nominative, rather than the addition of the suffix *-s*; that is, it appears that *c* is replaced with *x*. As always, we would rather have an analysis that lines up √duc with other roots. To do so, we must ignore spelling and instead concentrate on how the word is pronounced. If we represented the various forms of Ðduc phonetically, then the problem is not so difficult. First, it is necessary to remember that the Latin character *c* (as in *ducem*) represented the sound [k] and that the symbol *x* represents the sound sequence [ks]. If we then represent the various forms of *dux* phonetically, it is easy to see that it is inflected in the same manner as √urb (Table IV.8).

Table IV.8: Inflection of √duc

nominative	duks
accusative	dukem
genitive	dukis

This use of the single character *x* to represent the sequence [ks] was borrowed into English along with Latin words. In contrast, when Greek words are borrowed with this character, it can represent [ks] as in *exodus* but it is also used to represent [z]: as in *xylophone* and *xenophobia*.

Some of the characters in the early system served more than one function. For example, Latin had a [w] sound, but did not have a distinct character to represent it. Instead, the character *u* was used. There was never any difficulty in resolving the ambiguity, because the two sounds [u] and [w] were in complementary distribution. That is, whenever the character *u* appeared before a vowel, it represented the sound [w]. Otherwise, it represented the sound [u]. For example, the root that we find in borrowings such as *vivacious* was written in Latin as *uiuu* and pronounced [wiwu]. Similarly, Latin also had the sound [y] but did not use a distinct character to represent it. Instead, the character *i* was used. Again, there was never any problem recognizing when the character was representing [y] and when it was representing [i] because the two sounds were in complementary distribution. The sound [y] occurs only before vowels. Thus, *ius* "law" was pronounced as [yus].

Later Developments

The alphabet that is used by English and many other languages was adapted from the early Latin alphabet by creating new characters to meet the needs of each adopting language and to adapt to changes in the Latin language.

Of the characters that have been added, perhaps the most obvious is the reintroduction of *Z* at the end of the alphabetic sequence. This character was added because it became necessary to distinguish between [s] and [z]. Notice that if there is only the character *s*, as in the original Latin alphabet, then it is not possible to distinguish between *sip* and *zip* or *sap* and *zap*.

Of linguistic interest are the additions of *J, V, W,* and *Y*. As noted previously, *i* and *u* originally served double duty. As Latin changed and as other languages adopted the alphabet, this usage become unwieldy. The character *y* was first added to the alphabet eventually used by English in approximately 50 BCE. It was adapted from the Greek letter upsilon (Υυ) and used in Late Latin when transliterating Greek words such as *chrysanthemum* and *symphony*. The English innovation was to use it to represent the consonant [y]. In the Romance languages, on the other hand, the character *j* was created by elongating *i* to replace *i* when it had previously represented [y]. The character *j* was placed next to *i* in the alphabetic sequence. Thus, the characters *y* and *j* can be used as literal shibboleths to roughly determine the language family of the words containing them: words with *y* used to represent the consonant [y] are likely English while those with *j* are likely Latin and Romance. Occasional used of *y* in French words, such as *royal* and *loyal*, show that this rule in not perfect.

The close relationship between *y* and *i* in English spelling can be illustrated with two bits of evidence. One we can think of as a dialectal difference between British and North American spelling conventions. There is an occasional use of *y* in British spelling where North American would use *i*. For example, the British spelling *tyre* contrasts with the North American *tire*. Another case is found between different historical dialects. Before the spelling system for English was (more or less) fixed, the character *y* was often used where we now find *i*. For example, Blake's famous poem contemplating theodicy begins:

Tyger, tyger burning bright,
In the forests of the night[10]

Similarly, recall that Chaucer was able to use different spellings of *air* (as *eyre* and *aire*) to different effect (see page 6), indicating again the similar roles that these two characters play.

As an historical example of the period before the spelling conventions concerning *y* were fixed, notice that *royal* was originally borrowed from French as *roial*. *Merriam-Webster's* gives the etymology of *royal* as:

[ME *roial* fr. AF, real *roial* fr. L *regalis*, fr. *reg-*, *rex* king; akin to OIr *rí* (gen. *ríg*) king, Skt *rājan*, L *regere* to rule—more at RIGHT][11]

A second source of evidence is the frequent alternation of *i* and *y* in English spelling rules in contemporary English. For example, many adjectives formed

---

10 William Blake. *The Complete Poems.* Alicia Ostriker, ed. Harmondsworth, New York: Penguin, 1977, p. 125.
11 p. 1086.

with the suffixes -*ly* and -*y* can be nominalized[12] with the suffix -*ness*. In the nominalized form, the suffixes are spelled *i* rather than *y* (Table IV.9).

Table IV.9

clean	cleanly	cleanliness
cost	costly	costliness
coward	cowardly	cowardliness
dead	deadly	deadliness
kind	kindly	kindliness
lone	lonely	loneliness
man	manly	manliness
oil	oily	oiliness
shape	shapely	shapeliness
world	worldly	worldliness

Notice that these instances of *i* and *y* are both pronounced as (roughly) [i]. There is no phonetic reason for a different character, one or the other would suffice. The variation of *i* and *y* is a quirk of English spelling: At some point, it was decided that an English word could not end with *i* and that the character *y* would be used in that position instead.

One also finds the alternation between *i* and *y* in the conjugation of verbs and the declension of nouns (Table IV.10). The rule appears to be that English spelling conventions use the character *y* to represent vowels and diphthongs only when it is the final character of a word (*cry*) or in the interior of a word if the next character is *i* (*crying*) or when the previous character represents a vowel (*played*, but *cried* < *cry* + *ed*). One can also note that, correspondingly, the character *i* does not appear at the ends of words (so *cry* but not *cri*) but is instead replaced with *y*. Nor does it appear between vowels (so *played* not *plaied*).

Table IV.10

cry	cries	crying
die	dies	dying
fry	fries	frying

---

12 *Nominalize*: from the Latin *nomen*, "name". To nominalize is to create a noun.

fly	flies	flying
lie	lies	lying
pry	pries	prying
terrify	terrifies	terrifying
try	tries	trying
buy	buys	buying
play	plays	playing

There are two classes of exceptions to this observation. Neither contradicts it because there are good reasons why they shouldn't follow the rule. One is that this spelling rule does not hold for Greek words like *abyss, acetylic,* and *chrysanthemum*. As mentioned previously, this was the original use of *y*, representing the sound [ü], a high front tense rounded vowel (like [i] but rounded like [u]). This *y* doesn't follow the original rule because it is being used to represent a vowel from a different language. Once more, this illustrates again our point that rules, even spelling rules, are language specific. The rules governing the use of the characters *i* and *y* govern their use in English. When it comes time to represent other languages—which, remember, used a different orthography—these rules do not hold and the same characters can be used to different purposes.

The second group are compounds, words that are formed by combining two or more bases as in *wastebasket, screwdriver,* and *grandmother*. In compounds, a *y* that terminates the first member of the compound remains unchanged (Table IV.11). This is not entirely unexpected, because in some sense the *y* continues to be the last character of a word, namely the first word of the compound, and so obeys the rule.

Table IV.11

city	cityfolk
copy	copyright
belly	bellyache
cry	crybaby
ferry	ferryboat
fly	flypaper
heavy	heavyweight

lady	ladybug
any	anybody
pussy	pussyfoot

This discussion should go some way to explaining the familiar phrase that students learning English spelling must memorize: namely that the vowels of English are *a, e, i, o, u* and sometimes *y*. First, to be linguistically accurate, we should correct the phrase to be, the characters that represent the vowels of English are *a, e, i, o, u* and sometimes *y*. Of course, as we have just discussed, the character *y* sometimes represents a vowel (sometimes the vowel [i] and sometimes [ay] and in Greek words [ü]). Other times, it represents the sound [y] in words such as *year, young,* and *youth,* which, in the classification of sounds taught in grammar school, is grouped with consonants.

The character *u* has a similar story. It was observed earlier that Latin *uiuus* was pronounced [wiwus]. That is, sometimes the character *u* represented [u], but when it occurred before another vowel it represented [w]. In the evolution of Latin into the Romance languages, this [w] changed to [v], as can be observed in the borrowing *vivacious* from the root *uiuu*. The Romans had two forms of the letter *u*. The character *u* was used in writing, but when carved on a stele it was straightened out into *v*. The solution to the problem of how to represent the sound [v] was to take *v*, the alternate form of *u*, and assign it to the sound [v]. In English, on the other hand, the character *w* was created to distinguish between [u] and [w]. Its name—*double u*—betrays its origin.

To emphasize the cognate relationship between *v* or *j*, on the one hand, and *w* or *y*, on the other, compare Latinate words with *v* and *j* with their English cognates with *w* and *y* (Table IV.12).

Table IV.12

Latinate	English
vegetable	wake
revolve	walk
value	wield
vibrate	whip
juvenile	young
January	year
jaundice	yellow
jugular	yoke

This is not the end of the story for the system that the Romans developed. As different cultures adapt the alphabet to their languages, they again find that some of the symbols are unnecessary and that other symbols must be added. One of the common problems is that the Latin system of vowels *a, e, i, o, u* is inadequate for many languages. The English system uses various combinations of vowel symbols and the presence or absence of a final unpronounced *e*[13] to indicate its various vowels. Many other cultures have added diacritics to the vowels to augment the number of sounds that can be represented. For example, like English, German has the high front vowel found in *beet*. It also has a rounded version of the same vowel that the Roman alphabet cannot accommodate. Conventionally, this vowel is represented in the German version of the Roman alphabet by placing two dots above the character *u*: *ü*.

Spelling Rules
In the perfect system that an alphabet aims for, a sound is represented by a single character. For example, the sound [b] is unambiguously represented by the character *b*. However, as we have seen, languages change over time, and, as words are given new pronunciations, as new sounds are introduced into the language, or as new principles on how words are constructed are introduced, the original system must be adapted to accommodate these innovations.

Although it may initially seem that the best way to accommodate the development of a new sound in a language is to create a new symbol, in fact this is rarely the option selected, probably because it is expensive for both printers and the education system. Instead, it is cheaper to take a familiar symbol and mark it somehow to show that it is being used in a different way. One type of mark is a diacritic, such as a macron over a vowel to indicate that it is long, the German umlaut (as in *ü*) or the cedilla used in French under a *c* (*ç*) to indicate that it is pronounced [s].

Another kind of mark is to use another familiar symbol in conjunction with one felt to be closest to the new sound to indicate that it is being used in a new way. This sequence is called a *digraph*.[14] In English, the symbol *h* has been used this way in some instances, perhaps because it was already being similarly used when representing Greek words (e.g., *ph* in *telephone*, *th* in *thesis*, and *ch* in *chameleon*). When the sound [ʃ] entered the language, the digraph *sh* was created to represent it: e.g. *shoot* and *sheep*. Similarly, when the sound [tʃ] developed, the digraph *ch* was adapted from Greek transliteration: e.g. *church* (note the German cognate *Kirche* which shows that at some point and under the right conditions English had the rule k → tʃ).[15]

---

13 Notice the difference between *ride* (with the final *e*) and *rid* (without a final *e*).
14 *Digraph*: from the Greek *di-*, "two", and *graph*, "write".
15 The character *h* is used for various purposes in other languages. In Portuguese, a palatal nasal [ñ] developed. This is a nasal produced by the contact of the blade of the tongue with the palate, a nasal between [n] and [ŋ]. This nasal is represented in Portuguese orthography as *nh*. In Italian spelling, there are rules that specify how the sequence *gi* should be pronounced. To negate these rules, an *h* is inserted to create the sequence *ghi*.

The innovation of using sequences of letters to represent a single sound introduces the notion of a *spelling rule* to the system used to represent the sounds of the language. No longer are all sounds represented by a single character. Instead, some sounds are represented by a sequence of symbols, each of which individually represents different sounds. For example, when reading English it is necessary to know that the character *s* represents the sound [s] and the character *h* represents the sound [h] but that the digraph *sh* does not represent the sequence of sounds [sh] but the single sound [ʃ].

Another innovation is to use spelling rules as mimics of the phonological rules of the language. This trick is pervasive in the representation of English vowels. As mentioned previously, Old English made a distinction between long and short vowels. During the early Middle English period, two phonological rules affecting vowel length entered the language that correlated vowel length with syllable structure.

We would think it odd if a word consisted only of consonants and had no vowels. The reason for this intuition is that the phonetic contour of a word–the way a word sounds–is organized into syllables[16] and the basic unit of the syllable is a vowel.[17] A syllable consists of sequences of consonants organized around the vowel. Using C to represent one or more consonants and V to represent a vowel, a syllable can have the following structures:

    V
    CV
    CVC
    VC

Each language has a set of rules that determine how a word is divided into syllables. This division into contours around vowels is important to languages that have stress rules. For example, the stress rule for Old English was something like *stress the first syllable*. To work this rule, there must be a notion of syllable.

A starting point for dividing English words into syllables is the following set of rules:

1. A syllable can begin with either C or V (e.g., *bat* and *at*)
2. A syllable can end with either a C or V (e.g., *set* and *see*)
3. The sequence VCCV is divided as VC | CV (e.g., *into* = in | to)
4. The sequence VCV is divided as V | CV (e.g., *atop* = a | top not at | op)

---

16 *Syllable*: from the Greek *syn-*, "together", and *lamb*, "to hold".
17 This is actually simplistic but adequate for our purposes. In fact, consonants can often perform the same function as a vowel.

There is more to be said, but this is sufficient for the purposes of exploring English spelling.

Rule 2 acknowledges two different kinds of syllables distinguished by the last segment in the syllable. A syllable can end with either a consonant or a vowel. Those that end with a consonant, we will call *closed* syllables. Those that end with a vowel, we will call *open* syllables.

The two phonological rules of early Middle English that are of interest controlled the length of vowels depending on the type of syllable in which it appears. These rules are:

1. All vowels in closed syllables are short
2. All vowels in open syllables are long

Once these rules were established, vowel length was completely governed and consequently predicted by syllable structure.

Previously, in the spelling conventions for English, it was necessary to represent both long and short vowels. One method was to use double vowel characters as in *food* and *feed*. However, the fact that vowel length is predicated on syllable structure provided an alternative method: the spelling system could mimic the rules governing vowel length by creating orthographic open and closed syllables.

To create an orthographic closed syllable and thereby represent the preceding vowel as short, all that is necessary is to double the final consonant of the syllable. This method is commonly seen in verb conjugations. For example, the present participle is always formed in English with *-ing*. However, if this is directly added to a verb that ends with a single consonant, the length of the vowel of the root will be incorrectly represented because an open syllable will have been created. Notice that if *-ing* is added to the verb *stop* without any further changes, the syllable division (by Rule 4 above) is *stoping* → *sto | ping*. But this syllable division incorrectly represents the vowel *o* as long because *sto* is an open syllable. The solution is to double the consonant *p* so that the *orthographic* syllable division is *stopping* → *stop | ping*.[18] Now the orthography represents the syllable as closed and the vowel is correctly represented.

It was easy enough to use the orthography to mimic a closed syllable. Representing an open syllable is slightly harder. It is necessary to create the sequence *VCV*. If the second vowel does not already exist, then one must be created with

---

18 Of course, the actual pronunciation of *stopping* is roughly [stapǝn] and the syllable division is [sta | pǝn]. It is important to keep in mind that doubling the consonant is an orthographic trick to represent the vowel and that other phonetic facts, such as there really is only one consonant articulated and that the syllable is in reality open, are misrepresented.

the stipulation that it is not representing an actual vowel. In the end, the character *e* was selected as this second vowel and used to create an open syllable. Thus, the difference between *pin* and *pine* is that the latter has an *orthographic* open syllable, *pi | ne*, while the former does not. This difference captures the difference in their respective vowels.

This is the explanation of the *silent e* of English spelling. Its use mimics an actual phonological rule from Old English: vowels in open syllables are long. When an open syllable is naturally created, the *silent e* is not necessary and is omitted. For example, the *silent e* is required in *grope* but not in the present participle *groping*.

This spelling convention was created for English words. It was only intermittently applied to words of other languages. Often, the spelling conventions of another language contradict this particular English convention. Consider as examples the words in Table IV.13. In these words, the English spelling convention does not apply. These words have been borrowed from French and so this is not entirely surprising.

Table IV.13

chalice
crevice
avarice
lettuce
menace
novice
notice

If the *silent e* convention does not apply in these words, would it not be better to drop it? Table IV.14 gives this alternative spelling. Notice that if this spelling is adopted, the syllables are correctly represented as closed, but the final *c* character now represents the sound [k], not the sound [s] as it should. This is because there is a French spelling convention that the character *c* represents the sound [s] when it is followed by the characters *e* or *i*. So, to get the sound right for the character *c*, there must be a following *e*.

Table IV.14

chalic
crevic
avaric

lettuc

menac

novic

notic

As a general rule, the character *e* at the end of a word does not represent a sound but rather contributes to the representation of sounds by other characters. If the character *c* requires a following *e*, it is not bending the rules too much to allow it at the ends of words since it is not representing a sound there anyway. However, its use here is a French spelling rule, and it does conflict with its use in English spelling rules.

There are other cases when it is the vowel length rule that has priority and the rule governing the pronunciation of *c* before *e* must be avoided. Consider the pairs of words in Table IV.15. In this table, the left-hand column contains a set of verbs from which the nouns in the right-hand column are formed. An obvious question is why the verbs are spelled with *k* where the nouns use *c*.

Table IV.15

invoke	invocation
evoke	evocation
convoke	convocation
provoke	provocation
revoke	revocation

In fact, the character *c* was the original character used to spell both nouns and verbs. So, why are the verbs now spelled with *k*? Consider what would happen if the verbs were spelled with the original *c*. For example, *invoke* would be spelled as *invoce*. This spelling gets the pronunciation of the character *c* wrong. It is the French spelling rule that governs what sound the character *c* represents that is at work here. The final *e* following the *c* dictates that *c* represents [s].

To avoid the consequences of the French rule, the final *e* could be omitted. Then *invoke* would be spelled *invoc*. But, now, the representation of the vowel is wrong. The orthographic closed syllable incorrectly represents the vowel. So, the final *e* is necessary to get the pronunciation of the vowel right, and the switch to the character *k* is necessary to avoid the French spelling rule.

It is inconsistencies like this that occasionally prompt some to urge a spelling reform for English. After all, there is a certain arbitrariness to many of the conventions; there is no *a priori* reason why *y* should be used at the ends of words and *i* internally. Often a single character represents many different sounds (compare the *c* of *cook* and that of *city*) and the same sound is represented by different symbols (compare the first sound of *fine* and *phone* and the last sound of *rough*). It is argued that this inefficient system should be replaced with one that is closer to a true phonetic alphabet, in which each symbol unambiguously represents one sound and each word is spelled in a way that its pronunciation is obvious.

Contrasting with this view is another which argues that at least part of the function of a spelling system is to represent the relatedness among words. If we spelled words exactly as they are pronounced, we will loose this feature. To see what happens if a spelling strictly represents just how words are pronounced, start with an easy case; the words in the right hand column of Table IV.16 are clearly related to those in the left-hand column. It is does note take any sophisticated analysis to see that those in the right-hand column are formed by adding *-ment* to those in the left.

Table IV.16

govern	government
adorn	adornment
achieve	achievement
commit	commitment
contain	containment

Sometimes, when morphemes are added there are consequent changes in how the original forms are pronounced. When the decision has been made that the difference in pronunciation is so great that it must be represented, the relatedness of the words is obscured. The words in Table IV.17 offer examples where this has happened. The words in the right-hand column are clearly formed from those in the left, but it is not quite clear how. Chapter 9 will explore how these are related.

Table IV.17

divide	division
conclude	conclusion
delude	delusion
deride	derision

The difference in spelling between the related forms may be so great that it is not immediately obvious that the forms are related at all. This is especially true if, once the relatedness is no longer sensed, the meanings of one or both of the words change. Table IV.18 gives examples of pairs of words whose relatedness is, to varying degrees, not obvious and requires some analysis to see.

Table IV.18

food	fodder
goose	gosling
house	husband
out	utmost
home	hamlet
holy	Halloween

If English spelling is reformed so that pronunciation is unambiguously represented, the situation in Table IV.18 will be repeated through the lexicon.

Conclusion

The history of the alphabet is a story of various cultures attempting to adapt an ancient set of symbols to the particular sounds of their languages. The Greeks were the first to create a system in which both consonants and vowels were represented. The Romans borrowed the Greek alphabet and adapted it to Latin. Each culture in Europe and now the other continents has subsequently borrowed either the Greek or the Roman system and adapted it to its language by removing some of the characters, changing the existing characters, adding new ones, and adding diacritics to make the distinctions that are relevant to each language.

An example of the difficulty of adapting the alphabet to a new language is the problem of transliteration. When transliterating, one is attempting to represent a foreign word by matching the characters of one system, for example, the Thai alphabet, Japanese syllabaries, or the Semitic alphabet, to those of another like the Roman alphabet. To get a feel for how difficult this can be, consider the name of the leader of Libya at the time this is written. His name is something like Gadafi but as an Arabic name it contains many sounds that are not represented in the Roman alphabet. Table IV.19 gives some examples of attested transliterations of his name.[19]

---

19 There is a joke of someone asked to give the serial number on his computer: *PQKG213*. He responds, "P as in pneumonia, Q as in Qadafi, K as in Kadafi and G as in Gaddafi."

Table IV.19

Muammar Qaddafi	Mu'amar al-Kadafi	Moamar al-Gaddafi	Muamar Kaddafi
Mo'ammar Gadhafi	Muammar Ghaddafy	Mu'ammar Al Qathafi	Muammar Quathafi
Muammar Kaddafi	Muammar Ghadafi	Muammar Al Qathafi	Mohammer Q'udafi
Muammar Qadhafi	Muammar Ghaddafi	Mo'ammar el-Gadhafi	Muammar Gheddafi
Moammar El Kadhafi	Muamar Kaddafi	Moamar El Kadhafi	Muamar Al-Kaddafi
Muammar Gadafi	Muammar Quathafi	Muammar al-Qadhafi	Moammar Khadafy
Mu'ammar al-Qadafi	Mohammer Q'udafi	Mu'ammar al-Qadhdhafi	Moammar Qudhafi
Moamer El Kazzafi	Muammar Gheddafi	Mu'ammar Qadafi	Mu'ammar al-Qaddafi

Why is it necessary to review the alphabet? Because, aside from intrinsic interest, it is important to emphasize that the alphabet as it is used for English is a representation system that does not necessarily do the job that we need. It is a collection of characters that is used to represent words according to a variety of principles. In the case of English, these principles include those developed for English and others that were adopted from the various languages from which English has borrowed words.

Some of the rules that we will be exploring determine how words are pronounced. Since the representation system that English has adopted is not particularly efficient at representing pronunciation, it is not the appropriate system for representing or thinking about these rules. For example, the character *x* actually represents the sequence [ks]. We can observe this by noticing that the pair *tacks* and *tax* are pronounced identically. Representing [ks] as *x* has its disadvantages. One disadvantage is that it made the declension of *Đduc* obscure: it was necessary to recall that *x* represented [ks] before it was evident that *dux* had the same structure as *urbs*. Other problems generated by *x* will be encountered when Latin and Greek are considered in detail.

A further example of problems generated by a focus on orthography rather than phonetics is the frequency of questions such as "Is *j* voiced or voiceless?" This is an odd question because *j* is a character from the alphabet that English uses; it doesn't sound like anything at all. Often it is used in that system to represent the voiced affricate [dʒ] as in *judge* but also is used in words like *Johann* to represent the sound [y]. What is more, in the phonetic character set that we are using to represent consonants in this book, no sound is represented by the character *j*. The lesson is that it inappropriate to think of alphabetic characters as having phonetic properties. Rather, the purpose of the characters of an alphabet is to represent sounds and it is the sounds that have phonetic properties.

Further, an alphabetic system may or may not do a good job of representing the sound system of a language.

The salient point is that the way we think about words and the rules that apply to them is in terms of how they are pronounced, not how they are spelled. Sometimes, the way that they are spelled meets our needs. But it does not always.

In the presentation in the text, we will use plain English orthography when it agrees with the phonetic facts. However, when English orthography does not properly represent the facts, we will move to representing words phonetically.

Further Reading

Daniels, Peter, T. and Bright, William. *The World's Writing Systems*. New York: Oxford University Press, 1996.

Diamond, Jared. *Guns, Germs, and Steel*. New York: W. W. Norton & Company, 1999.

Ouaknin, Marc-Alain. *Mysteries of the Alphabet*. Translated by Josephine Baker. New York: Abbeville Press, 1999.

Sacks, David. *Language Visible: Unravelling the Mystery of the Alphabet from A to Z*. Toronto: Alfred K. Knopf Canada, 2003.

5 The Structure of Words

Introduction

One of the interesting problems in linguistics is defining the concept of *sentence*. It seems that this unit is an important one in the structure of a language. When we read and write, we tend to do so by organizing our ideas into sentences and then into larger units. The sentence seems to be the unit that we use to express our ideas. But what is it?

It is likely that any definition or description of a sentence would include the observation that it is composed of words. But what is a word? For those who have not studied linguistics, this seems like a trivial question. Surely it is obvious what a word is.

As obvious as it may seem, the concept of word has resisted a satisfying definition. To give just one example, one of the most popular definitions, originally proposed by the linguist Leonard Bloomfield, is:

A word is a minimal free form.

Although perhaps not initially enlightening, this definition does get at what we mean by *word*. The definition is intended to get at the notions that

1. A word is a linguistic unit (a *form*);
2. A word can be used by itself (it is *free*), as opposed to other units like the -*s* of *cats*, which is a unit that carries a plural meaning that cannot be used by itself;
3. A word is the smallest unit (it is *minimal*) that can be used by itself, in contrast to phrases like *a large cat*.

For example, it is easy to imagine situations in which a word like *dogs* occurs in isolation.

> A: What are those over there?
> B: Dogs

In this way, it contrasts with forms like the plural *s* that was added to *dog* to form *dogs*, which cannot be used by itself.

Furthermore, the word is the smallest unit (the minimal form) that can occur in isolation. It contrasts with phrases and sentences, which are larger forms than the word and also appear in isolation but are composed of words.

The definition is a nice one because it places the concept of *word* as an intermediate between *morpheme* (units that may or may not occur freely and are atomic) and *phrases* (units that occur freely but are composed of units that can also occur freely). Words are the smallest units that can occur freely.

Unfortunately, it is easy to think of examples that do not fit the definition. For example. the following is perfectly plausible:

> A: Did you say *clear* or *unclear*?
> B: *Un*

We don't want to say that *un* is a word because it is not normally used in the ways that clear-cut cases of words are, but here and in other situations that can be easily constructed, it is.

There have been many other attempts to define *word*, none of which has survived counter-arguments. So, what seems like an obvious concept turns out to be quite slippery. It is so slippery that many languages don't have a word for *word*. That may seem surprising, but English was once one of those languages. The contemporary notion of word is a new one in English. The word *word* was recruited for this idea. Originally, *word* did not refer to the concept we think is obvious but cannot define; it referred to speech. This reference is evident in English idioms:

by word of mouth	orally
in the beginning was the word	a reference to the deity speaking the world into existence
have words with	to argue

The Map Is Not the Territory

Many think that the problem of defining *word* has already been solved. For example, those who have a learned a language like English, which uses the Roman orthography, may look to how we represent words in that orthography for an answer: words are those strings that are set off by spaces. There are several problems with this idea, and it is useful to explore these to reveal some of the properties of words that we need to keep in mind.

As we discussed previously, orthography is a representation of the language; it is not the language itself. The representation used for English has a long history and was not originally designed for English. Although this representation is called the Roman orthography, because it was borrowed from the system used to represent Latin, it was not originally invented by the Romans. They borrowed it from the Greeks. The Greeks did not invent it but borrowed it from the Sumerians. The Sumerians would not recognize what had happened to the system they had used. Not only does it not look like the system that they had developed, it does not even operate on the same principles.

The main innovation introduced by the Greeks and later adopted and used by the Romans was the use of symbols to represent sounds only. The set used by the Sumerians was a complex and unsystematic use of symbols used to represent ideas, syllables and sounds. The Greeks created a standard system that related symbols to unique sounds. However, just as the Roman numeral system (I, II, III, IV, V, etc.) did not have a symbol for *o*, the Greek orthography did not have a space. The Greek system, and later the Roman system, did not originally set off words with spaces or other punctuation.

The space was added to the system English now uses later in history of this system. Possibly as a result of its more recent introduction or perhaps because native speakers are not entirely comfortable with the notion of *word*, the space is not used systematically to delimit words. To illustrate this, we consider a class of words that are known as compounds.

Compounds are composed of units that we might recognize as also being words. Examples include *blackbird* and *wastebasket*. One way we can demonstrate that these are single words is to compare their stress patterns with strings that we know are words or phrases.

Stress is the relative force used to utter a syllable or the loudness of the syllable. In a word like *detergent*, the middle syllable *-ter-* receives greater stress than the other two. Stress is not all or nothing; there are degrees of stress. For example, in the word *photograph*, the first syllable *pho* receives the greatest stress, the last syllable *graph* the second greatest and the middle syllable *to* the least. For our purposes, we can distinguish between primary and secondary stress. We will mark these with superscript digits. Thus *photograph* is stressed as *pho¹togra²ph*.

To emphasize the differences in the stress of syllables in a word, note what happens to the stress placement when we add *-er* to *photograph*. The primary stress shifts to the *-to-* syllable: *photo¹graphe²r*.

A difference between multisyllabic words, on the one hand, and phrases, on the other, is the stress pattern assigned to each. As we can see above, many words in English have a 1-2 stress pattern. The first stressed syllable receives primary stress and the second stressed syllable receives secondary stress. In a phrase, on the other hand, each words is stressed separately. Consider the difference between the word *blackbird* and the phrase *black bird*.

> The phrase that describes a bird that is black is stressed as bláck bírd; both words receive primary stress.

> The name of the bird is stressed as bláckbìrd; the first syllable receives primary stress, and the second receives secondary stress.

Note that in examples like *blackbird* and *wastebasket*, the compounds are distinguished from phrases by removing the space (thus adhering to our putative rule for distinguishing words). However, this is not always the case. Consider the American name for the frankfurter: *hot dog*. On examination, it has a stress pattern like the compound *blackbird*, i.e., $ho^1t\ do^2g$, not like the phrase *black bird* (a bird which is black). If *hot dog* is given phrasal stress, it no longer refers to a frankfurter but rather to a canine with a high temperature.[1] Examples of compounds that have a space are endless: consider $ha^1rd\ dri^2ve$—a piece of computer equipment—and $co^1p\ ca^2r$, $wi^1ndow\ si^2ll$, etc.

The example of compounds demonstrates that English orthography is not a reliable criterion for determining the words in a sentence. Worse, there are many languages for which this criterion is irrelevant. We can distinguish two classes of such languages. The first emerges from the many cultures that have not developed orthographic representations for their languages. Although they have no writing system, the languages of these cultures certainly contain words. The second class are languages like Thai and Ancient Greek. Both of these cultures developed writing systems, but these writing systems did not originally contain spaces or punctuation and did not delimit words in the orthography except by the beginnings and ends of lines. Clearly for languages such as this, relying on the orthography to determine what the words are in a sentence will not work.[2]

Inflection

Imagine that your employer gives you the job of writing a computer program to extract all the words from a book and create an index for the book. It is easy enough to extract every string that is delimited by spaces. As we have seen, you would likely break up a lot of words like *hard drive* into their components incorrectly. However, supposing that you have solved this problem, you would

---

[1] Notice that the sentence *Even hot dogs eat hot dogs* is sensible with the right stress.
[2] In fact, a rather lot of effort in Thai computational linguistics is spent developing software that can pick out words in a sentence.

still have a lot of words that probably don't need indexing: words like *to, in, the* and *that*. It would be possible to make a list of these and remove them from the list.[3] Having done this, you would still find yourself with an odd problem: the list contains many words that are similar to each other and have almost the same meaning, and the ways in which they do differ in meaning and form are very predictable.

For example, in a technical document it is possible to find *compute, computes, computed* and *computing*. It is redundant to index each of these separately, because, in some sense, they are all different forms of the same word: COMPUTE. In fact, if we look for these words in an actual dictionary, we find only COMPUTE. The other forms are sometimes listed as variations as in *Merriam-Webster's* which begins the entry as:

com•pute ... -puted ... -puting[4]

After giving the citation form in bold, the entry includes the spelling of some of the related forms.

We now have two different senses of *word*: there are units like *compute, computes, computed,* and *computing* that we use when we speak and write, and there is the abstract unit that we find in the dictionary. Both of these objects are interesting, but it is awkward to use the same term for both because they have quite different properties.

We will retain the term *word* for the objects that we can observe on the page or hear when someone speaks. The abstract item found in a dictionary is often called a *lexeme* or *lexical entry*. Both these terms refer to the objects' home in the *lexicon*.[5]

Compute, computes, computed, and *computing* differ only by being different inflected forms of the lexeme COMPUTE. Another way of phrasing this is to say that *compute, computes, computed,* and *computing* are members of the paradigm of the lexeme COMPUTE. A *paradigm* is the complete set of inflected forms of a lexeme. Each word inherits its core meaning from the lexeme and is created by a separate inflectional rule that has added grammatical information. This observations gives us an opportunity to start to define *word*:

A word is an inflected form of a lexeme.

This definition will only work for lexemes that can be inflected but that is enough for us to make the point. The classes of lexemes that can be inflected in

---

3 This list of words that shouldn't influence the indexing of a document is called a *stop list*.
4 p. 256.
5 *Lexicon*: ultimately from the Greek *logos*, "word". A lexicon is a dictionary.

English are verbs, count nouns, adjectives, the auxiliaries *be* and *have*, and perhaps some prepositions like *near*.[6] There are other classes that do not inflect—such as most prepositions such as *to* and *from*, determiners like *the* and *an*, and conjunctions like *and* and *but*. This definition will not cover them.

As we have seen (Table II.5), the inflected forms of the verb are 3rd singular present tense, non 3rd singular present tense, past tense, present participle and past participle. Count nouns are inflected for number: singular and plural. Adjectives are inflected for positive, comparative, and superlative (see Table V.1).

Table V.1: The Inflected Forms of the Adjective *big*

positive	big
comparative	bigger
superlative	biggest

This analysis assumes that there is a set of rules that will build words. Imagine that your task is to take a list of lexemes and write a computer program that will generate a list of words from these lexemes. You will need to write rules of the form

$$\text{Word} \Rightarrow \text{Lex} + \text{infl}$$

This rule reads that a word consists of a lexeme plus an inflectional suffix. The *Lex* will provide the core meaning of the word, the *infl* will provide the grammatical meaning. For verbs, your program will contain rules such as the following:

$$\text{Word}_{V[+3sg]} \Rightarrow \text{Lex}_V + s$$
$$\text{Word}_{V[pres\ part]} \Rightarrow \text{Lex}_V + ing$$

The first rule states that it is possible to create a word with the category V (for verb) that is inflected for the 3rd singular (present tense) by adding *s* to the end of a lexeme of category V. The second states that a word of category V that is inflected for the present participle consists of a lexeme of category V and *ing*.

Rules of this sort can also be represented as tree diagrams. In a tree diagram, the information that appears to the left of the arrow in the rule appears as the top node. The information on the right of the arrow appears as leaves on branches in the tree (see Figure V.1).

---

6 Notice *near, nearer, nearest*.

Figure V.1: Tree Diagrams

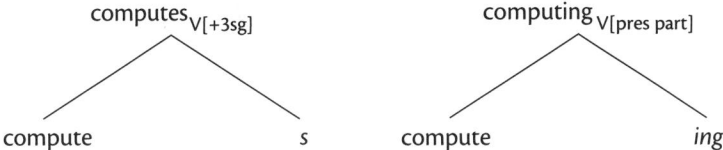

A tree diagram is a useful way of graphically representing the structure of a word or lexeme.

What kind of rule generates the non3rd singular *compute*? The rules given previously are binary[7] rules; that is, they are equivalent to trees that have two branches. For words that do not have explicit inflectional endings, we propose unary rules. The non 3rd singular rule looks like this:

$$\text{Word}_{V[-3sg]} \Rightarrow \text{Lex}_V$$

If we return to the original problem—how to create a computer program to generate all the inflected forms of a lexeme—we see that the rules that we are proposing will almost do the job. Once we have written all the rules that we need (and hired a clever computer programmer who will turn them into computer code), we will generate a set of inflected forms for every lexeme we have in our dictionary. But will they all be correct?

Consider the rule

$$\text{Word}_{V[pres\,part]} \Rightarrow \text{Lex}_V + ing$$

If we think that the lexeme is COMPUTE, then this rule will create COMPUTE+*ing*. When we remove the boundary marker "+" we get ⁽computeing.[8] Clearly, this is not right. We need some additional rule that will fix the spelling.

We have previously (and briefly) discussed phonological rules and saw that they are responsible for adjustments in how words are pronounced. For the purposes of illustration, we adopt the same mechanism to the spelling change that we require.

What sort of rule do we need to ensure that our computer program spells *computing* correctly? For one thing, it must be general because it must ensure that *concluding, providing,* and many others are also correctly spelled. When we compare the lexemes with the present participles that we want to create (Table V.2), we immediately observe that we need to delete *e* before *ing*.

---

7   *Binary*: from the Latin *binarius* "two".
8   The "¢" is used to mark incorrect forms.

Table V.2: Lexemes and Present Participles

COMPUTE	computing
CONCLUDE	concluding
PROVIDE	providing

We will express this by the rule:

$$e + i \rightarrow i$$

This rule describes the deletion of *e* when it is followed by *i*. We don't want to delete every *e* when followed by *i* because there are lots of sequences of *ei* that are fine: for example, *conceive* and *perceive*. That is why we include "+" between *e* and *i* in the rule. The "+" indicates that the *e* is the end of something and that the *i* is the beginning of something else. We now have the machinery in place to solve the original problem: generating all inflected forms of a set of lexemes. The derivation in Table V.3 illustrates how this will work. First we apply the "$\Rightarrow$" rules to a lexeme to build a word, then we apply the "$\rightarrow$" rules.

Table V.3: Deriving Words

COMPUTE$_V$	COMPUTE$_V$	
	[compute + s]$_{V[+3sg]}$	Word$_{V[+3sg]}$ $\Rightarrow$ Lex$_V$ + s
[compute+ing]$_{V[\text{pres part}]}$		Word$_{V[\text{pres part}]}$ $\Rightarrow$ Lex$_V$ + ing
[comput+ing]$_{V[\text{pres part}]}$	"	$e + i \rightarrow i$
[computing]$_{V[\text{pres part}]}$	[computes]$_{V[+3sg]}$	Remove "+"

Notice that we need the "$\rightarrow$" rule because we proposed that the lexeme would be *compute*. If we thought that the lexemes was COMPUT there would be no problem with adding -*ing*. However, we would get *computs when we applied the -*s* rule. If we went with this analysis, we would need a rule that inserted an *e* after the root unless it was followed by -*ing*. So, one way or another, we need "$\rightarrow$" rules to handle the problem with the *e* that appears at the end of so many English words.[9]

Relatedness of Words

We also need to explain how words are related to each other. The machinery that we described in the preceding section will explain how inflected words like

---

9 Notice that this problem is created by the "silent e" discussed in Chapter 4.

computes and *computing* are related: they are derived from the same lexeme by different rules. But there is another sort of relatedness to explain.

Consider the word *antidisestablishmentarianism*. As we examine the word, we can extract elements that we have seen before:

1. The word ends with *-ism* which usually indicates a system of beliefs, (as in *Calvinism* and *nationalism*);
2. It begins with *anti-* which we recognize as meaning something like "opposed to", as in *antidemocratic* or *anti-ballistic missile*;
3. Next to *-ism* is *-arian* which creates adjectives that refer to occupations, ages, or sects, as in *antiquarian*, *octogenarian*, and *vegetarian*;
4. After *anti-*, we note *dis-* which means something like "the opposite or reverse of", which can also be found in *disable* and *disadvantage*;
5. Inside *-arian* and *-ism* is *-ment* which seems to create nouns from verbs, as in *government*.

In the end, we are left with *establish*. Even here, we might suspect a connection with *stable* although it is not clear what the remaining *e-* and *-ish* mean.

The kind of relatedness that we want to understand is that between *antidisestablishmentarian* and *antidisestablishmentarianism*, or *advantage* and *disadvantage*. Clearly, the first pair of words are related by a rule that adds *-ism* to *antidisestablishmentarian*, the second by a rule that adds *dis-* to *advantage*. But these rules do not create different words from the same lexeme, as do the inflectional rules that we discussed in the previous section. Instead, these rules create new lexemes.

We have, then, two kinds of rules. Those which map lexemes onto words we call *inflectional rules*. Those which create new lexemes we will call *derivational rules*. The distinction is an important one. Inflectional rules add information that the grammar of the language requires, such as marks for subject/verb agreement or the number of a noun. These rules must apply if words are to be used correctly. Derivational rules are a mechanism by which the lexicon of a language can be enriched in response to the invention of new artifacts and ideas. For example, in the early days of the communication industry it was popular to use *tele-* to create new lexemes: see. *telephone* < *tele* (far) + *phone* (sound)[10], *television* < *tele* + *vision*, and *telegram* < *tele* + *gram* (write).

Derivational rules have two possible consequences that are different from inflectional rules. First, a derivational rule might, but not necessarily, create a lexeme with a meaning different from the meaning of the basic form. This contrasts with inflectional rules which only add grammatical information. Compare the difference between the inflectional rules that create singular

---

10 The operator "<" is read as "is derived from".

table and plural *tables*, and the derivational rule that creates *antibacterial* from *bacterial*. The inflectional rule adds information about number to the original lexeme. The derivational rule creates a new lexeme with a very different meaning from the original *bacterial*.

The second consequence that a derivational rule can have is the change of grammatical category. For example, given adjectives like *clear* and *quick*, it is possible to create the adverbs *clearly* and *quickly* by adding *-ly*. Inflectional rules, since they elaborate the paradigm of a lexeme, do not change grammatical category.

In addition to different functions, inflectional and derivational rules have different structural properties as well. The example of *antidisestablishmentarianism* demonstrates that derivational rules can apply to lexemes that have been created by previous derivational rules. However, the same cannot be said for inflectional rules (in English). Once we have created a word from a lexeme by applying an inflectional rule, we cannot apply another inflectional rule. For example, if we apply the 3rd singular rule to create *governs*, we cannot then apply the present participle rule to create *ᵉgovernsing*.

The application of an inflectional rule also seems to block any further application of derivational rules. For example, if we apply the present participle rule to *govern* to create *governing*, we cannot then add *-ment* to create *ᵉgoverningment*, even though we can create *government*.[11]

In a sense, inflected words on our definition are morphologically inert; they cannot be subject to any further rule. To return to our computer program analogy, when we add derivational rules to our program we will need to find a way to ensure that derivational rules apply *inside* inflectional rules. In a computer program, we do this by creating blocks of instructions that are ordered with respect to each other. Once a block of instructions has been executed, it is finished unless some other part of the program routes control back to it. The structure of a program that builds words would be like that in Figure V.2.

There are several things to note about the structure of our computer program.

1. As we want, derivational morphology will apply inside inflectional morphology. This is because there is no way to get back to derivational morphology once inflectional morphological rules have applied.
2. Derivational morphology creates lexemes and can be consulted as many times as we like. For example, after creating *government* by a rule that adds *-ment* to certain kinds of verbs, we can re-enter the derivational morphology module and create the adjective *governmental*.

---

11 This may be peculiar to Indo-European languages.

3. Once we have inflected a word, we will apply phonological rules much as we saw in Table V.3 to create its phonetic form.[12]

Figure V.2: Word Building

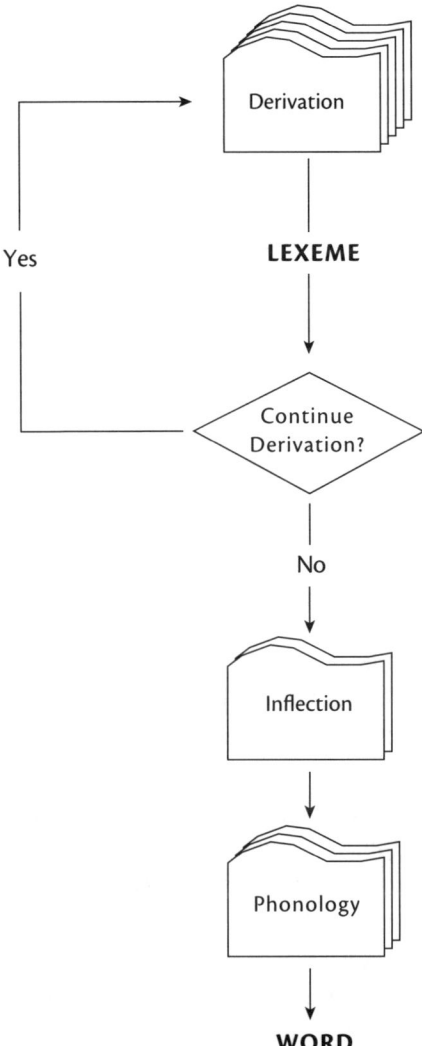

Terminology
We are now in a position to make some finer distinctions and examine some concepts that are useful when analyzing words. Consider a simple case like *unreadable*. Clearly, two derivational rules have applied: one has added *un-*

---

12 In Chapter 6, we will see that there are reasons to review where phonology fits in this scheme.

and the other has added *-able*. The unit to which they have been added is *read*. These units—*read*, *un-*, and *-able*—are *morphemes*.[13]

The morpheme is the unit used to build lexemes and words. It is sometimes defined as follows:

> The morpheme is the smallest meaningful unit.

This definition highlights the atomic property of morphemes: they are the building blocks of words and lexemes, and if we try to break them down further, we will not find anything meaningful.

For example, we analyzed *unreadable* as consisting of *un-*, *read*, and *-able*. We can identify a meaning for each of these (Table V.4).

Table V.4: *unreadable*

un-	not
read	interpret written text
-able	capable of performing an action

However, if we try to break down any of these morphemes further, we end with nonsense. For example, we might try to analyze *-able* as *ab* + *1e*. This doesn't work because neither of the components means anything. The idea that the components of words should in some sense be meaningful and should therefore be encountered often is one that we use unconsciously all the time. For example, when confronted with the word *misled*, we recognize it as the past tense form of *mislead* and not the past tense form of *misle*—as *filed* is the past tense for of *file*—because *misle* is not an actual word. Similarly, I recently encountered a company named *Saferide* and parsed the name as *safe* + *ride* and not as *safer* + *ide* with the expectation that there could be a *Safeide* and a *Safestide*, because *ide* is meaningless.

The notion that morphemes are meaningful forces us to think a bit more about meaning. It seems that we can acknowledge different kinds of meaning. There is the sort that we likely think of immediately, which we can call *lexical* meaning. This is the kind that we think that lexemes such as *dog* or *beauty* carry, the kind that we think that dictionaries normally deal with.

Morphemes, such as *un-* and *-able*, which must normally attach to a lexeme and cannot appear in isolation, carry lexical meaning as well.

---

13 *Morpheme*: from the Greek *morphos*, "shape". Some science fiction stories have characters who can "morph". That is, they can change their shape.

A second kind of meaning is found the plural *-s* in *trees* and the *-s* of *likes* in the sentence *Mary likes piano sonatas*. These morphemes perform a different function from those that carry lexical meaning. They are inflectional and are required by the grammar. As a consequence, we could say that they carry *grammatical* meaning.

Finally, morphemes such as the *-ly* of *quickly* and *clearly* don't seem to carry either lexical or grammatical meaning, but they clearly have a function: they signal that the lexemes they have created are adverbs. These we can say carry *categorical* meaning. They signal the category of the lexeme. English has a large number of morphemes that carry both categorical and lexical meaning. For example, *-ment* carries the categorical meaning of *noun* when it is added to verbs. Notice that *enchantment* is created from the verb *enchant*. In addition, one of the meanings that it can contribute is the state resulting from having had the action of the verb applied. Enchantment is the state of having been enchanted.

The definition of *morpheme* as "the smallest meaningful unit" is serviceable, but occasionally creates problems. For example, most of us would want to say that *speedometer* has internal structure because we recognize the morphemes *speed* and *meter*. But what does *-o-* mean? It doesn't mean anything at all. Instead, it seems to have been inserted on analogy with *thermometer, chronometer, odometer,* etc. because next to them *speedmeter* sounds odd.

This is a technical problem that shouldn't detract from the main point. Morphemes are the basic units that are used to build lexemes and words.

When we scan the morphemes that compose *unreadable*, we note that not all morphemes are created equal. One of them—*read*—seems to supply the core meaning while the others are attached to it. In fact, I have been suggesting this is the case when I represent the other morphemes as *un-* and *-able*, with dashes indicating whether they are added before or after the core morpheme.

So, our first distinction among morphemes is between the *root* of a lexeme or word and its *affixes*.[14] A root is the fundamental component of the lexeme. Typically, it will carry the core meaning of the lexeme. An affix is a morpheme that is added to a lexeme. We can further subdivide affixes into those which are added to the beginning of the lexeme—*prefixes*—and those that are added at the end of a lexeme—*suffixes*.

We now have a structural taxonomy of morphemes (Figure V.3). A taxonomy is a classification based on a set of criteria. A structural taxonomy is a taxonomy based on the structural properties of the morphemes.

---

14 *Affix*: from the Latin *ad*, "to" + *figere*, "attach". An affix is a morpheme that is attached to something else.

Figure V.3: Structural Taxonomy of Morphemes

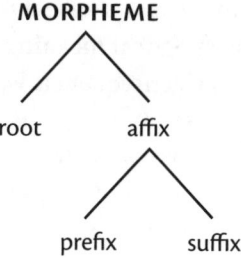

We have also created a functional taxonomy of affixes, although we did not mention it at the time. Affixes have two functions: they are either derivational and create new lexemes, or they are inflectional and create words (Figure V.4).

Figure V.4: Functional Taxonomy of Affixes

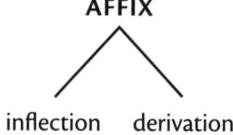

Derivational Rules

We return now to derivational rules. The properties of these rules are interesting. To investigate them, we consider the grammatical categories of *read* and *readable*. To determine the grammatical category of a word, we can use it in a sentence and then determine how it is used.

> Sandy reads philosophical books.

Quite clearly, *read* is used as a verb. Equally clearly, *readable* is not a verb. We can see that if we substitute it for *read* in the preceding sentence.

> ᵉSandy readable philosophical books.

If *readable* was a verb, then it should be possible to substitute it for other verbs and obtain a plausible sentence. Instead, we get gibberish. Not only does the string of words make no sense, it is not close to being an English sentence.

What category is *readable*? To determine this we first use it in a grammatical and sensible sentence.

> Sandy enjoys readable books.

Here it is used as an adjective to modify *books*. We can demonstrate that it is an adjective by substituting a *bona fide* adjective like *big*.

Sandy enjoys big books.

Thus, one of the properties of *-able* is that it is used to create adjectives. A second property is that it can only be added to verbs. To demonstrate that the latter restriction is accurate, try to add it to words that are not verbs. For example, *table* is a noun and cannot accept it: $^{\varepsilon}$*tableable*. Similarly, *beautiful* is an adjective and cannot accept it: $^{\varepsilon}$*beautifulable*.

In conclusion, *-able* is a suffix that creates adjectives from verbs. We can now build a rule that will add *-able* to the appropriate forms to create an adjective:

$$\text{Lex}_A \Rightarrow \text{Lex}_V + able$$

This rule states that when *-able* is added to a lexeme of category V, a new lexeme of category A (for adjective) is created.

Consider next the prefix *un-*. What sorts of lexemes can it attach to? To answer this question, we uncover another subtlety about morphemes. Consider the words in Table V.5.

Table V.5: The Prefix *un-*

	Root	Root Category
unclean	clean	adjective
uncover	cover	verb
unfold	fold	verb
unfriendly	friendly	adjective
unholy	holy	adjective
unbind	bind	verb

At first it appears that *un-* can be added to both adjectives and verbs.

We must be careful here. Note that when *un-* is added to an adjective it means "not". *Unclean* literally means "not clean". But does *uncover* mean "not cover"? No, it means "remove the cover". Similarly, while *unholy* means "not holy", *unbind* does not mean "not bind" but rather "remove the binding". Our first impression that *un-* can be added to both adjectives and verbs needs clarification. The *un-* that means "not"—call it *un-*^{1}—can only be added to adjectives.

The *un-* that means something like "reverse X" where "X" is the verb to which it is added—call it *un-²*—can only be added to verbs.

So, in fact, we have not one but two morphemes: *un-¹* and *un-²*. We know that they are two morphemes because they do not mean the same thing. This establishes an important principle about morphemes:

> A persisting property of a morpheme is its meaning. A morpheme carries the same meaning each time it is used.

If two identical strings have the same meaning, then they are instances of the same morpheme. Thus, the prefixes of *unclean* and *unholy* are instances of the same morpheme. If two identical strings are not used with the same meaning, then they must be instances of different morphemes. Thus, the prefixes of *uncover* and *unclean* are not instances of the same morpheme.

The morpheme in which we are first interested is *un-¹*. This morpheme is added to adjectives to create adjectives the meaning of which is the negation of the original adjective.[15]

Negative: $Lex_A \Rightarrow un + Lex_A$

On the other hand, *un-²* is added to verbs to create new verbs that mean something like "reverse X" where "X" is the original verb.

Reverse: $Lex_V \Rightarrow un + Lex_V$

We now have the rules necessary to create *unreadable*:

$Lex_A \Rightarrow Lex_V + able$

Negative: $Lex_A \Rightarrow un + Lex_A$

Can these rules apply in any order? That is, can we create *unreadable* simply by applying the rules to *read* as we wish or do we have to pay attention to the forms that they apply to and the forms that they create?

Some thought suggests that there is only one order that will work. We have seen that *un-¹* can be added only to adjectives. As a consequence, it cannot be added to *read* because *read* is a verb: this explains why *ᶜunread* meaning "not performing the act of reading" is not a possible English word. However, *-able* will create an adjective from a verb, in this case, *readable*. Thus, the *-able* rule

---

15 There appear to be examples where *un-1* is added to nouns: words like *Uncola* and *undead*. We will consider these to be exceptions that have explanations in advertising and Hollywood.

Relatedness of Words 117

must apply before the *un-¹* rule. The *-able* rule creates an adjective to which *un-¹* can be added.

Another way of thinking of this is to notice that *unreadable* has internal structure. It is not simply a sequence of morphemes. The tree diagram for *unreadable* makes this apparent. Notice that each application of a rule creates a new level of structure. Since we used two rules to create *unreadable*, it has two layers of structure. Notice that this kind of structure is what the computer program we designed in Figure V.2 will create. On the first entry through the derivational morphological module, a rule that adds *-able* will create the adjective *readable*. The **Continue?** module sends control back into the derivational morphological module where a rule adding *un-* to adjectives creates *unreadable*.

Figure V.5: Tree Diagram for *unreadable*

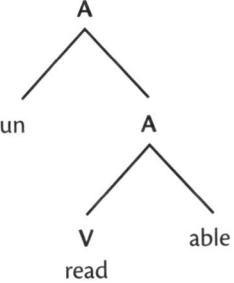

The power and utility of representing the structure of words with tree diagrams can be illustrated by considering words like *unfoldable*. This word is ambiguous: it can be interpreted in more than more way. One interpretation is "not capable of being folded"; we could attribute this of a piece of lumber. It is not possible to fold a piece of lumber. Call this *unfoldable¹*. On the other hand, it can also be interpreted as "capable of being unfolded"; we could attribute this of a highway map. Highway maps are typically folded and must be unfolded to be used and are, therefore, capable of being unfolded. Call this *unfoldable²*.

Notice that *unfoldable¹* contains the negative prefix *un-¹*. Something that is unfoldable in this sense is *not* foldable. Now *unfoldable²* contains *un-²*. Something that is unfoldable in this sense is something whose folds are able to be *reversed*.

A tree diagram illustrates how a word is put together and which parts modify which. As a consequence, they can be used to illustrate how ambiguous strings like *unfoldable* can be interpreted in different ways. *Unfoldable¹* has the same structure as *unreadable* in Figure V.5. Notice that this is the only structure possible. The prefix *un-¹* can only be added to adjectives. Since *fold* is a verb, *un-¹* cannot be added to it. Instead, the suffix *-able* is added first to create the lexeme *foldable*. Since *foldable* is an adjective, it can be negated with *un-¹*. Notice that *un-¹* negates the adjective *foldable*, not the verb *fold*. Thus, a simple meaning representation of *unfoldable¹* could be [not [foldable]] (Figure V.6).

Figure V.6: Tree Diagram for *unfoldable¹*

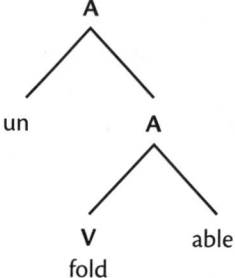

Turning to *unfoldable²*, we note that the prefix in this case is *un-²*. This prefix can only be added to verbs. Thus, it cannot be added to the adjective *foldable*. Instead, it must be added to the verb *fold* to create the lexeme *unfold*. The suffix *-able* can be added to this lexeme because it is a verb. Thus, a simple meaning representation of *unfoldable²* could be [[unfold] able to] (Figure V.7).

Figure V.7: Tree Diagram for *unfoldable²*

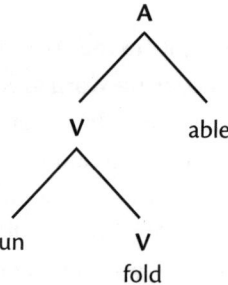

Conclusion: On the Notion of Word

We began this chapter questioning the definition of *word*. It should by now be clear that this is not as easy to answer as it might have seemed.

To begin with, we have seen that we must distinguish between what we are calling *word* and *lexeme*. A lexeme is an abstract unit that resides in a lexicon. We can think of a lexicon as a paper dictionary or, more interestingly, as the dictionary that resides in our minds. We are assuming that we do not memorize every inflected form of a noun or verb but instead internalize rules that generate these forms from the lexeme. In our sense of the term, a word is an inflected form of a lexeme.

There is evidence to suggest that the assumption that we internalize rules is correct. First, we are always able to correctly inflect new words. We don't invent new inflections for each new word that is created. Native English speakers know immediately that the plural of *wump* is *wumps* (not *wumpi*) and that the plural of *gutch* is *gutches* even though these are not actual words.

Second, and most interestingly, when children are acquiring language they will produce words that they have never heard before, words that are not English but perhaps should be. Words like *goed*, *comed*, and *foots*. Note that in each case, the correct form (*went*, *came*, and *feet*) is irregular. What seems to be happening is that the children have learned a rule and apply it universally. Only later do they learn that some words behave exceptionally.

It should be evident that the question "How many words are there in the English (or French, etc.)?" is not an easy one to answer. The appropriate first response is "Do you mean inflected forms or lexemes?" Different answers to this question will result in radically different answers to the first question.

The second property of words that should now be apparent is that they can have internal structure. This internal structure can be represented by tree diagrams. In a tree diagram, the leaves of the tree represent the morphemes. The nodes of the tree represent the new lexeme or word that has been created. Typically, this node will be marked with the syntactic category of the new lexeme or word and any grammatical information that has been added.

For example, when we begin to draw the tree diagram for the word *uncovered* as in the sentence *I uncovered Superman's secret identity*, we note that it has the derivational prefix *un-²*, the root *cover* and the past tense inflectional suffix *-ed*. In what order do the rules that add the affixes apply?

Earlier, we noted that a property of inflectional rules is that the word that they create is morphologically inert; nothing else can be added to it. Therefore, the prefix must be added before the inflectional suffix. Consequently, the tree diagram for *uncovered* will be like that in Figure V.8.

Figure V.8: Tree Diagram for *uncovered*

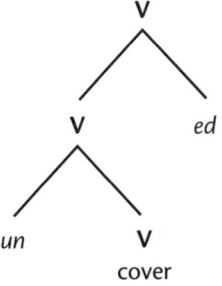

Finally, the passage from lexeme to word is mediated by a set of morphological rules. The derivational component of the lexicon creates new lexemes and can in principle apply as often as we like. The inflectional component creates inflected words from lexemes. Our concern in this book is with the derivational component of the English lexicon.

6 Integration

Introduction

In the previous chapters, we introduced three concepts that are central to our study:

1. *Change.* We have seen by comparing Old English and Contemporary English and by examining the Indo-European languages that languages change over time. We have also seen an example of a spelling change to a lexeme when a morpheme is added in the instance of COMPUTE+*ing* > *computing*.
2. *Structure.* Our preliminary examination of the problem of defining a word revealed that words have internal structure. In fact, this internal structure can be quite complex. As part of our explanation of this structure, we have proposed morphological rules of different types that can build lexemes and words.
3. *Borrowing.* Languages contain words from other languages. They have been borrowed because a culture needed words for concepts, objects, and artifacts that it either only recently discovered or invented, or because there is a tradition within the culture to use words from other languages for new technologies (as in English), or because the culture needs foreign words for taboo subjects.

In this chapter, we integrate these three concepts to provide the tools we require for the analysis of the English lexicon.

Structure and Borrowing

It is not unusual when writing on technically or conceptually sophisticated subjects to be stuck for a moment looking for the proper plural form of a word: Is criteria a singular or plural? What is the correct plural of medium: media or mediums? Why is formulas the plural of formula, except in logic and mathematics, where it is formulae? What is the plural of alumnus? If English nouns generally form the plural by adding -s, as in *tree/trees*, why does *phenomenons* sound odd?

If we investigate by determining the language of origin of these words, we discover that those that give us trouble are not English words. Usually they have either Latin or Greek origin.

Table VI.1: Foreign and English Plurals

Latin	Greek	Foreign Plural	English Plural
	phenomenon	phenomena	
	criterion	criteria	
formula		formulae	formulas
medium		media	mediums
alumnus		alumni	
pendulum		pendula	pendulums
vacuum		vacua	vacuums
	thesis	theses	
	index	indices	indexes

Two things become apparent when we examine Table VI.1. First, the true plural form is that from the original language. Often, this is the only plural form. Second, some words have become naturalized so that they are now receiving the native English plural.

The naturalization process is an interesting one and worth comment. In some cases, we can imagine that the naturalized form will replace the foreign form. This is likely for *vacuums* and for *formulas* outside of the specialized discourse of logic and mathematics. In some cases, both the foreign and naturalized forms continue to persist although with different meanings. Compare *media* and *mediums*. The former refers to the environments in which creatures live, the substances with which art is produced, etc. The latter refers to those who claim to be able to contact the supernatural world. Note also that *media* has also become a noun often used in the singular and referring to the means of communication for conveying news, entertainment, and advertising. Finally, some words seem resistant to naturalization. It is unlikely that *thesis* will be naturalized because it is only used in specialized contexts and the naturalized plural *thesises* is awkward.

Figure VI.1: Word Building, Revision 1

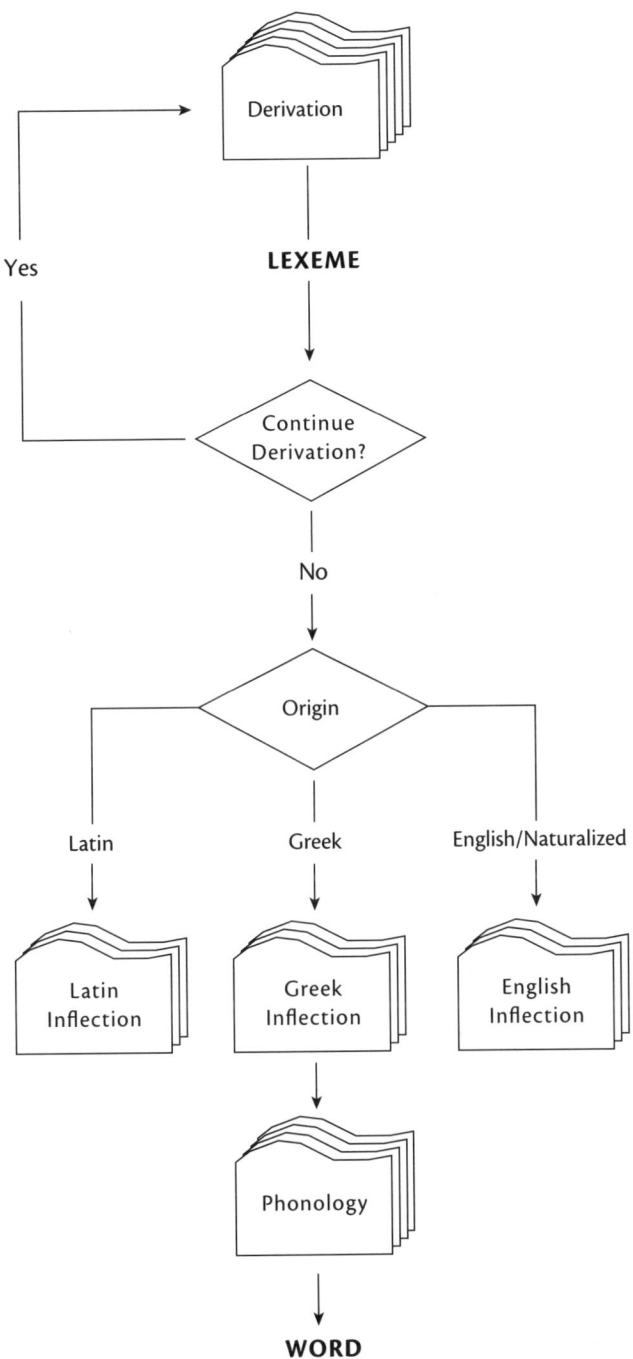

These considerations should make us reconsider the computer program we designed in Figure V.2. There, we proposed a single module for inflection. This won't do, because there are different ways to inflect a noun for plural, depending on whether it is a Latin, Greek, or English or naturalized noun. We need to revise the program so that we will have separate modules for inflecting words depending on their origin (Figure VI.1). In this revised version of the program, each lexeme will be marked with its language of origin. Before the lexeme is inflected, this mark is first examined so that the lexeme will be inflected by the appropriate inflection module. Each module contains just the rules for inflecting a word from that language.

If it is true that inflectional rules must be localized to the language of origin, it is reasonable to question whether the same is not true of derivational rules. The best method for testing whether rules are local to particular languages is to try to apply them to a selection of words from various languages. The idea is that if we create ungrammatical words by breaking the rules, then the rules must exist.[1] For example, consider the rule:

$$\text{Lex}_N \Rightarrow \text{Lex}_V + ion$$

This rule will create nouns from verbs by adding -ion. Table VI.2 gives examples of lexemes that can be created with this rule and some that cannot. What distinguishes the successful applications of the rule from the unsuccessful applications? To answer this question, we must return to a dictionary and determine what each group has in common.

Table VI.2

Verb	Noun
opine	opinion
complete	completion
produce	production
prevent	prevention
open	¢openion
break	¢breakion
fall	¢fallion

---

[1] The aphorism *the exception that proves the rule* is usually used to mean that is it possible to establish a rule by finding instances that do not obey the rule. This is an odd notion. In fact, *prove* is descended from *probe* and has this meaning in the aphorism. The aphorism should be *the exception that tests the rule*; that is, the exception tests whether the rule is correct.

Merriam-Webster's provides the following etymologies for the words in Table VI.2:

> *Opine*: [ME fr. MF & L fr. MF *opiner*, fr. L *opinari* to have an opinion]
> *Complete*: [ME *complet*, fr. L *completus*, fr. pp. of *complēre*]
> *Produce*: [ME (Sc), fr. L *producere*, fr. *pro-* forward + *ducere* to lead—more at TOW]
> *Prevent*: [ME, to anticipate, fr. L *praeventus*, pp. of *praevenire* to come before, anticipate, forestall, fr. *prae-* + *venire* to come—more at COME]
> *Open*: [ME, fr. OE; *akin* to OHG *offan* open, OE *ūp* up]
> *Break*: [ME *breken*, fr. OE *brecan*; akin to OHG *brehhan* to break, L *frangere*]
> *Fall*: [ME, fr. OE *feallan*; akin to OHG *fallan* to fall and perh. to Lith *pulti*][2]

Notice that whenever it is possible to apply the -ion rule, the lexeme that takes the suffix is Latinate. In the examples we have considered, the lexemes that cannot take the suffix are of English heritage. There are many other reasons why a lexeme cannot take this suffix, but the one constant is that if a lexeme does take this suffix, it must be Latinate.

Considerations such as these indicate that we should again reconsider the computer program illustrated in Figure VI.1. This version still assumes that there is a single derivational module that builds lexemes. However, as we have seen, we need to create blocks of rules that apply only to lexemes of particular languages. Figure VI.2 illustrates how this will be accomplished. Just as we had separate inflectional modules, we will have separate derivational modules. This means that we must index the rules by language so that they will be applied only when appropriate. For example, the -ion rule will now be:

$$[\text{Lex}_N \Rightarrow \text{Lex}_V + ion]_{\text{Latin}}$$

Hybrids

In the simplest of worlds, all words would be "derivationally pure". That is, words should be derivationally Latin, Greek, or English, but not a mixture. For most derivational processes, this is true. However, occasionally hybrids are created. A hybrid is a lexeme that contains elements from more than one language.

It is important to note that the existence of hybrids is itself evidence that at least one of the elements from which they have been created has been borrowed into the language. For example, the parts of hypertension are *hyper* and *tension*. The first is Greek and the last is Latin. Clearly, wherever this word was coined (Latin, Greek, or English), it borrowed one or both of the parts.

---

2 pp. 870, 254, 991, 984, 868, 151, 450.

Figure VI.2: Word Building, Revision 2

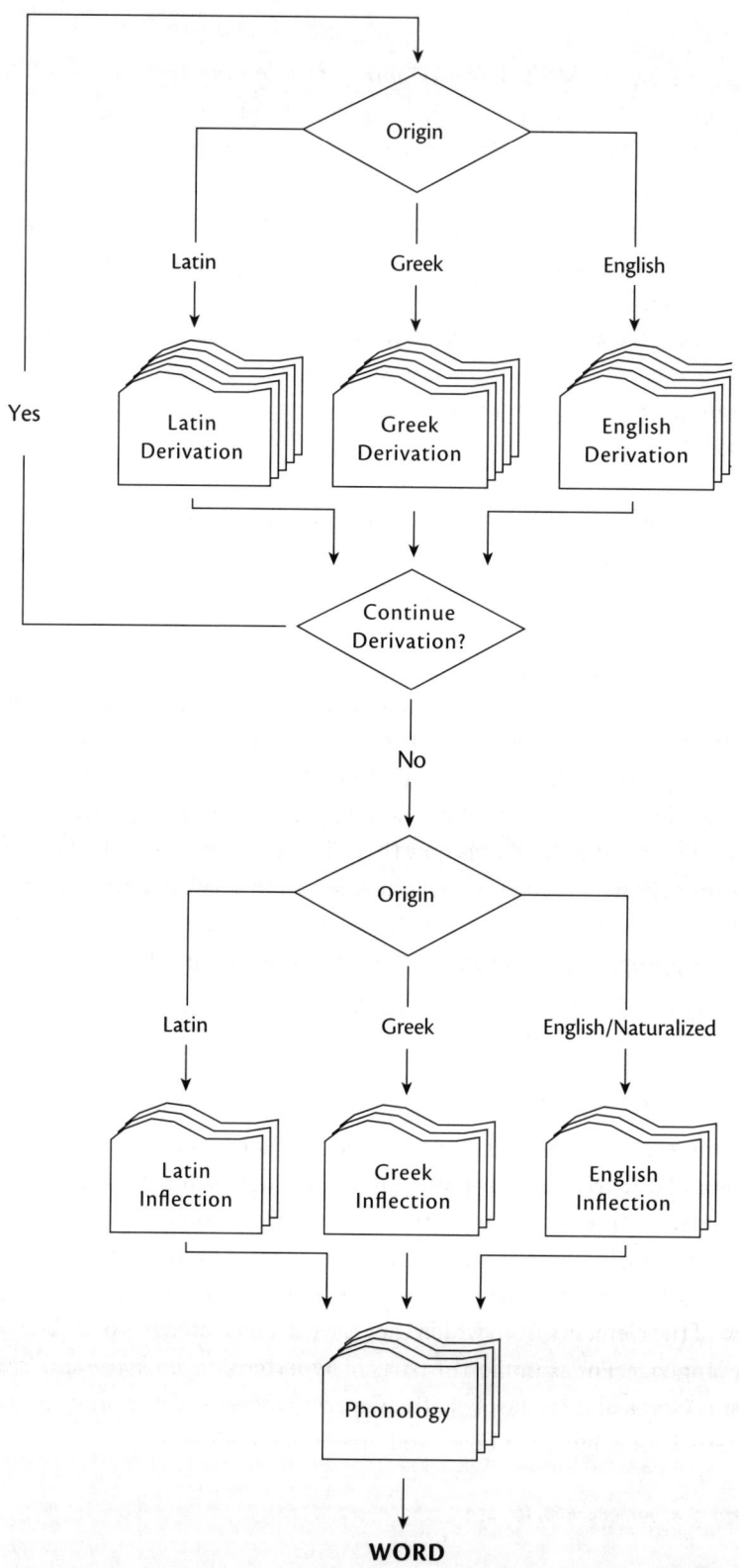

Our computer program in Figure VI.2 will not permit us to create hybrids unless we reconsider the language of origin each time we attempt to create a lexeme. If we want to create hybrids, we will need to include a mechanism that directs lexemes to other derivational modules. Hybrids are created for many of the same reasons we described in the discussion of borrowings. Often, a new concept is created and no word for it exists in any language. Ethical philosophers had this problem when they began to investigate whether it was possible to behave in a way that is neither moral nor immoral. How could they refer to this behaviour? The problem they had was that the negative form of *moral* already exists as *immoral* and it does not have the meaning that they were looking for. To create a new word for this new concept, they used the negative prefix from Greek and attached it to the Latin lexeme *moral* to create *amoral*.

Another more recent hybrid that now has common currency is dysfunction. The etymology of the prefix *dys-* is given in *Merriam-Webster's* as:

> [L *dys-*, fr. Gk; akin to OE *tō—*, *te—* apart, Skt *dus-* bad difficult][3]

The origin of *function*, on the other hand, is Latinate.

Latin has a prefix that is cognate with the Greek *dys-*. This is the prefix *dis-* found in *dissemble* and *dissimilar*. Those who coined the word *dysfunction* did not use the Latin prefix because it no longer has the meaning that they wanted. It now means something like "apart, away". These are not the concepts that were sought when *dysfunction* was coined.

If those who had coined *dysfunction* had used the Latin prefix *dis-* instead, what would the word look like? Think of words like *different* and *difficult*.

Another reason that hybrids are created is that one of the elements has become naturalized. We have been treating borrowings from a language as though they are a single indistinguishable class of words or lexemes. However, the longer an element has been in a language, the more it resembles native words. For example, although no one would be surprised to discover that *anaerobic*, *apotheosis*, *turbulent*, and *vociferous* are not native English words, most would be surprised to learn that neither are *beautiful*, *chair*, *clear*, or *wagon*. To the novice, these look like perfectly good English words, but all have been borrowed. They look English-like because they have been in the language much longer that the others cited above and have been in much more common usage. As a consequence, their rough edges have been smoothed off and they have come to resemble English lexemes.

---

3 p. 389.

A similar process has occurred with the suffix *-able*. It was originally imported into English on the ends of lexemes such as *dependable, capable,* and *remarkable*. Eventually, it was detached and viewed as an English suffix and can now be attached to virtually any English verb: *readable, workable, laughable,* etc.

The examples in Table VI.1 and the analysis of inflection implicit in Figure VI.1 suggest a problem that needs to be addressed: how are singular nouns inflected? If one is teaching English to someone and needs to explain how to create plural nouns, a naive analysis might lead to the suggestion that plural English nouns are created by adding *-s* to the singular. But that is not what the program diagrammed in Figure VI.2 describes. It describes a process by which words are created from the lexemes and a singular noun is a word, not a lexeme. It is not possible to create the plural by an operation on a singular word.

One proposal is to include two rules for nouns in our English inflection module. One is the rule that creates plural nouns from lexemes by adding *s*:

$$[\text{Word}_{N[pl]} \Rightarrow \text{Lex}_N + s]_{\text{English}}$$

The second rule will create a singular noun from a lexeme by adding nothing at all:

$$[\text{Word}_{N[sg]} \Rightarrow \text{Lex}_N + \emptyset]_{\text{English}}$$

One advantage to this proposal is that it corresponds to our definition of a word's paradigm as the set of inflected forms of a lexeme. This proposal claims that the paradigm of a noun lexeme is created by the two rules given above. in contrast, the naive view that plurals are formed from singulars, not from lexemes, does not correspond either to the program in Figure VI.1 or to the definition of *paradigm*.

The Latin and Greek examples in Table VI.1 provide further evidence that using rules to generate both plurals and singulars from lexemes is the right way. Table VI.1 contains several different classes of nouns, each class forming the singular and plural in a unique way. We will focus on just one class to illustrate the argument. The singulars and plurals from a Latin class are given in Table VI.3.

Table VI.3: Latin Plurals

Singular	Plural
medium	media
pendulum	pendula
vacuum	vacua

The first thing that we note is that the heuristic[4] that some have proposed for English—form the plural from the singular—will not work in Latin. We cannot form *media* by adding something to *medium*. Instead, we must discover the lexeme and specific markers for the singular and plural. When we scan the other words in Table VI.3, we note that they all end in *-um* in the singular and *-a* in the plural. It appears that the lexemes are *medi-*, *pendul-*, and *vacu-*. To generate the singular and plural words, the Latin inflectional module requires two rules:

$[\text{Word}_{N[sg]} \Rightarrow \text{Lex}_N + um]_{\text{Latin}}$

$[\text{Word}_{N[p]} \Rightarrow \text{Lex}_N + a]_{\text{Latin}}$

Notice that this is the same configuration of rules that we proposed for English. The inflectional bits differ, but that is expected from language to language. What remains the same (and has been inherited from the Indo-European parent language) is the configuration of rules. Contemporary English differs from Latin in that it no longer adds anything to the lexeme to form the singular, but both languages have rules that create singular and plural words from lexemes

Summary
The essential point of this section is that when we investigate word structure, we must be aware of the language of origin. Conversely, if we want to discover the parent language of a word, recognizing the parts of the word is very helpful.

Change and Structure
We have previously noted changes in English and its ancestors through history. There is a subtler sort of change that we have already touched upon without comment. In Chapter 5, we designed a computer program that could generate words. In addition to derivational and inflectional rules that build up lexemes and words respectively, we proposed a different sort of rule that applied after the inflectional rules to "clean up" and create the form with which we are familiar.

For example, to create the word computing we add -ing to COMPUTE. But, this creates the form COMPUTE+ing. Once the "+" is removed, the resulting form is ᶜcomputeing. To generate the correct form, we proposed a rule "e + i → i" to delete the "e". This rule is really just a spelling rule, borrowed from our discussion of historical change and introduced to get the form *computing* right. But there are good reasons to keep the idea of this kind of rule in our computer program. Consider the data in Table VI.4. It should be immediately apparent that all the words are formed by adding a prefix to a lexeme. Interestingly, this prefix in each column negates the adjective to which it has been added.

---

4   *Heuristic*: from Greek *eureka* "I found it". A heuristic is a method for discovery.

Table VI.4: Negative Prefix

inactive	illegal	irreplaceable
intolerant	illegible	irredeemable
intractable	illicit	irregular
inflexible	illegitimate	irrelevant

Our first attempt to understand these data could be to propose three rules:

$$\text{Lex}_A \Rightarrow in + \text{Lex}_A$$

$$\text{Lex}_A \Rightarrow il + \text{Lex}_A$$

$$\text{Lex}_A \Rightarrow ir + \text{Lex}_A$$

But now we have a problem of constraining these rules so that they apply only to the right lexemes. For example, the *il-* rule never applies to lexemes that begin with t, as in *¢ilterminable* instead of *interminable* or *f*, as in *¢ilfinite* instead of *infinite*; the *ir-* rule never applies to lexemes that begin with *a*, as in *¢iranimate* instead of *inanimate*.

A quick scan of Table VI.4 shows that *il-* appears only when the lexeme to which it is added begins with *l*, and *ir-* appears only when the lexeme begins with *r*. So far, our machinery for word and lexeme building hasn't given us a method for expressing this. But perhaps we should ask if we want it to.

By proposing three different rules, we are claiming that there are three different negative morphemes illustrated in Table VI.4. Recall that we noted that an important property of morphemes is the persistence of meaning. Conversely, this property suggests that when we discover different forms with the same meaning we must consider whether they are synonyms[5] or different forms of the same morpheme. In the case we are considering, the variants are very similar in form and their differences are completely predictable. The *il-* and *ir-* forms are predictable. The in- form seems to occur in a variety of unpredictable places (before *a, t, c, f,* etc.) that have nothing in common.

An alternative explanation that linguists always look for is one which proposes a single morpheme with a single lexeme building rule. Since we cannot predict where the in- variant will occur, we select it as representative of the morpheme. We will generate the other forms of the morpheme by using the "→"

---

[5] *Synonym*: from the Greek *syn-*, "with", and *onym*, "name". Synonyms are forms that have the same or very similar meaning.

rules that we have previously suggested are necessary for getting spelling right. From now on, we will refer to these rules as phonological rules. Phonological rules are responsible for adjusting how morphemes are pronounced given the context that morphological rules have created.

An illustrative analogy can be found in chemistry. Just as we can study morphemes and morphological structure in isolation, it is possible to study atoms and atomic structure. For example, we could study hydrogen (H) and oxygen (O) and learn about properties such as atomic weight. However, when we combine them in the appropriate quantities, we get H_2O, which has a different set of properties. Similarly, when morphemes are combined, contexts are created for changes in the units that compose morphemes. The rules that govern these changes are phonological rules.

Our analysis of the negative prefix proposes the single morphological rule:

$$Lex_A \Rightarrow in + Lex_A$$

In addition, we need two rules to generate the variants of in-:

$$n + l \rightarrow l + l$$

$$n + r \rightarrow r + r$$

Examples of how this rule complex operates to create the forms that we are familiar with are given in Table VI.5.

Table VI.5: Deriving Negative Adjectives

active	legal	regular	
in + active	in + legal	in + regular	$Lex_A \Rightarrow in + Lex_A$
"	il + legal	"	n+l → l+l
"	"	ir + regular	n+r → r+r
inactive	illegal	irregular	Remove "+"

As always and as illustrated by our computer program, the lexeme building rules apply first. After the lexeme (and word) have been built, the phonological rules apply to readjust how components of the morphemes are pronounced given the new context they are found in.

Phonological rules like those above are called *assimilation*[6] *rules*. In an assimilation rule, one sound becomes similar or identical to a neighbouring sound. In the rules above, *n* assimilates to *l* and *r*. In these rules, *n* assimilates completely and so the sound becomes identical to *l* and *r*. There are other cases where a sound assimilates only partially.

Consider the data in Table VI.6. When we scan the first four rows, we note a prefix *im-*. This prefix is added to adjectives to create an adjective whose meaning is the negative of the original. The similarity in form and meaning to the in- prefix above suggests that this new prefix is somehow related to it. If we assume that the *immature* is *in* + *mature*, then it is clear that we require the phonological rule:

n + m → m + m

Table VI.6: Negative Prefix *im-*

moral	immoral
measurable	immeasurable
mobile	immobile
mature	immature
possible	impossible
practical	impractical
precise	imprecise
potent	impotent

We should recognize immediately that this, too, is an assimilation rule: *n* has completely assimilated to a following *m*. But what of words like *impossible*? This word seems to contain a prefix *im-*. Again, this prefix is added to adjectives to create adjectives whose meaning negates the original, so we assume that it another form of the prefix *in-*. To make this analysis work, we require another phonological rule:

n + p → m + p

---

6 *Assimilation*: from the Latin *ad-*, "to", and *similare* "make similar to". In the linguistic context, to assimilate to something is to become similar to it.

What kind of a rule is this? Most linguists are uncomfortable if a phonological rule does not have a "natural" feel to it. Assimilation rules like those above have this characteristic: there is an underlying explanation for the change, in that one sound is becoming more like another. Can we show that this rule is also "natural"?

In order to see the naturalness of this rule, we need to review the properties of consonants from the Consonant Chart in Figure III.3. There we note that whereas *n* is an dental nasal, both *m* and *p* are labials. Thus, the rule above is another example of assimilation: *n* has partially assimilated to the following *p*. It is still a nasal, but now is articulated in the same position as *p*.

To this point, we have relied on English orthography to illustrate assimilation. We can get away with this because the characters *l*, *r*, and *m* (roughly) represent the sounds [*l*], [*r*] and [*m*] respectively. But, consider the data in Table VI.7. At first, these look to be simple examples of adding the negative prefix in- to a lexeme. However, this is one case where English orthography fails us.

Table VI.7

complete	incomplete
calculable	incalculable
competent	incompetent
conclusive	inconclusive
convenient	inconvenient

In fact, in normal speech the nasal represented by the character n is pronounced as [ŋ], the velar nasal not the dental nasal [n]. To discover why this should be, it is necessary to consider the phonetic properties of the first consonant of the lexeme to which the prefix is added, just as we did in the other cases. Once again, English orthography is not particularly helpful. Instead, it is necessary to consider what consonant the character *c* represents in these lexemes. Some experimentation should convince you that the character *c* represents the consonant [k]. Thus, there appears to be a rule:

n + k → ŋ + k

If you refer to the Consonant Chart, you can verify that both [ŋ] and [k] are velar consonants. Therefore, this rule is also an assimilation rule.

We expect that phonological rules have a sort of generality. They are not proposed to get the various forms of a single morpheme right. Instead, they are supposed to apply regularly throughout the language. Thus, one way we can justify our analysis of the prefix *in-* and our phonological rules is to demonstrate that these rules apply in other places. That these rules meet the criterion of generality should be evident from an examination of the data in Table VI.8.

Table VI.8: The Prefix *con-*

form	conform	respond	correspond	mission	commission
duct	conduct	relate	correlate	measure	commeasurable
test	contest	lateral	collateral	press	compress
genial	congenial	lapse	collapse	pact	compact
strict	constrict	labor	collaborate	patriot	compatriot
sign	consign			passion	compassion
join	conjoin				
figure	configure				
verge	converge				

In left columns of Table VI.8, we note a prefix *con-* that is added to a variety of different grammatical classes. In other columns and rows, we note that other instances of *col-*, *cor-*, and *com-*. These other instances appear in just those environments that our phonological rules predict. Consequently, it is not necessary to create more than one new morphological rule for con-:[7]

---

[7] Actually, this is not quite accurate. Words like *comestible* <com + estible, "edible", and *comity* <com + i + ty, "politeness", suggest that the prefix is actually com- not con-. This is because the roots that the prefix is added to here begin with a vowel. Therefore, if the prefix were *con-* there is no consonant to which the *n* could assimilate and the prefix should remain *con-*. But, in these words it doesn't appear as *con-*, it appears as *com-* indicating that *com-* is the actual prefix.

This is the historically accurate analysis. However, there is reason to continue with the analysis that the prefix is *con-*, aside from the fact that the pedagogical point is easier to see if we take the prefix to be *con-* rather than *com-*.

First, if the prefix is actually *com-*, the assimilation to *n* before *f* and *v*, consonants made with lips and teeth, as in *configure* and *converge*, is not obvious. We would expect *ᶜcomfigure* and *ᶜcomverge*. Notice that the intensifier com- shows the correct form in *comfort* <L com-, + fortis, strong> (*Merriam-Webster's* p. 248). Second, a recent form such as *conurbation*, "densely populated urban area" (created in 1915), shows n before a vowel. This indicates that the morpheme has, indeed, been reanalyzed as *con-*.

The analysis that we will go with is that while the prefix was originally *com-*, it was reanalyzed as *con-*, and our phonological rules apply to this form.

Notice, that after being borrowed into English, the prefix was further reanalyzed as *co-*. Evidence for this reanalysis are words like *coworker*, *codefendent*, etc.

Lex ⇒ *con* + Lex

The phonological rules that were created to account for the various forms of *in-* will look after the rest. Another way of looking at it is that the various forms of *con-* justify the phonological rules we have proposed. They are independent evidence in favour of these rules.

Summary
The function of morphology is to create lexemes and words. By combining morphemes, morphological rules bring together sounds that may create contexts for change. The rules that govern this change are phonological rules. These rules adjust the pronunciation of morphemes given their new contexts and apply after morphological rules have constructed lexemes and words.

Change and Borrowing
The criterion of generality requires that a phonological rule potentially applies to every word in the language. The only reason that a rule won't apply is that the sounds to which it is sensitive do not appear in the word. On this initial understanding of the criterion, there appear to be numerous examples that show that the phonological rules that we have been proposing are incorrect.

Consider the examples in Table VI.9. The right hand columns demonstrate that there is a prefix *un-* that is added to adjectives to create adjectives whose meaning negates that of the original. Although this prefix superficially resembles the negative prefix *in-*, we cannot treat it as a variant. First, there is no way to predict the vowel; that is, we cannot propose a natural phonological rule that changes i to u in the right circumstances. Second, and most important for our purposes, it does not behave the same way: the n in un- does not assimilate to a following *l, r, m,* or *p*. On this basis we can propose a morphological rule:

$[Lex_A \Rightarrow un + Lex_A]_{English}$

Table VI.9: The Negative Prefix un-

		happy	unhappy
		conditional	unconditional
		deniable	undeniable
legal	illegal	lawful	unlawful

redeemable	irredeemable	readable	unreadable
		ripe	unripe
mature	immature	manly	unmanly
possible	impossible	pleasant	unpleasant

The failure of assimilation to apply to *un-* initially seems to contradict the criterion of generality. To put it another way, if we maintain that the criterion is correct, then these words seem to indicate that the phonological rules that we have proposed are wrong, because they do not apply where they apparently should.

The solution to this dilemma is found when we examine the historical origins of the words in Tables VI.4, VI.6, and VI.9. The prefix *in-* is always attached to words of Latin origin. This prefix was borrowed into English when the Latin words to which it is attached were borrowed. On the other hand, the prefix *un-* is an English prefix and is added to English words or borrowed words that have been naturalized.

Just as morphemes can be identified with particular languages, phonological rules can also be categorized by their language of origin. The assimilation rules that we have been examining are Latin rules and as a consequence do not apply to English morphemes, such as un-.

To provide further illustration of the localization of phonological rules, consider the words in Table VI.10. The forms on the left illustrate the base to which a prefix has been added. The first few examples suggest that the prefix is *an-* and that it is added to an adjective to create an adjective whose meaning negates the original. Again, it is quite similar to the *in-* negative prefix. However, we cannot predict when the vowel is *a* and when *i*. We suppose instead that this is a different prefix:

$$\text{Lex}_A \Rightarrow an + \text{Lex}_A$$

Table VI.10: Greek Negative Prefix *an-*

aerobic	anaerobic
matriarchy	anarchy
isotropic	anisotropic
oxygen	anoxic
isometric	anisometric
urine	anuria

theist	atheist
gnostic	agnostic
pathetic	apathetic
phonic	aphonic
rhythmic	arhythmic
static	astatic

As we scan the other words in the list, we note that the n of this prefix does not assimilate. Instead, we seem to have a variant *a-* appearing. Our task is to discover a phonological rule that will predict when the morpheme appears as *an-* and when as *a-*.

It should be evident that the prefix is *an-* before vowels and *a-* before consonants. Continuing with our analysis of the prefix as *an-*, we require a phonological rule that will delete *n* before consonants. Using "C" to represent any consonant, we write:

$$n + C \rightarrow + C$$

This rule creates further problems. Why do some instances of *n* assimilate, some do nothing, and some delete? The answer lies in the language of origin. We have seen that the assimilating *n* is Latinate and the inert *n* is English. The *n* that deletes is Greek. Thus, our morphological and deletion rules should be:

$$[\text{Lex}_A \Rightarrow an + \text{Lex}_A]_{\text{Greek}}$$

$$[n + C \rightarrow C]_{\text{Greek}}$$

To completely account for sensitivity to language of origin, we need to make a final revision to the structure of our computer program for generating words. We have already localized morphological rules to their respective languages. We will also localize phonological rules. After derivational rules apply, the phonological rules of the originating language will also apply to adjust sounds according to their new context. This is pictured in Figure VI.3.

138　INTEGRATION

Figure VI.3: Word Building: Final Version

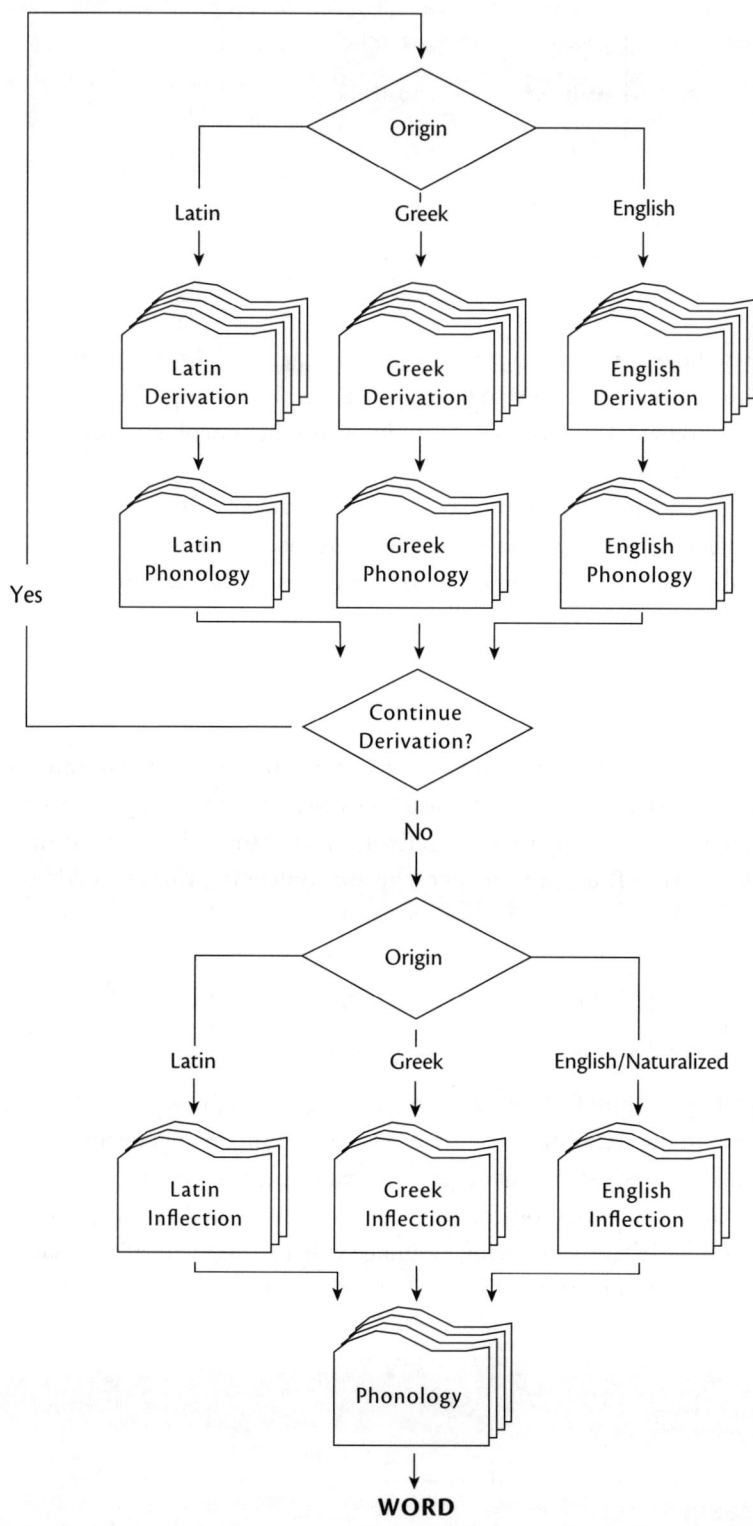

The rule

$$n + C \rightarrow C$$

should look familiar, since it applies in English to the indefinite article *an*. One of the rules that an English speaker must learn is that the article is *an* before words that begin with vowels and *a* before words that begin with consonants; notice that it is *an apple* but *a consonant*. The alternation is explained by proposing that the article is just *an* but that a rule deletes *n* before consonants, as with the Greek negative.

This observation can be used to emphasize that phonological rules are sensitive to the phonetic structure of a word, not to the way it is spelled. Notice that although the rule claims that the indefinite article is *an* before words that begin with a vowel, we find sequences like *a ukulele, a uniform* and *a union*. Do these examples force us to reconsider our rule? Is it possible that the rule is wrong?

If we pronounce these words carefully, we note that they do not begin with a vowel but with the consonant [y]. For example, *union* is pronounced [yunyən]. The rule is correct if it applies to the phonetic form of a word and not the spelling of the word.

Another example is *a hippopotamus*, but *an hour*. If one concentrates on pronunciation, it should be noticeable that there is an initial consonant [h] in *hippopotamus* but no consonant [h] in *hour*.

As discussed previously, the orthography of a language is not always an accurate clue to its structure.

Throughout this discussion we have commented on the similarities among the prefixes *in-*, *un-*, and *an-*. Why do Latin, Greek, and English all have a negative prefix that is added to adjectives and why are these prefixes so similar in form? Recalling that these are sister languages, the answer should be evident. These prefixes are cognates; they are descended from a single Proto-Indo-European prefix (Figure VI.4).

Figure VI.4

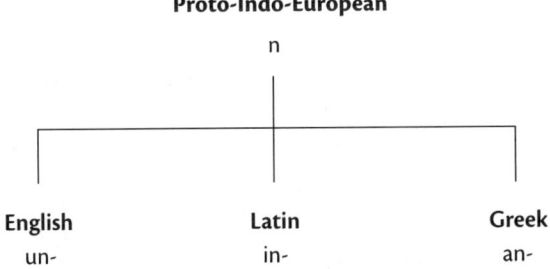

A Complete Analysis of the Negative Prefixes

We end by considering a final set of data to complete our analysis of the negative prefixes used in English. Consider first the data in Table VI.11. There is something odd about these terms that we have not previously seen. Consider the contrast between *noble* and *ignoble*. It is clear that there is a negative prefix, but it is not clear what this prefix is.

Table VI.11: Latin Negatives II

noble	ignoble
norm[1]	ignorant

We could propose that the prefix is *ig-*. A look in a dictionary reveals that *noble* was borrowed from Latin, and so it is susceptible to Latin morphological rules. A possible rule could be:

$$[\text{Lex}_A \Rightarrow ig + \text{Lex}_A]_{\text{Latin}}$$

Unfortunately, this won't do because we cannot tell when to use this rule and when to use the rule that we have previously proposed (and in which we presumably have more confidence):

$$[\text{Lex}_A \Rightarrow in + \text{Lex}_A]_{\text{Latin}}$$

This is the same problem that arose when we initially proposed rules like:

$$\text{Lex}_A \Rightarrow in + \text{Lex}_A$$

$$\text{Lex}_A \Rightarrow il + \text{Lex}_A$$

$$\text{Lex}_A \Rightarrow ir + \text{Lex}_A$$

Then, it was noted that it wasn't possible to predict when to use one or the other, except on phonological grounds. The problem here is somewhat worse: there is no way to predict at all when to add *ig-* and when to add *in-*, except that *ig-* is added to *noble* and a root that appears to be √nor. Notice that both these roots begin with n so we might suppose that this is somehow important. But there is also a root √noc meaning "injury", as in *noxious*,[8] which is found

---

8 Remember that x = [ks] and that the character c represents [k].

negated in *innocent* and *innocuous*. This fact proves that one cannot predict a prefix *ig-* based on the root beginning with *n*.

Suppose, instead, we propose that our usual rule is the right one and that the g is created by a phonological rule, such as:

$$[n + n \rightarrow g + n]_{Latin}$$

On this analysis, we would derive *noble* and *ignoble* as in Table VI.12.

Table VI.12: Deriving *ignoble* I

noble	noble	
"	in + noble	$[Lex_A \Rightarrow in + Lex_A]_{Latin}$
"	ig + noble	$[n + n \rightarrow g + n]_{Latin}$
noble	ignoble	remove "+"

Unfortunately, our phonological rule can't be right because there are examples where the sequence of n + n does not convert to g + n. For example, when we negate the now rare adjective *nocent* (which means "guilty"), we produce *innocent* "not guilty", not *ᶜignocent*. Additionally, the same root √noc appears in *innocuous* "not harmful" without the predicted g.

Whenever the solution to a problem is elusive like this, it is useful to review our assumptions. Sometimes, assumptions are unstated and when made explicit can be re-examined. One of our assumptions, apparent in Table VI.12, is that the lexeme to which the prefix is added is *noble*. Suppose that this is incorrect, and the lexeme is instead *gnoble*? This lexeme never appears by itself: we need a rule that creates *noble* from *gnoble*. Suppose that *g* is deleted when it appears with n at the beginning of a word. Using a convention from phonology, we write this as:

$$[\# gn \rightarrow \# n]_{Latin}$$

The crosshatch "#" is used here to indicate that there is no material before gn; that is, the *gn* string must appear at the beginning of a word.[9] This rule explains why *noble* does not begin with *g*.

Now, we consider *ignoble*. If the lexeme to which *in-* is added is *gnoble*, then the structure of *ignoble* is *in + gnoble*. To successfully derive *ignoble*, we require

---

9   If we wanted to say that this rule could only apply at the end of a word, we would write *gn # → n #*.

a rule that will delete the *n* of *in-*. This rule must be restricted to just those lexemes in which the prefix is added to a lexeme that begins with *gn* because the *n* does not delete in, for example, *inglorious*, in which the prefix is added to a lexeme that begins with *gl*.

$$[n + gn \rightarrow + gn]_{Latin}$$

When we combine these rules, we can successfully derive both *noble* and *ignoble* as in Table VI.13.

Table VI.13: Deriving *ignoble* II

gnoble	gnoble	
"	in + gnoble	$[Lex_A \Rightarrow in + Lex_A]_{Latin}$
noble	"	$[\# gn \rightarrow \# n]_{Latin}$
"	i + gnoble	$[n + gn \rightarrow + gn]_{Latin}$
noble	ignoble	Remove "+"

How can we tell if this last analysis is the right one? We will use two sorts of evidence: that from other Latin borrowings and evidence from cognates in Greek and English.

The lexemes *ignoble* and *ignorant* are based on a Latin form *gn*. It was used to create words that denoted aspects of knowledge (and, by extension, esteem in *noble*). Thus, we find *ignorant* "not knowing". Latin had another form that alternated between *gn* and *gen* and refers to acts of birth and production. The *gen* version is apparent in *generate* and *genus* among many other words. The *gn* form is most readily apparent in *pregnant* from *pre* "before" + *gn* "birth".[10] Let us refer to this form as gn^2 and the form referring to knowledge as gn^1.

We will use gn^2 to demonstrate that we need the phonological rules that we proposed to explain *noble* and *ignoble* for other purposes. To do so, we consider the forms *natal* and *cognate*. These words are semantically related: *natal* refers to birth, and cognate words are born from the same parent word. Clearly, in *cognate*, a prefix has been added to *gnate*. We know from previous discussion that the prefix is *con-*. Thus, the morphological structure of *cognate* is *con + gnate*. We have already proposed a rule that predicts—correctly—that the *n* of *con-* will delete before *gn*. That this prediction is correct for different prefixes and lexemes is evidence in favour of the rule.

---

10 This root also appears in *malign* and *malignant*.

That the lexeme *natal* is derived from the form *gn²* is clear from its meaning and similarity of form (it is missing only the initial *g*). If the lexeme is *gnatal*, the rule we proposed for *noble* will convert it to the correct *natal* (Table VI.13).

Table VI.14: Deriving *cognate*

gnatal	gnate	
"	con + gnate	$[Lex_A \Rightarrow con + Lex_A]_{Latin}$
natal	"	$[\# gn \to \# n]_{Latin}$
"	co + gnate	$[n + gn \to + gn]_{Latin}$
natal	cognate	Remove "+"

That the rules we need for lexemes created from *gn¹* are also needed for lexemes created from *gn²* is strong evidence that these rules are correct.

We can also verify that we are right that *ignoble* is formed from *gn¹* "know" by examining cognates from other languages. In Table VI.15, Greek and English words and structural cognates are provided. If we examine the Greek words first, we note immediately that *gn¹* in Greek is more immediately obvious than in Latin. The reason for this is that Greek lacks the rule that deletes g before n at the beginning of words. The lack of *n* in agnostic is predicted by the deletion we have already proposed for Greek (an + C → a + C).

Table VI.15: *know*

Latin		Greek		English	
noble	ignoble	gnostic	agnostic	knowable	unknowable
(norm)	ignorant				

The English example presents an interesting case. Whereas the Latin and Greek forms begin with *gn*, the English form begins with *kn*. If we recall our discussion of Grimm's Law, voiced stops became voiceless stops in Germanic languages like English and, in particular, *g* became *k*. Thus, English *know* is predicted from Latin *gno* and Greek *gno*. However, English know is pronounced as (approximately) [no] and particularly not as [kno]. Our explanation is that English has had in its history an Anglicized version of the rule in Latin that deletes velars before a nasal:[11]

---

11 For a reminder of the meaning of these phonetic terms, see Figure III.3.

$[kn \rightarrow n]_{English}$

Whereas, in Latin this rule applies only to a string at the beginning of the word, in English the rule applies everywhere. This explains why (the pronunciation) of the English words know and unknowable do not show the alternation found in noble and ignoble but instead the root is [no] in both.[12]

Conclusion

The English lexicon is partitioned into different sections, each of which is responsible for word building according to a set of principles different from the other sections. To this point, we see that we need to divide the lexicon into partitions for Latin, Greek, and English words. Later, we will add a significant partition for French.

The principles that govern word building are expressed as morphological rules and phonological rules. The former are responsible for combining morphemes into lexemes and words. The latter adjust how morphemes are pronounced when they appear in different contexts.

Each partition contains a unique set of morphological and phonological rules. The principle of generality requires that each phonological rule applies regularly within the relevant partition.

Further Reading

Partridge, Eric. *Origins: A Short Etymological Dictionary of Modern English.* New York: Greenwich House, 1983.

---

12 An interesting counter-example to the rule is *acknowledge* which does not show the deletion of *k*.

7 Identifying Morphemes

Introduction

We have identified two properties that are integral to the notion of *morpheme*:

1. Each instance of a morpheme must convey the same meaning as that proposed for its lexical entry. We might permit some fuzziness to this principle — that is, in some cases we might agree that a morpheme is used in different ways or may not have an identifiable meaning — but usually it will be possible to identify a core meaning common to all the instances of a morpheme.

2. A morpheme might vary its shape—as does the Latin negative prefix among *in*, *im*, *i*, *ir*, and *il*—but the variants are predicted by phonological rules.

The various instances of a morpheme are its *allomorphs*.[1] Parallel to the distinction between lexeme and word is that between morpheme and allomorph. A morpheme is an object in a lexicon, perhaps one's mental dictionary. An allomorph is the use of that morpheme in context. *Morpheme* is a more abstract concept than *allomorph* in the sense that we can observe allomorphs but must deduce the form of a morpheme.

In the case of the Latin negative, we can say that there is a morpheme IN which has allomorphs *in*, *im*, *i*, *ir*, and *il*.

In this chapter, we explore these properties in more detail.

---

[1] *Allomorph*: from the Greek *allo*, "other" and *morph*, "shape".

Homonyms[2]

Consider the data in Table VII.1.

Table VII.1

genius	ingenious
flection	inflection
toxic	intoxicate
luminous	illuminate
lustrous	illustrious
pact	impact
pregnant	impregnate
radiate	irradiate
rupture	irruption

It seems clear that the forms in the right-hand column are formed from those on the left by, in part, adding a prefix. The prefix appears to be the Latin negative prefix *-in*. Equally, we can note that the pattern of variation in the prefix is identical to that which we have seen with the Latin negative prefix: it appears as *il* before *l*, as *ir* before *r*, as *im* before *p*, and as *in* before other characters.

Are we justified in concluding that these words also contain instances of the Latin negative prefix?

Two things should alert us that this is not the negative prefix. First, whereas our previous examples of the negative prefix were restricted to adjectives, the examples in Table VII.1 do not line up so tidily. If we want to save our neat rule for the Latin negative prefix, we would prefer that these examples be something else.

When we examine the meaning of this prefix, it is clear that it cannot be a negative prefix. This becomes obvious when we contrast *impregnable* with *impregnate*. One of the meanings of the former (and the meaning that interests us) is "not capable of being captured"; we can describe a fortress as being impregnable. Clearly, this is formed by adding the negative prefix *in-* to *pregnable*. In contrast, *impregnate* means "to make pregnant"; it in no way implies

---

2 *Homonym*: from the Greek *homo* "same" and *onyma* "name". Homonyms are forms that have the same spelling (and usually the same pronunciation) but different meanings such as *butter*, the milk product, and *butter*, "one who butts". Unfortunately, *homonym* is often used for words that are pronounced similarly but spelled differently like *to*, *two*, and *too*. These latter are more properly called *homophones*.

the negation of *pregnant*. The prefix of *impregnate* is not the negative prefix, but one that could be glossed as "in"; that is, it refers to a location. We will consequently call it the locative[3] prefix. Notice that

- to be *intoxicated* is to have a toxin inside oneself;
- to *irradiate* something is to direct radiation into it;
- to be *ingenious* is to have genius inside;
- to *illuminate* something is to shine light on it.

Notice that the principle that we appeal to here is that from property 1 above: each instance of a morpheme must carry the same meaning. Since these instances are not negative, they must be instances of a different morpheme. Since they share roughly the same meaning of "in", we propose that they are all instances of the same morpheme, the locative.

Another point that is important to make is that this morpheme is susceptible to the same rules as the Latin negative morpheme. This provides further evidence that we were correct when we proposed these rules. They were not designed for just the negative prefix. They apply to the locative and to *con-* as well.

There is yet another instance of *in-*, although it is little used. Table VII.2 gives examples

Table VII.2

flammable	inflammable
regardless	irregardless

It is clear that *inflammable* is not the negative form of *flammable*. Not only is an inflammable thing likely to burst into flame, it is perhaps more likely to do so than is a flammable thing. Similarly, those who use a word like *irregardless* do so to emphasize the meaning of *regardless*. This *in-* is clearly neither negative or locative. It is, instead, an intensifier.

Synonyms

English Locative

Now that we have established the locative morpheme, we can examine other examples in Table VII.3. These, too, seem to illustrate a morpheme with locative meaning. Are we justified in proposing that the morpheme *in-* in Table VII.3 is the same morpheme as that illustrated in Table VII.1?

---

3 *Locative*: from the Latin *loc-*, "place".

Table VII.3: Locatives

born	inborn
built	inbuilt
come	income
deed	indeed
door	indoor
put	input
let	inlet
lay	inlay
road	inroad
rush	inrush
set	inset
sight	insight

We should notice that this morpheme does not behave the same way as that in Table VII.1. Notice that in, for example, *inlay* the *n* does not assimilate to the following *l* as expected. According to Principle 2 above, each variant of the morpheme must be predictable by rule. Since these are not predicted by the rules that we have created for Latin, they cannot be instances of the Latin locative morpheme.

If we examine the origins of the words in Table VII.3, we discover that they are all English. Thus, the locative morpheme illustrated in this table is an English morpheme. Its Englishness explains why it does not assimilate. The assimilation rules are Latin rules and apply only to Latin constructions.

Greek Locative

Since both English and Latin have a locative morpheme, it should not surprise us that we can find examples of a Greek locative. Table VII.4 contains some examples of the Greek locative with explanations of the Greek root.

Table VII.4: Greek Locative

encyclopedia	en + cyclo + paedia	circle + teach
enema	en + heina	send
endemic	en + demos	people
energy	en + erg	work
ellipsis	en + leip	leave
empyrean	en + pyre	fire
emblem	en + ball	throw
embolism	en + ball	throw

Notice that the Greek locative is susceptible to a set of assimilation rules similar to those in Latin. In Greek, the *n* of the locative prefix assimilates completely to a following *l* and partially to a following *p* or *b*.

Summary

We have seen that there are two intersecting properties of a morpheme: its meaning and its pronunciation. Together with its grammatical properties (what it can be added to and what the effect of this is), these properties constitute the morpheme's definition. Strings may sound alike but cannot be instances of the same morpheme if they do not carry the same meaning. Similarly, strings that carry the same meaning cannot be instances of the same morpheme if they do not have the same phonological characteristics.

We illustrate the results of our research in Table VII.5, together with the phonological rules that apply to the morphemes.

Table VII.5: Summary

	English	Latin	Greek
Locative	in	in Assimilation	en Assimilation
Negative	un	in Assimilation Deletion	an Deletion

The Latin Partition

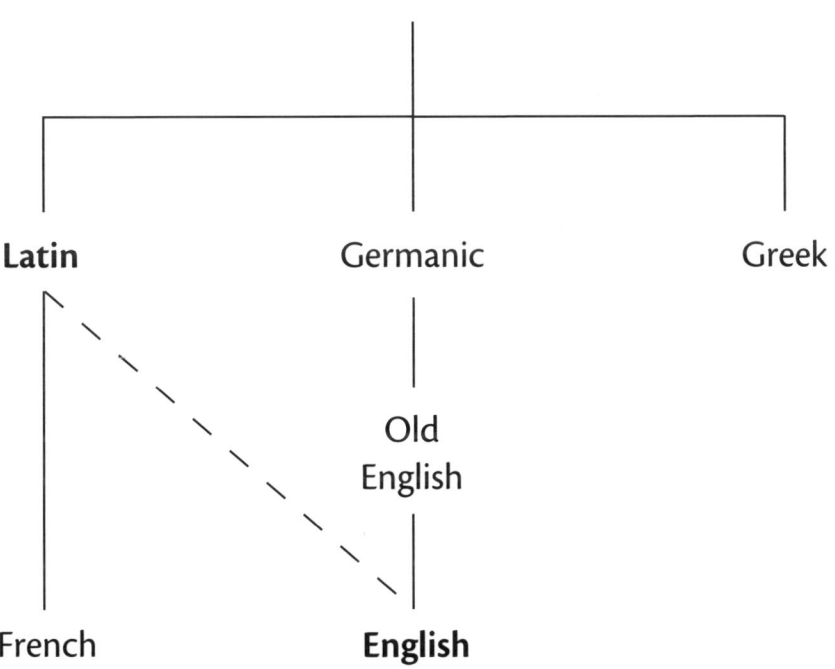

8 The Latin Verb

Introduction

Latin was an inflecting language. By this we mean that many of the grammatical notions that a language like English or Cantonese would express by separate words are expressed, instead, in the inflectional paradigms of, *inter alia*, nouns and verbs. Table VIII.1 gives an example by comparing English words and phrases with their counterparts in Latin. Notice that whereas English often requires several words to express a set of grammatical concepts, Latin requires but one; information about person, number, tense, mood, and aspect are part of the inflectional system of the verb.[1]

Table VIII.1: Examples of Latin Verb Inflection

I love	amō	first person singular, present tense, indicative mood, active voice
I loved	amāvī	first person singular, past tense, perfect aspect, indicative mood, active voice
I was loving	amābam	first person singular, past tense, imperfect aspect, indicative mood, active voice
I will love	amābō	first person singular, future tense, indicative mood, active voice
loved	amātus	past perfect participle
loving	amantus	present participle

---

1 Notice that Latin, like Old English, made a distinction between long and short vowels. Long vowels are indicated by a macron over the vowel. This distinction will be important later in this chapter, so we will continue to make it, but keep in mind that this distinction has been lost in Contemporary English.

It is worth reviewing elementary grammar to be clear what is meant by some of the terms used above. *Person* designates the referent of a pronoun or the agreement marking on a verb and takes the values of *first* (the speaker), *second* (the hearer), or *third* (a third party who is spoken of). Latin and English both distinguish between singular and plural referents. Some languages distinguish other categories of number including dual (two) and paucal (a few). In the plural of the first person, Latin and English have a single pronoun or verb marker. Many languages distinguish between first person plural inclusive (i.e. "we" including the hearer) and first person plural exclusive (i.e., "we", excluding the hearer).

Tense refers to the time or state of the action. *Present tense* locates the action designated by the verb in the present, *past tense* in the past. *Perfect aspect* indicates that the action has been completed and, hence, locates it prior to the time of reference. *Imperfect aspect* locates an action prior to the time of reference and indicates that it is incomplete, continuous, ongoing, customary, or contemporaneous with another action.

Mood refers to the speaker's attitude toward the action. The *indicative mood* indicates that the statement is considered fact. The *subjunctive mood* marks the statement as a supposition or statement of possibility.

Voice marks the relation of the grammatical subject of the sentence to the verb. In *active voice*, the grammatical subject is usually the agent (as in <u>The child</u> broke the toy). In the *passive voice*, the grammatical subject is usually the object upon which the agent acts (as in <u>The toy</u> was broken by the child).

English did not borrow much of this inflectional structure when it borrowed Latin verbs, but it did borrow some. Latin had a derivational morphology that acted on different parts of the verb. For example, *amateur* was created from the past perfect participle of the verb illustrated in Table VIII.1[2] and the proper name *Amanda* from the present participle, both with the same root $\sqrt{am}$ "love". In the next section, we will examine how a Latin verb is constructed. In subsequent sections, we will explore the derivational rules that English has borrowed.

The Structure of the Verb

The regular verbs of Latin are usually arranged into four conjugations.[3] Each conjugation is a general description of the paradigms of the verbs that are its members. It is usually easy to determine which conjugation a verb belongs to by looking at the infinitive[4] because it displays a *thematic vowel*. Table VIII.2

---

2 The past participle is *amat-*. The suffix *-us* is an inflectional ending.
3 *Conjugation*: From the Latin *con-*, "together" and *jug*, "join". A conjugation is a pattern of inflection, literally a joining together of morphemes (in a regular pattern).
4 The infinitive is *nonfinite*, meaning that it is not inflected for person, number, or tense.

gives examples of the four conjugation classes. From these, it should be possible to determine the basic structure of the infinitive.

Table VIII.2: The Thematic Vowel

| amāre | to love | monēre | to warn | regere | to rule | audīre | to hear |
| creāre | to create | credēre | to believe | legere | to read | finīre | to finish |

It should be evident, first, that the infinitive is formed by adding *-re* to something.

Table VIII.3: The Thematic Vowel II

| amā + re | to love | monē + re | to warn | rege + re | to rule | audī + re | to hear |
| creā + re | to create | credē + re | to believe | lege + re | to read | finī + re | to finish |

As we scan the remainder of the words, we note that the bit that *-re* is added to always ends in a vowel.

If we had time to examine all the regular verbs in Latin, we would find that a very large class of them form the infinitive in this way: adding *-re* to a form that ends in a vowel and that vowel is always one of the four in Table VIII.2. This vowel is called the *thematic vowel* because it determines the theme of how the paradigm of the verb will be constructed, its conjugation. Table VIII.4 shows that structure of these verbs. Note that there are four thematic vowels: ā, ē, e and ī.

Table VIII.4: The Thematic Vowel III

am + ā + re	to love	mon + ē + re	to warn
reg + e + re	to rule	aud + ī + re	to hear
cre + ā + re	to create	cred + ē + re	to believe
doc + e + re	to teach	fin + ī + re	to finish

The general pattern for forming a verb in Latin is to begin with a root, such as *am*, and add its thematic vowel. We will call the form that consists of a bare root and a thematic vowel the *thematic stem*. To this thematic stem, inflectional endings are added.

Obviously, English did not borrow Latin inflection, so we are not much interested in that aspect of Latin morphology. However, in Latin, derivational rules could apply to both the thematic stem and other forms created from the thematic stem. And, English did borrow forms created by these rules.

Derivation from Latin Verbs

The first step to create a verb in Latin is adding a thematic vowel to a root to create the thematic stem. We must propose, then, the following rule:[5]

$$[\text{Stem}_{theme} \Rightarrow \text{Root} + V_{theme}]_{Latin}$$

Notice that it is possible to form words from just the verb root. Table VIII.5 gives some examples of English words borrowed from Latin or created in English from Latin forms that are formed simply from the root and do not contain the thematic vowel.

Table VIII.5: Derivations from Roots

Root	Verb	Gloss	English Borrowing
√leg	legere	to read	college
√doc	docere	to teach	docile
√am	amāre	to love	amorous
√fac	facere	to make, do	faculty
√rap	rapere	to seize	rapture
√prob	probāre	to test	probe
√frig	frigere	be cold	frigid
√put	putāre	to reckon	compute

Latin has a large number of morphological rules that build lexemes from the past participle stem, so we will start with it and return the present participle later.

Past Participle Stems

The past participle stem is formed by adding -t- to the thematic stem. In many cases, that is all there is to say. Having formed the past participle, other

---

5 Here, "V" is an abbreviation for *vowel*. Thus V_{theme} signifies one of the thematic vowels.

Derivation from Latin Verbs 157

suffixes may be added to form new lexemes. To see how this works, consider the root from Table VIII.5 √prob, "to test". We first add the thematic vowel to form the thematic stem:

prob + ā   [Stem$_{theme}$ ⇒ Root + V$_{theme}$]$_{Latin}$

From the thematic stem, we create the past participle stem by adding the past participle suffix -t-:

prob + ā + t   [Stem$_{ppp}$ ⇒ Stem$_{theme}$ + t]$_{Latin}$

From these two forms, it is possible to create a number of words. Table VIII.6 gives a few examples.

Notice that the -ion suffix is a very common addition to the past participle stem. It is sometimes stated that the suffix is in fact -tion. This cannot be correct for several reasons. First, the -t- can occur without -ion as in probate. We know from facts about Latin inflectional morphology that this -t- is in fact the past participle suffix. Second, sometimes the -ion suffix occurs without the -t- as in opinion < opin "to think" + -ion.

Table VIII.6: Derivation from √prob

Stem$_{theme}$	Stem$_{ppp}$
probable	probate
probabilistic	probation
probability	probationary

As a useful review, we can consider the tree diagrams for words derived from the thematic stem and the past participle stem. Figure VIII.1 gives the tree diagram for *probable*. We can see that it is formed from the thematic stem by adding *-ble*. This suffix forms adjectives and consequently, the tree is rooted at Lex$_A$.

Figure VIII.1: *probable*

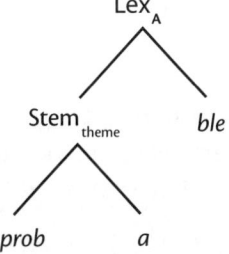

By way of comparison, Figure VIII.2 is the tree diagram for *probation*. Formed from the same root, it has an extra layer of structure: the suffix *-ion* is added to the past participle stem rather than the thematic stem.

Figure VIII.2: *probation*

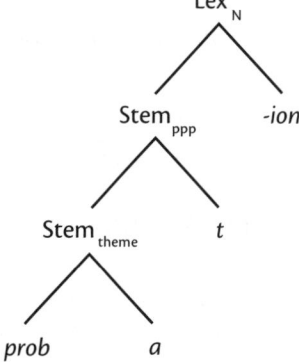

It is a useful exercise to consider a list of Latin roots, construct their stems, and determine which lexemes English has borrowed or constructed off these stems and the original root. Table VIII.7 gives some examples. Notice that it is not always the case that English has constructed words off both stem types.

Table VIII.7: Derivations from Roots and Stems

Root	Gloss	Borrowing	Stem$_{theme}$	Borrowing	Stem$_{ppp}$	Borrowing
√cre	create		cre + ā		cre + ā + t	create
√aud	hear		aud + ī	audible	aud + ī + t	audit
√put	reckon		put + ā	computable	put + ā + t	putative
√spir	breathe	inspire	spir + ā		spir + ā + t	inspiration
√turb	to disorder	disturb	turb + ā	imperturbable	turb + ā + t	
√greg	flock		greg + ā	gregarious	greg + ā + t	congregation
√voc	voice	vocal	voc + ā	vocable	voc + ā + t	vocation
√dur	last		dur + ā	durable	dur + ā + t	duration
√fin	finish	final	fin + ī		fin + ī + t	finite

Notice that our previous observation that the *-ion* rule frequently applies to the past participle stem is demonstrated in Table VIII.7. Furthermore, it should be apparent the frequent *-ble* formation is created from the thematic stem. Notice that there is a variation between *-ible* and *-able*, as in *audible* and *durable*. It should be clear that the vowel is actually the thematic vowel and that the suffix is just *-ble*.

The Phonology of the Past Participle

To this point, we have been able to illustrate the past participle and the types of words that are formed from it without considering any phonological changes that may be triggered by this construction. As we know from previous chapters, it is more usual that morphology creates conditions for phonological change. The past participle is no exception.

To begin, we consider a simple case: the past participles of verbs that take -ē- as the thematic vowel. Table VIII.8 gives some examples.

Table VIII.8: ē Theme Derivations

Root	Gloss	Borrowing	Stem$_{theme}$	Borrowing	Stem$_{ppp}$	Borrowing
√mon	warn	monument	mon + ē		mon + ē + t	monitor
√cred	believe		cred + ē	credence	cred + ē + t	credit
√hab	have		hab + ē	habilitate	hab + ē + t	habit
√deb	owe		deb + ē		deb + ē + t	debit
√fug	flee	refuge	fug + ē		fug + ē + t	fugitive

It should be evident that the thematic vowel changes to *-i-* in derivations from the past participle stem (and sometimes in the thematic stem). This is quite regular among borrowings in English, and so we can record a rule:

$$[+ \bar{e} + t \rightarrow + i + t]_{Latin}$$

The most drastic changes applied to past participles of verbs with thematic *-e-*. Table VIII.9 lists the first set that we will consider.

As we scan derivations from the past participle, we note that the thematic vowel deletes in the past participle. Thus, *fact* is derived from *fac + e + t* by deleting the thematic vowel *e*.

$$[+ e + t \rightarrow + t]_{Latin}$$

One might ask why we suppose that *fact* is derived from *fac + e + t* and that a rule deletes the *e*. It might seem, at first sight, that it would be easier to derive it from *fac + t*. To see that the ease of deriving *fact* from *fac + t* is illusory, recall our computer program metaphor. We wish to create a set of rules that will correctly derive the vocabulary of English. We have already seen that we require this morphological rule when building the past participle:

$$[\text{Stem}_{ppp} \Rightarrow \text{Stem}_{theme} + t]_{Latin}$$

If we suppose that the verbs with thematic *e* are formed differently, then we will need a separate morphological rule just for those verbs. But then we would need to introduce a mechanism to restrict this rule to just *e*-theme verbs. To do this, we would need to introduce extra machinery to allow us to restrict morphological rules to particular words or classes of words. This significantly complicates our morphology. Perhaps this is necessary, but for now it is actually easier to keep our morphology regular and include a phonological rule that deletes *e* in the appropriate places.

Table VIII.9: e Theme Derivations

Root	Gloss	Borrowing	Stem$_{theme}$	Borrowing	Stem$_{ppp}$	Borrowing
√fac	make, do	facile	fac + ie	effi<u>c</u>ient	fac + e + t	fact
√doc	teach	docile	doc + e		doc + e + t	doctor
√dic	say		dic + e		dic + e + t	diction
√pig	paint	pigment	pig + e		pig + e + t	picture
√spec	see	specimen	spec + e		spec + e + t	spectacle
√rup	break		rup + e		rup + e + t	rupture
√reg	rule	regular	reg + e	regent	reg + e + t	correct
√leg	read	college	leg + e	legend	leg + e + t	collect
√ag	drive	agile	ag + e	agent	ag + e + t	act
√frag	break	fragile	frag + e		frag + e + t	fracture
√fig	mold	figment	fig + e		fig + e + t	fiction

As we scan further through Table VIII.9, we note that when the root ends in g, this character is replaced with c in the past participle. In order to understand what has happened, we need to consider what speech sounds the letters g and c are intended to represent in these words.

The character *g* represents several different sounds in the English spelling system. The character was originally introduced into the orthography to represent [g]. That is the sound that is of interest to this problem.

Derivation from Latin Verbs

What does the character *c* represent in words like *correct* and *collect*? It represents a voiceless velar stop which we represent as [k]. Thus, the change that we are interested in is

g → k

In strictly phonetic terms, this is a change of a voiced velar stop to a voiceless velar stop. Why does this happen? If we examine where this change occurs, we note that it happens before the past participle morpheme *t*. What is special about *t* that it triggers this change? To see, we remind ourself that [t] is a voiceless dental stop. Thus, the change that we are interested in is:

g + t → k + t

This is the change of a voiced velar stop to a voiceless velar stop before a voiceless dental stop. What is happening is that the velar stop is becoming more like the dental stop. This is another example of assimilation, the process by which sounds change to resemble neighbouring sounds. We have previously seen that the Latin negative and locative prefixes will assimilate to a following *r* or *l*. In that case, the assimilation was complete. In the case under examination here, the assimilation is partial. The sound [g] does not assimilate completely to [t] but only partially by becoming voiceless.

In Italian, the assimilation process continued and generalized. Consider as an example, the root √*dic*, "say". The past participle in Latin is *dictus*, "said". In English, we find borrowings like *diction* and *predict*. In Italian, *dictus* becomes *detto* which was borrowed into English as *ditto*. In Italian, assimilation becomes complete: [kt] → [tt].

When someone says "Ditto" or uses ditto marks they are etymologically saying "(Already) said".

To discover if this idea is correct, that voiced stops assimilate to voiceless stops, we look to roots that end in voiced stops other than [g]. One other voiced stop is [b]. An odd property of early Indo-European languages is that [b] appears in very few words. But there is one root in Latin that ends in [b]. And this root shows exactly the behaviour that we expect if our rule that voiced stops assimilate to voiceless stops is correct (Table VIII.10).

Table VIII.10: *e* Theme Derivations II

Root	Gloss	Borrowing	Stem$_{theme}$	Borrowing	Stem$_{ppp}$	Borrowing
√scrib	write	scribble	scrib + e		scrib + e + t	description

We seem to have two rules

$$g + t \rightarrow k + t$$
$$b + t \rightarrow p + t$$

In fact, these rules accomplish the same thing: they assimilate a voiced stop to a following voiceless stop. Perhaps there is only one rule:

voiced stop + voiceless stop → voiceless stop + voiceless stop

---

This rule assimilates a voiced stop to a following voiceless stop. The curious might wonder what happens if the situation is reversed; that is, what happens if a voiceless stop is followed by a voiced stop? It turns out that this situation is difficult to investigate if we look only at roots. In Chapter 10, we will encounter data that answers this and a larger question: does voicing assimilation apply only to stops?

In the meantime, consider the data in Table VIII.11. These data demonstrate voicing assimilation of [k] to a following [m] in *segment* < *sek + ment*. Recall that [m] is voiced. Thus the [g] of *segment* is a voiced reflex of [k], created by a rule that ensures that a stop agrees in voicing with a following stop or nasal. Contrasting with the root √sec, which shows voicing assimilation in *segment* < *sek + ment*, but not *section*, are roots such as √pig, which show voicing assimilation in *picture* < *pig + e + t + ure*, but not in *pigment*.

Table VIII.11: Voicing Assimilation

Root	Gloss	Root	Stem$_{PPP}$	√ + ment
√pig	paint		picture	pigment
√sec	cut	secant	section	segment
√frag	break	fragile	fracture	fragment

Thus, the rule that is proposed above is likely too specific. On the one hand, it does not address assimilation of voiceless stops to voiced consonants. On the other hand, it does not comment on assimilation of voiced stops to other voiceless consonants, such as [s]. In a fully articulated analysis, we would investigate all possible structures that juxtapose stops with following consonants and determine what happens. As we will see later, sometimes they assimilate completely, sometimes partially.

We will keep in mind opportunities to exploit voicing assimilation when we examine roots that end in the dentals [t] and [d]. The changes are somewhat exotic. Again, we examine verbs that take the thematic vowel *e* (see Table VIII.12).

Table VIII.12: *e* Theme Derivations with Dental Roots

Root	Gloss	Borrowing	Stem$_{theme}$	Borrowing	Stem$_{PPP}$	Borrowing
√vīd	see		vīd + e	evident	vīd + e + t	vision
√sed	sit	sediment	sed + e	sedentary	sed + e + t	session
√cād	fall		cād + e	cadence	cād + e + t	occasion
√cīd	cut	suicide	cīd + e		cīd + e + t	incision
√claud	close	conclude	claud + e		claud + e + t	clause
√mit	send	permit	mit + e		mit + e + t	permission
√pat	suffer		pat + ie	patient	pat + e + t	passion
√pot	be able		pot + e	potent	pot + e + t	possible
√lūd	play	delude	lūd + e	ludicrous	lūd + e + t	delusion
√suad	sweet	persuade	suad + e		suad + e + t	persuasion
√rīd	laugh	ridicule	rīd + e		rīd + e + t	derision
√rōd	gnaw		rōd + e	rodent	ex + rōd + e + t	erosion

In these forms we note that the cluster that results—either *t* + *t* or *d* + *t*—converts to *ss* or *s*. How many rules are required to get the right results? And can we determine when the result is *ss* or *s*?

If we work backwards, we note that the reflex of *ss* or *s* seems to depend on the length of the vowel in the Latin root. Recall that the macron over a vowel signifies length. If the vowel is long, then the reflex is *s*; if the vowel is short, then the reflex is *ss*. However, the reflex is also *s* if the root contains two vowels as in *suasion*, or a diphthong, as in *conclusion* with the root √claud. If we interpret a long vowel as a sequence of two vowels, then we can collapse all instances as the rule:

$$VV + ss \rightarrow VV + s$$

Of course, the vowel length is not apparent in English. Since this is Latin rule, it is sensitive to the properties that the morphemes had when they originally appeared in Latin.

Long vowels have often presented a problem of representation. What is the correct way to represent a long vowel and distinguish it from a short vowel? We have seen that Latin orthography, and Old English after it, represented long vowels by the usual vowel characters superscripted with a macron. So a long [e] is represented as ē. However, there are other possible representations. For example, one of the other representations that we have seen is that used in the history of English: instead of using a macron, long vowels are represented as a sequence of two vowels.

This latter representation seems to have some merit. It appears that in Latin, at least, long vowels have the same influence as a sequence of two different vowels. In particular, *ss* converts to *s* when preceded by either a long vowel or a sequence of two different vowels. When long vowels are represented as a sequence of two identical vowels, this similarity of patterning is captured in a single rule.

Note that we are assuming that the direction of change is from *ss* to *s* and not from *s* to *ss*. This makes sense because we will be beginning with a cluster of two consonants, for example $t + t$. Consider the derivation of *possible*. Its structure will be *pot+e+t+ible*. After the thematic vowel is deleted, the result is $pot + t + ible$. To create the final result we need a rule to convert the $t + t$ sequence to *ss*:

$$[t + t \rightarrow ss]_{Latin}$$

How do we derive *vision* from a root that ends in *d*? Do we need another rule that converts $d + t$ into *ss*? If we recall that our voicing assimilation rule proposed that all voiced stops will assimilate to a following voiceless stop, we note that $d + t$ should convert to $t + t$. From this point, we have all the necessary rules.

We put all this together in Table VIII.13. In the morphology, the thematic stem is first created by adding the thematic vowel *e*. From this, the past participle stem is created by adding *t*. Finally, a lexeme of category *N* (i.e., a noun) is created by adding the suffix *-ion*.

In the phonology section, the thematic vowel is first deleted (as we saw it must in words like *doctor*). This creates the environment for voicing assimilation and the *d* of *vision* assimilates to *t*. Note that this rule was originally proposed for words like *correct* and *script* with the roots √*reg* and √*scrib*. After the rule that converts $t + t$ to *ss* has applied, the shortening rule applies when the original Latin root had a long vowel.

It is worth noting that a word like *vision* has precisely the same structure as *probation* (see Figure VIII.2). The single difference is the thematic vowel that each takes. But, this difference has dramatic consequences because, whereas the structure of *probation* is obvious (once one learns to recognize thematic

Table VIII.13: Derivation of *mission* and *vision*

mit	vīd	
mit + e	vīd + e	[Stem$_{theme}$ ⇒ Root + V$_{theme}$]$_{Latin}$
mit + e + t	vīd + e + t	[Stem$_{ppp}$ ⇒ Stem$_{theme}$ + t]$_{Latin}$
mit + e + t + ion	vīd + e + t + ion	[Lex$_N$ ⇒ Stem + ion]$_{Latin}$
mit + t + ion	vīd + t + ion	+ e + t → + t
"	vīt+ t + ion	Voicing Assimilation
mission	vīssion	t + t → ss
"	vīsion	VV ss → VV s
mission	vision	English Spelling

and past participle stems), the thematic vowel of *vision* deletes, which triggers a cascade of phonological rules that obscures the underlying structure of *vision*.

The last group of dental roots that we will examine in this section are those that end in more than one consonant (Table VIII.14). Note that the past participle has a single *s*.

Table VIII.14: Consonant Cluster Roots

Root	Gloss	Borrowing	Stem$_{theme}$	Borrowing	Stem$_{ppp}$	Borrowing
√vert	turn	convert	vert + e	convertible	vert + e + t	version
√scand	climb	descend	scand + e	scandent	scand + e + t	ascension
√tend	stretch	extend	tend + e	tendency	tend + e + t	tension
√spond	promise	correspond	spond + e	correspondent	spond + e + t	sponsor
√pend	hang	pend	pend + e	dependent	pend + e + t	pension

We could ensure that our computer program correctly analyses these words by proposing that *ss* converts to *s* when there is a preceding consonant:[6]

$$VC + ss \rightarrow VC + s \text{ (e.g., tenssion > tension)}$$

---

6 The character "C" is used as shorthand for *consonant*.

However, we would be missing something interesting if we stopped there. We should note that this rule is very similar to the other rule that we have proposed for shortening *ss*:

VV + ss → VV + s (e.g., vīssion > vision)

It seems clear that there should be some way to collapse these two rules into a single rule. In fact, that would be desirable. They have the same effect—shortening *ss* to *s*—and they are almost identical. One way to approach this is to introduce another variable into our notation for writing rules. To this point, we have used "V" to represent any vowel and "C" to represent any consonant. We could introduce "X" to represent any sound at all. With this innovation, the two rules can be rewritten as:

[VX + ss → VX + s]$_{Latin}$

This rule describes a change by which *ss* shortens to *s* if it is preceded by a vowel and either another vowel or a consonant. This rule shows some insight into what is happening and suggests further research, namely why VV and VC behave similarly.

Although the etymological structure of a word like *vision* is not obvious, this is because it has been obscured by phonological rules. In fact, it is identical to that of *probation*. Compare the structure of *probation*, as illustrated in Figure VIII.2, with that of *vision* in Figure VIII.3.

Figure VIII.3: *vision*

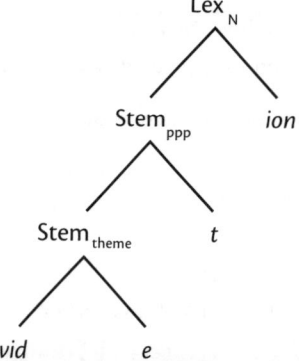

The last forms that we will consider are illustrated in Table VIII.15. The importance of these roots is that they highlight the difference between orthography and phonetics. The problem that these roots represent (if we pay attention to the orthography instead of phonetics) is the appearance of *x* in *annex* and *reflex*. Where did this come from and what sort of rule do we need to insert it?

Table VIII.15

Root	Gloss	Borrowing	Stem$_{theme}$	Borrowing	Stem$_{ppp}$	Borrowing
√nect	tie	connect	nect + e		nect + e + t	annex
√flect	bend	inflect	flect + e		flect + e + t	reflex

If we ignore the *x* for a moment and ask what is expected, the answer to the problem should become clear. First, note that the etymological structure of *annex* is that which we usually expect: *annect + e + t*.[7] The root has been augmented with a thematic vowel to form the thematic stem. The thematic stem has, in turn, been augmented with the morpheme *t* to form the past participle stem.

We know that the thematic vowel will delete because it is the short [e] theme. This will produce:

annect + t

The next rule that applies converts *t + t* to *ss*:

annecss

Finally, the rule discussed above will delete one *s* from the sequence *ss* because it is preceded by a consonant:

annecs

It may appear that we have failed to generate the correct form, since what we want is *annex*. However, if we recall that the character *c* represents the sound [k] then the actual form that has been generated is:

anne[ks]

Recall that the sequence [ks] was represented in Latin by the character *x*. Do the conversion of [ks] to *x* and it is clear that what was generated is, in fact, *annex*.

A continuing problem is that we are using the Roman orthography to represent roots and affixes. Doing so works most of the time. But the Roman orth-

---

7 We are ignoring the prefix.

ography does not always provide a good phonetic representation. The *annex* case is one where the Roman orthography fails us: it represents two sounds with one character. By doing so, it obscures the phonetic structure of the word and makes something look like a problem when it is not.[8]

This problem becomes more apparent when we consider the past participles of *reflect* and *connect*. It should be clear how *reflex* is derived. However, when we add the nominalizing *-ion*, we get *reflection* and *connection*. These appear to be exceptions to the rule that *-ion* is added to past participles. In fact, these seem to be North American aberrations. *Reflect* and *connect* have been re-analyzed as *re + flec + t* and *con + nec + t*. That is, the root final *t* is perceived as the past participle and so the nominal forms follow naturally as *reflection* and *connection*. Notice, however, that the British spelling of these words is *reflexion* and *connexion*. These demonstrate the correct etymology.

Exceptions

The American linguist Edward Sapir famously said, "All grammars leak." By this he meant that while the task of the linguist is to find regularities in language, there are always exceptions. In our case, these are lexemes that do not obey the rules or do obey rules that they shouldn't. Anyone who has formally learned a second language is familiar with the dismay of learning that the effort of internalizing a rule must be followed by a period of memorizing all the forms that do not follow the rule.

The reasons why a form does not line up with the rule-governed members of the lexicon need not be linguistic but can often be external to the language. For example, we are not surprised when borrowed words do not obey English rules.

This tension between the regularity of language and external influences is common in theorizing about language. In the 19th century, two schools that participated in this debate were the Atomists and the *Junggrammatiker*. Each group was interested in charting the history of the Indo-European languages. The Atomists took as their slogan,

> Every word has a history.

---

8   The incorrect interpretation of an orthography can have unfortunate consequences. As an example, the Thai language has both aspirated and unaspirated stops. An aspirated stop is one followed by a puff of air; an unaspirated stop is not. When Thai is transliterated into English, aspirated stops are represented as the stop character—*k*, for example—followed by an *h*: e.g. *kh*. One of the famous beach resorts in the south of Thailand is a beautiful island called *Phuket* which English speakers give an unfortunate pronunciation if they are not aware of this spelling convention.

By this they meant that each word was subject to a unique set of influences and no regular set of rules could be constructed that could describe an interestingly large group.

The *Junggrammatiker* (so-called because they were the students of the original Indo-Europeanists and were looking to form their own paradigm of research: *Junggrammatiker* can be translated from the German as *New Grammarians*) took as their slogan,

> No exception without a rule.

This captured their belief that all language (or an interestingly large part of it) was regular. If a group of exceptions were discovered that apparently contradicted a proposed rule, the *Junggrammatiker* proposed that either the rule was incorrect and further research was necessary to discover the correct formulation or, more interestingly, there was a second rule that intersected with the first to produce the apparent exceptions. It was the discovery of explanations for a group of exceptions to Grimm's Law that convinced many that the Atomists' position was, if not wrong, at least too extreme and that the *Junggrammatiker* position was fruitful.

The data in Table VIII.16 are examples of English words that seem to violate Grimm's Law or are exceptions to it. Each English word is paired with its Latin cognate. Notice that in Latin, each word has a [t]. From Grimm's Law, we expect that this [t] will shift to [θ]. Inexplicably, it does not. At first, this seemed to support the Atomists' position that there is no general rule governing language change. It was Karl Verner who noticed that there is an explanation for these and other exceptions, namely, that Grimm's Law fails when the voiceless stop is preceded by [s].

Table VIII.16

Latin	English
host	guest
stellar	star
stale	still
statue	stand
stratum	straw

With this in mind, let us note that the picture of the Latin past participle presented here is a tidy one. Everything seems to line up according to a discernible set of rules. For the majority of verbs, this picture works. Unfortunately, there are numerous irregularities hinging primarily on what happens to the thematic vowel and what form it takes. This should not be too surprising because little is known of the origin, function, or history of the thematic vowel. Consequently, it is entirely possible that there are rules that have not been discovered that will explain these irregularities. Alternatively, we could adopt the position that there are no regularities, that there are no rules.

For the purposes of this section, we will highlight the regularity that has been proposed for the fate of the -thematic vowel in the past participle, namely, that the short [e] deletes and the long vowels remain. Generally, this is true. But among verbs borrowed into English, there are exceptions, as highlighted in Table VIII.17. In these verbs, the thematic vowel deletes in the past participle although it is the long vowel [ī].

Table VIII.17: Deletion of long themes

Root	Gloss	Borrowing	Stem$_{theme}$	Borrowing	Stem$_{PPP}$	Borrowing
√ven	come	convene	ven + ī	convenient	ven + ī + t	convent
√sent	feel	consent	sent + ī	sentiment	sent + ī + t	sense

Unfortunately, there is not much more to be said except that these are exceptions to the regularity that we have proposed: namely, that only the short [e] theme vowel deletes. This is the odd fact about exceptions: true exceptions are not very interesting because there is not much more to say about them. If we could discover more about them, if we could say more, then we could eventually explain them and they wouldn't be exceptions.

There is another class of exceptions that are more interesting. Table VIII.18 gives a few examples that should strike one as odd.

Table VIII.18

cessation
compensation
conversation
dictation
improvisation
sensation

To get at the peculiarity of these, try to find the root. It is clear that each of these has been nominalized with the familiar morpheme *-ion*. We expect that this is added to past participles and, in each case, it is possible to find the past participle *t* immediately before the nominalizer. This implies that the preceding vowel *a* is the thematic vowel. Thus, a first guess at the structure of these words would be that in Table VIII.19.

Table VIII.19

cess + a + t + ion
con + pens + a + t + ion
con + vers + a + t + ion
dict + a + t + ion
in + pro + vis + a + t + ion
sens + a + t + ion

At this point, something should stand out as peculiar. Scanning the resulting proposals for roots, some of them should look familiar. For example, given the lexeme *converse*, it is fairly straightforward in light of the rules discussed previously to discover the root √vert. But the proposal in Table VIII.19 is that the root is, in fact, √vers. Similarly, given *improvise*, the root should be √vid, not √vis; given *process*, the analysis should give the root as √ced, not √cess; and given *sense*, we should see that the root is √sent. In fact, what is odd is that *improvise*, *process*, and *sense* are clearly derived from the past participle. And yet, there seems to be a second past participle added to create *improvisation*, *cessation*, and *sensation*. It appears that the actual structure of these lexemes is that in Table VIII.20.

Table VIII.20

[ced + e + t] + a + t + ion
con + [pend + e + t] + a + t + ion
con + [vert + e + t] + a + t + ion
[dic + e + t] + a + t + ion
in + pro + [vid + e + t] + a + t + ion
[sent + i + t] + a + t + ion

The original past participle stem is enclosed in brackets. What seems to have happened is that the phonology obscured the internal structure of these past participles and new verbs were formed off them, often with subtly different meaning. These new verbs, of course, have their own past participles. What is striking is that whenever new verbs were formed in Latin, they were always formed with the thematic vowel *a*.[9]

The Latin past participle originally functioned as an adjective. Many of the English borrowings preserve this function: note *desolate, content, separate,* and so forth. But, English can also convert adjectives into verbs without any morphological change: note *to busy (oneself)* from *busy, to dry* from *dry*. Similarly, English began converting Latin past participles to verbs as well.

Together, the formation of new past participles with the theme *a* and the ability to convert past participles to verbs provide a mechanism for creating new verbs: a new morpheme *-ate*. Orthographically, this morpheme is a fusion of the thematic vowel *a*, the past participle *t*, and the English spelling rule that adds *e* to indicate how to pronounce the preceding vowel. For example, the word *vaccine* was formed off the Latin noun *vacca* "cow" because the original vaccines were developed from cowpox. The verb is formed by adding *-ate* to form *vaccinate*.

Present Participle Stems

The present participle in English is formed by adding *-ing* to the verb. Thus, *breaking* is the present participle of *break*. In Latin, the present participle stem is created by adding *-nt* to the thematic stem. Table VIII.21 gives some examples.

Table VIII.21: Present Participles

Root	Gloss	Borrowing	Stem$_{theme}$	Stem$_{pp}$	Borrowing
√pend	hang	pendulum	pend + e	pend + e + nt	dependent
√sci	know		sci + e	sci + e + nt	scientist
√vid	see	provide	vīd + e	vīd + e + nt	evident
√sed	sit	sediment	sed + e	sed + e + nt	sedentary
√pot	be able		pot + e	pot + e + nt	potent
√ag	drive, do	agile	ag + e	ag + e + nt	agent
√reg	rule	regular	reg + e	reg + e + nt	regent

---

9 This is a practice that seems to have continued in the Romance languages. When each Romance creates new verbs, it does so in the conjugation that is the reflex of the *ā* theme Latin conjugation. A Latin exception to this observation is *expedite/expedition* which clearly has the nominal root √ped "foot".

Derivation from Latin Verbs 173

Root	Gloss	Borrowing	Stem$_{theme}$	Stem$_{pp}$	Borrowing
√err	wander	error	err + a	err + a + nt	errant
√plic	fold		plic + a	plic + a + nt	applicant
√rog	ask		rog + a	rog + a + nt	arrogant
√sta	stand		sta	sta + nt	instant
√merc	trade	commerce	merc + a	merc + a + nt	mercantile

These lexemes are created by the morphological rule that creates the present participle:

$$[Lex_{pp} \Rightarrow Stem_{theme} + nt]_{Latin}$$

Lexemes like those in Table VIII.21 have structures like that of *potent* given in Figure VIII.4

Figure VIII.4: *potent*

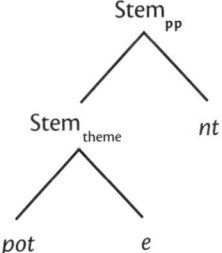

Sometimes, the vowel of the present participle appears as *ie*, as in Table VIII.22. In some of these, the *i* is the thematic vowel and it is augmented with *e* (e.g., *convenient*); sometimes, the *i* was part of the root and the *e* is the thematic vowel (e.g., *scientist*); and sometimes the thematic vowel is *e* and is augmented with *i* (e.g., *gradient*).

Table VIII.22: Present Participles

Root	Gloss	Stem$_{pp}$	Borrowing
√ven	come	ven + ī + e + nt	convenient
√sci	know	sci + e + nt	scientist
√pat	feel	pat + ie + nt	patient
√grad	step	grad + ie + nt	gradient

Assibilation

A common suffix added to the present participle stem in Latin was *-ia* which would create a noun. Lexemes derived with this suffix are not normally borrowed directly into English except in Latinate phrases like *in absentia*. However, these lexemes did develop into French and were then borrowed. For example, the lexeme *absentia* developed into a form that was borrowed into English as *absence*. Thus, we find for the first time a bit of French phonology in English. The rule is:

$$[t + iV \rightarrow s + iV]_{French}$$

Notice that the [t] has changed to [s] (although spelled with *c*) and that the following vowels have been deleted in French (Table VIII.23). This rule is called *assibilation*[10] and is the conversion of a sound (often a stop) to a sibilant. When we examine French further, we will note that it is a very common rule.

To see the assibilation rule at work elsewhere, consider the problem of teaching someone about English spelling. You would like to explain to them when the character *c* is pronounced as [k] and when as [s]. What is the rule? If you make two columns putting words with the [k] version of the character *c* in one column and the [s] version of the character *c* in the other, the answer should jump out at you.

The assibilation rule provides another set of present participle borrowings.

Table VIII.23: Assibilated Present Participles

Root	Gloss	Assibilated	Unassibilated
√aud	hear	audience	
√ī	go	ambience	ambient
√fid	trust	confidence	confident
√sci	know	science	scientist
√pat	feel	patience	patient
√curr	run	currency	current
√pend	hang, weigh	dependence	dependent
√tend	stretch	tendency	

---

10 *Assibilation:* From the Latin *ad-*, "to" and *sibil*, "hiss". Sibilants are sounds like [s] and [z].

Root	Gloss	Assibilated	Unassibilated
√ag	drive, do	agency	agent
√pot	be able	potency	potent
√solu	free	solvency	solvent
√vīd	see	evidence	evident
√her	stick	adherence	adherent
√flu	flow	confluence	confluent
√urg	urge	urgency	urgent
√sent	feel	sentience	sentient
√radi	root	radiance	radiant

Another form of this rule explains the pronunciation of past participles that have nominalized with *-ion*. Notice that the *t* of *nation, creation, probation, attention*, etc. is not now pronounced as [t] but as [ʃ]. In Latin, it was pronounced as [t], but it has assibilated when followed by [i] and another vowel, although the assibilated reflex is different from those in the present participles.

Productivity

A key to understanding much of the Latin partition of the English lexicon is being able to recognize roots and stems. Latin had a very productive derivational morphology and was able to create many words from the root, the thematic stem, the past participle stem, and the present participle stem. Once the basic elements and these lexical structures are learned, it is very easy to generate many words from a single root and to recognize that root in its various forms.

Table VIII.24 lists some of the lexemes in the English lexicon formed from the root √*scrib*, "write", together with approximate structure. The basic pattern should be evident. Lexemes are formed by adding prefixes and/or suffixes to the root or stems. It is a deceptively simple process, but a very powerful one. This process permits us to use resources that are already available to create new lexemes when they are required.

Table VIII.24

ascribable	ad + scrib ;+ able	prescribe	pre + scrib
ascribe	ad + scrib	prescript	pre + scrib + e + t
ascription	ad + scrib + e + t + ion	prescription	pre + scrib + e + t + ion
circumscribe	circum + scrib	prescriptive	pre + scrib + e + t + ive
circumscription	circum + scrib + e + t + ion	proscribe	pro + scrib
conscript	con + scrib + e + t	proscription	pro + scrib + e + t + ion
conscription	con + scrib + e + t + ion	scribe	scrib
describe	de + scrib	script	scrib + e + t
description	de + scrib + e + t + ion	scriptural	scrib + e + t + ur + al
descriptive	de + scrib + e + t + ive	scripture	scrib + e + t + ure
descriptively	de + scrib + e + t + ive + ly	subscribe	sub + scrib
indescribable	in + de + scrib + able	subscriber	sub + scrib + er
indescribably	in + de + scrib + able + ly	subscript	sub + scrib + e + t
inscribe	in + scrib	subscription	sub + scrib + e + t + ion
inscription	in + scrib + e + t + ion	superscription	super + scrib + e + t + ion
manuscript	manu + scrib + e + t	transcribe	trans + scrib
nondescript	non + de + scrib + e + t	transcript	trans + scrib + e + t
postscript	post + scrib + e + t	transcription	trans + scrib + e + t + + ion

The process of creating new lexemes from resources that already exist also provides a method for dealing with unfamiliar words when they are encountered. If we have an good understanding of Latin roots (and their meanings), of Latin prefixes and suffixes, and of the phonology that applies to them, we can often unpack unfamiliar words to determine what they are likely to mean. For example, knowing that *post* means "behind, after", it is possible to surmise that a *postscript* is something written after the main text.

Is the prefix of *inscribe* and *inscription* the negative or locative? If you know the meaning of *inscription*, it is possible to determine the meaning of the prefix. On the other hand, you should be able to determine the likely meaning of *inscription* from the meaning of its parts.

Summary

In this chapter, we have used the tools and concepts developed in previous chapters to analyze a portion of the English lexicon. We have developed three main concepts: structure, change, and representation, and used them in the analysis.

Structure
Although a word like *agent* might appear to be atomic, it should now be apparent that it is composed of several morphemes. The root is $\sqrt{ag}$. Using this root, the thematic stem *ag + e* has been created by the rule:

$$[\text{Stem}_{\text{theme}} \Rightarrow \text{Root} + V_{\text{theme}}]_{\text{Latin}}$$

From the root, the present participle form *agent* is created by the rule:

$$[\text{Stem}_{\text{pp}} \Rightarrow \text{Stem}_{\text{theme}} + nt]_{\text{Latin}}$$

Change
By combining morphemes, morphological rules juxtapose sounds that may react to the combination. The rules that govern these reactions are phonological rules. For example, when the past participle is created with the root $\sqrt{ag}$, the resulting structure is *ag + e + t*. The thematic vowel *e* deletes bringing *g* and *t* into contact. Latin requires that consonants agree in voicing under these conditions and so the resulting word is *act*, not *ᶜagt*.

Representation
Often, the act of solving a problem requires creating a system for representing its various facets. A good representation will sometimes solve the problem itself. We certainly have not reached that point. However, we have noted that the representation will sometimes provide solutions that are more satisfying that others. For example, we have seen on several occasions that what superficially appears to be different rules could be instead manifestations of the same, more general, rule.

Conclusion
From a comparatively small number of Latin roots, a significantly large number of words have been created, each based on the meaning of its root, but modified by adding prefixes and suffixes. In some cases, these roots are frozen, petrified, and unusable except in the words that English has inherited from Latin. Others are still transparent and available for use in the creation of new words.

One test to see if a Latin root or stem is still productive is to look for hybrids, or invent them and feel their naturalness. Consider the stem *script*. From this, the hybrid *unscripted* has been produced. We could also imagine describing an unlikely event as *unscriptable*.

> How do we know that *unscripted* and *unscriptable* are hybrids?

We know that words like this must have been created in English (thereby showing the *script* is productive) because they contain English bits which did not exist during the Roman period.

9 Latin Prefixes

Introduction

As we have seen, a key to understanding the Latin partition of the English lexicon is being able to recognize the roots of words of Latin origin. Part of this ability rests in knowledge of the rules that transform roots when suffixes are added. It is also important to be able to recognize Latin prefixes. In part, the prefixes add meaning and understanding that meaning is integral to understanding the meaning of the word. In addition, recognizing prefixes is part of the process of recognizing the root of a word.

In the following sections, we review the Latin prefixes that have been borrowed into English. We have already examined the negative *in-*, the locative *in-*, and the collective *con-*. Some of the others are already familiar; these are prefixes that have become naturalized and are productive in English. The prefix *re-* is an example. If you have already opened something, you can re-open it; if you have read a book, you can reread it; if you have written a letter, you can rewrite it, and so on.

Prefixes

In this chapter, we will review the prefixes that have been borrowed from Latin. At the same time, we will illustrate them with various Latin roots, some of which are new. In every case, we will illustrate the root with other words. In general, this is a useful practice. When learning a new root, try to generate as many words with it as possible.

Each of these prefixes presupposes a morphological rule of the form:

$$\text{Lex} \Rightarrow \textit{prefix} + \text{Lex}$$

In Latin, prefixes are category preserving. By this, we mean that when a prefix is added to a lexeme, the resulting lexeme is of the same category as the original. So, the rules will look like the following:

LATIN PREFIXES

$$\text{Lex}_N \Rightarrow \textit{prefix} + \text{Lex}_N$$
$$\text{Lex}_V \Rightarrow \textit{prefix} + \text{Lex}_V$$
$$\text{Lex}_A \Rightarrow \textit{prefix} + \text{Lex}_A$$

We embellish our formalism to express this as:

$$\text{Lex}_X \Rightarrow \textit{prefix} + \text{Lex}_X$$

where "X" represents the category.

The ordering of the rules that add prefixes and suffixes is a difficult issue to tease apart. It appears that when prefixes are added to lexemes derived from the past participle, they are added before the nominalizer *-ion*. Evidence for this is that lexemes like *correct* and *correction* exist, but *ᵉrection* does not. If the nominalizer *-ion* was added first, we would expect to find *ᵉrection*. In fact, it appears that for many Latin verbal roots (though not all), it is necessary to attach a prefix to a stem in order to create a lexeme that can be inflected. As illustration, the structure of *correction* is given in Figure IX.1.

Figure IX.1: *correction*

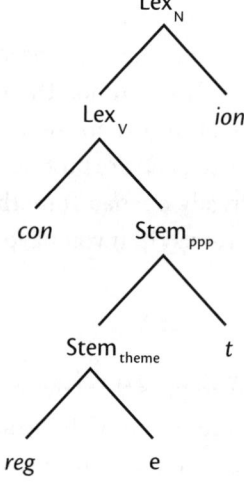

ad- (to)

Table IX.1: *ad-*

adit	ad + ī + t	√i	go	exit
adjunct	ad + jung + e + t	√jug	bind	junction
admit	ad + mit	√mit	send	permit
addict	ad + dic + e + t	√dic	say	dictionary

adduce	ad + duc	√duc	lead	conduct
admonition	ad + mon + ē + t + ion	√mon	warn	monitorh
adopt	ad + opt	√opt	choose	option
adoration	ad + or + ā + t + ion	√or	speak	orate
adorn	ad + orn	√orn	wear	ornament
adventure	ad + ven + ī + t + ure	√ven	come	convent
advertise	ad + vert + ise	√vert	turn	universe
advocate	ad + voc + ā + t	√voc	call	vocal

The prefix *ad-* is another that is susceptible to assimilation to the following consonant. Table IX.1 provides examples where its form is transparent. Table IX.2 gives examples of assimilation to [l], [r], [n], [f], [p], [b], [g], and [k].[1] Assimilation to [l] and [r] is familiar from our discussions of the Latin negative *in-* and locative *in-*. We will also accept assimilation to [n], [f], and [s] without comment. Thus, we propose the following rules:

$$[d + l \rightarrow l + l]_{Latin}$$
$$[d + r \rightarrow r + r]_{Latin}$$
$$[d + n \rightarrow n + n]_{Latin}$$
$$[d + f \rightarrow f + f]_{Latin}$$
$$[d + s \rightarrow s + s]_{Latin}$$

Table IX.2: *ad-* II

allude	ad + lūd	√lūd	play	ludicrous
allocate	ad + loc + ā + t	√loc	place	location
alleviate	ad + lev + iā + t	√lev	light	levitate
allegation	ad + leg + ā + t + ion	√leg	law	legal
arrest	ad + re + st	√sta	stand	statue
affable	ad + fa + able	√fa	speak	ineffable
affiliate	ad + fili + ā + t	√fili	son	filial
affinity	ad + fin + ī + t + y	√fin	end	infinite
affirmation	ad + firm + ā + t + ion	√firm	support	firm

---

1 Recall that [k] is represented as *c* in the spelling system that was used for Latin.

affix	ad + fig + s	√fig	attach	prefix
afflict	ad + flig + e + t	√flig	strike	inflict
affluent	ad + flu + e + nt	√flu	flow	fluid
affront	ad + front	√front	forehead	frontier
annihilate	ad + nihil + a + t	√nihil	nothing	nihilism
annex	ad + nect + e + t	√nect	tie	connect
assent	ad + sent	√sent	feel	sense
assess	ad + sed + e + t	√sed	sit	sediment
assimilate	ad + sim + il + ā + t	√sim	same	similar
append	ad + pend	√pend	hang, weigh	pending
applaud	ad + plaud	√plaud	applaud	plausible
applicant	ad + plic + ā + nt	√plic	fold	implicate
abbreviate	ad + brev + iā + t	√brev	brief	brevity
agglutinate	ad + gluten + ā + t	√gluten	glue	glutinous
aggregate	ad + greg + ā + t	√greg	flock	gregarious
aggravate	ad + grav + ā + t	√grav	heavy	gravity
accommodate	ad + con + mod + ā + t	√mod	mode	moderate
accord	ad + cord	√cord	heart	cordial

If we examine words like *append* and *abbreviate*, we note that they are examples of complete assimilation. Our problem is how to write the rule for this most efficiently. We could write:

$$d + p \rightarrow p + p$$
$$d + b \rightarrow b + b$$

But this isn't quite right. The only difference between [b] and [p] is voicing and this small difference shouldn't require us to write two separate rules.

If we recall that we already have a voicing assimilation rule that converts voiced stops to voiceless stops when followed by a voiceless stop, then we don't have to worry about the voicing. This rule will ensure that a sequence of two stops agree in voicing. We can then collapse the two rules above into a single rule:

$$[\text{dental stop} + \text{labial stop} \rightarrow \text{labial stop} + \text{labial stop}]_{\text{Latin}}$$

Together, this rule and the voicing assimilation rule will ensure that [d] assimilates to [p] before [p] and to [b] before [b]. By utilizing the voicing assimilation rule, we can restrict this rule to just place of articulation (dental vs. labial).

When we examine words like *aggregate* and *accord*, we note that we are presented with the same problem: [d] assimilates to [g] before [g] and to [k] before [k].[2] The only difference between [g] and [k] is voicing. Thus, we can include the rule following assimilation rule in our set:

[dental stop + velar stop → velar stop + velar stop]$_{\text{Latin}}$

Finally, we should note that these two rules are really two aspects of a single rule. That rule should say something like "A dental stop assimilates to a following stop." It is left as an exercise to think about how one could write such a rule with the notation that we have developed to this point. The solution to this problem should suggest how to collapse this rule with assimilation before [l] and [r] (assimilation to a following liquid) and assimilation before [f] and [s] (assimilation to a following fricative).

There is a group of lexemes that should be troubling. These contain roots that begin with a dental. We had previously proposed that the sequence $d + t$ will first assimilate to $t + t$ and then assibilate to $s + s$. This sequence of rules accounts for past participles like *passion* with the root √pat and *vision* with the root √vid. However, as is evident from Table IX.3, although assimilation (particularly voicing assimilation) applies, assibilation does not.

Table IX.3: Dental Stems

attenuate	ad + tenu + a + t + ion	√tenu	thin	tenuous
attend	ad + tend	√tend	stretch	tension
attest	ad + test	√test	witness	testify

The kind of explanation that we can give for this relies on the distinction between new and old words. We stratify both morphological and phonological rules so that phonological rules are paired with morphological structures.

The first thing we note is that the set of morphological rules that add prefixes are relatively new in the history of Latin. Evidence for their newness is that most of the prefixes were originally separate words, typically prepositions. For example *ad* is a preposition, meaning "to", and a prefix. It is clear that it

---

2   Remember that the character *c* represents the sound [k] in the original Latin spelling system.

was first a preposition and, over time, became phonologically attached to the word following it. Conversely, the past participle is an ancient structure. We know this because it is found in other related languages. The past participle rule appears to have originated early in the history of Indo-European, but the prefix rule is probably a Latin innovation.

The assibilation rule that is found in the past participle is also probably ancient. For example, a fossil of the rule remains in English and is found in the pair *wit*[3] and *wise*.

The way we explain the failure of assibilation in *attend*, etc. is that since assibilation is an old rule it applies only to old structures. It applies to the past participle but not to prefixes which are new structures.

Interestingly, voicing assimilation is one rule that persists through all stages of Latin.

The final group that we want to examine are those formed with roots that begin with [s] followed by other consonants (Table IX.4). Usually, when a root begins with [s], [d] assimilates to [s]. In these words, the [d] has disappeared.

Table IX.4: *ad-* III

aspire	ad + spire	√spir	breathe	inspire
aspect	ad + spec + e + t	√spec	look, see	inspect

We could propose that there is a rule:

$$d + sC \rightarrow sC$$

but this would not be enlightening. We would want to ask why [d] is deleted in this situation only. If instead we assume that the general assimilation rule applies, then the result would be:

as + spire
as + spect

The difference between forms like this and words such as *assent* and *assimilate* with *ss* is that *aspire* and *aspect* with a single *s* have a following consonant. The rule appears to be:

$$[s + s \text{ consonant} \rightarrow + s \text{ consonant}]_{Latin}$$

---

3 Note that *wit* is cognate with Latin √*vid*.

This sort of rule is called Cluster Simplification because it simplifies a cluster of consonants. The general idea is that clusters of consonants are unstable and likely to be broken up in some way. For example, it seems that the final consonant clusters in *bristle* and *thistle* have been simplified, if their spelling is taken as representative of how they were once pronounced. It makes a kind of sense that *ss* should simplify when followed by a consonant.

dis- (off, away, opposite)

This prefix originates from the Indo-European form **dwis*, which, if we recall Grimm's law, is cognate with English *two*. Thus, metaphorically, the image is of two different events or objects: that of the original and that indicated by its opposite or the result of moving away (Table IX.5).

Table IX.5: *dis-*

discord	dis + cord	√cord	heart	cordial
distend	dis + tend	√tend	stretch	tense
dispel	dis + pell	√pell	drive (away)	repel
dispense	dis + pend + e + t	√pend	hang, weigh	pendent
dispute	dis + put	√put	think, reckon	computer

As always, when this prefix is added to some roots there are consequent changes. For example, when added to roots that begin with [f], the [s] assimilates to the following [f]. We recognize this as an assimilation rule (Table IX.6).

Table IX.6: *dis-* II

different	dis + fer + e + nt	√fer	carry	Lucifer
diffident	dis + fid + e + nt	√fid	trust	fidelity
diffract	dis + frag + e + t	√frag	break	fragile

$$[s + f \rightarrow f + f]_{Latin}$$

Of particular interest is the loss of the [s] in certain words (Table IX.7). The problem here is determining what distinguishes the words in Table IX.5, where [s] does not delete, from those in Table IX.7. If we examine the first consonant in the root of the lexemes in Table IX.5, we note that they are all voiceless stops.

However, in Table IX.7, the first consonant is always voiced. This seems to be the critical distinction: [s] deletes before voiced consonants:

$$[s + \text{voiced consonant} \rightarrow \text{voiced consonant}]_{Latin}$$

Table IX.7: *dis-* III

digest	dis + ges + e + t	√ges	*carry*	gestation
dilapidated	dis + lapid + ā + t + ed	√lapid	*stone*	lapidary
dimension	dis + met + n + e + t + ion	√met	*measure*	metric
direct	dis + reg + e + t	√reg	*rule*	regal
divest	dis + vest	√vest	*dress*	vestment

A rule of this sort is not particularly interesting because there is no obvious reason why [s] should remain before voiceless consonants but delete before voiced consonants. A step in the direction of an explanation is the recognition that the voicing assimilation rule predicts that [s] should convert to [z] before voiced consonants. This event predicts that it is not [s] which deletes but [z]. Thus another rule would be:

$$[z\, C \rightarrow C]_{Latin}$$

This is somewhat better because it distinguishes between [s] and [z] and suggests that voicing is the difference between deleting and maintaining a consonant.

Notice that a rule like this is also part of the explanation for why Latin removed Z *zeta* from the alphabet: If all instances of [z] deleted, then Latin had no need of this character.

Naturalization and the Age of Words

The prefix *dis-* has been naturalized to some extent in English. One bit of evidence for this is that it appears in hybrids in English. That is, it has been attached to roots that are not Latin: *disband*, *disbar*, and *disbelief* are examples. These words could not have been created in Latin because the roots did not exist in Latin. Another bit of evidence that this prefix has been naturalized is that its behaviour no longer corresponds to the Latin rules that we have proposed for it. Notice that in *disband*, *disbar* and *disbelief*, the [s] appears before a voiced consonant.

The design of the morphology and English that we proposed in Figure VI.3 gets this exactly right. There we proposed that naturalized words are processed by the English phonology. Since the rule to delete [s] is a Latin rule, it will not apply to the naturalized use of *dis-*.

Table IX.8 provides other words where one would expect the deletion rule to apply.

Table IX.8

disgust	dis + gust	√gust	taste	gustatory
dismiss	dis + mit + e + t	√mit	send	permit
dismember	dis + member			
disrepute	dis + re + put	√put	think, reckon	putative
disrespect	dis + re + spec + e + t	√spec	see	spectacle
disrobe	dis + robe			

If we examine when these were created (Table IX.9), the explanation for the failure of the rule to apply is apparent. Notice that none of these words were created in Latin. Since they are not Latin words, although they may contain bits of Latin, Latin rules will not apply to them. Thus, we do not expect that the [s] will delete.

Table IX.9

disgust	Middle French
dismiss	Medieval Latin
dismember	Old French
disrepute	English
disrespect	English
disrobe	English

ex- (out)
Table IX.10 provides some examples of this prefix.

Table IX.10

exit	ex + i + t	√i	go	transition
exact	ex + ag + e + t	√ag	act, drive	agent
extract	ex + trag + e + t	√trag	drag	tractor
excision	ex + cid + e + t + ion	√cīd	cut	circumcise
exclamation	ex + clam + a + t + ion	√clam	cry	proclamation
exclude	ex + clud	√claud	close	include
exempt	ex + em + e + t	√em	buy	redemption
expend	ex + pend	√pend	hang, weight	depend
export	ex + port	√port	carry	import
extend	ex + tend	√tend	stretch	tense

The first problem that we want to explain occurs when this prefix is added to a root that begins with *s* (Table IX.11).

Table IX.11

expect	ex + spec + e + t	√spec	see	spectacle
expire	ex + spir	√spir	breathe	inspire

It appears that the *s* of the root disappears with the addition of the suffix. It is easy enough to write a rule that deletes *s* after *x*, but that would miss what is really happening.

The first step in the solution to this problem is to consider what sound or sounds the letter *x* represents. If we were to remove the letter *x* from the English alphabet, how would we spell the prefix *ex-*? Most would agree that *eks* is a serviceable spelling. In fact, the sequence *ks* is often substituted for *x* in advertising and *x* is often substituted for *ks*. The character *x* represents the sequence of sounds [ks].

With this in mind, we can note that we have already solved this problem. A word like *expect* is derived from

eks + spec + e + t

We have earlier proposed a rule that will delete one of the sequence *ss* if it is followed by another consonant. This is exactly the situation above.

This example highlights the importance of remembering that phonological rules apply to sounds, not to the orthography.

The data in Table IX.12 illustrate another variant of *ex-*. In these lexemes, the prefix has been reduced to *e-*.

Table IX.12: Simplification of *ex-*

educate	ex + duc + a + t	√duc	lead	deduce
emerge	ex + merg	√merg	sink	submerge
egregious	ex + greg + i + ous	√greg	flock	gregarious
elect	ex + leg + e + t	√leg	select	legislate
elevate	ex + lev + a + t	√lev	light	levity
erect	ex + reg + e + t	√reg	rule	regal

When we compare these forms with the previous ones, it should be clear that the *e-* variant appears when the root begins with a voiced consonant. This is similar to the instance when *s* deleted before a voiced consonant. We could write a similar rule such as

[ks + voiced consonant → voiced consonant]$_{Latin}$

but this doesn't explain the similarity between this case and the previous when the *s* of *dis-* deleted before voiced consonants. One way to think about the problem is to compare a case where deletion occurs with one where it does not, for example, *extend* and *educate*, where [t] and [d] differ only in voicing.

eks + tend
eks + duc + a + t

The problem becomes explaining why [k] deletes before [s] followed by a voiced stop but not before [s] followed by a voiceless stop. The stop seems too far away to be of any influence. Recall that we have already proposed a voicing assimilation rule for Latin which says the voiced stops assimilate in voicing to a voiceless stop. If we generalize this rule so that it applies in both directions, then we have a neat solution.[4]

[stops and fricatives assimilate in voicing to a following consonant]$_{Latin}$

---

4 This rule holds only when across morpheme boundaries. When a sequence of consonants is part of a single morpheme, there is no assimilation.

Notice that this rule will create a crucial difference between the two forms:

eks + tend
eks + duc + a + t → egz + duc + a + t

Now the rules are easy to write because they apply to [g] and [z]. First, we have a cluster simplification rule that applies to [g]:

$[g\ C\ C \to C\ C]_{Latin}$

This rule deletes [g] if it is followed by more than 1 consonant. Next, the rule deleting [z] applies:

$[z\ C \to C]_{Latin}$

Notice that these rules have provided an explanation for the disappearance of *s* in the prefix *dis*, as well. The [s] assimilates to the following voiced consonant to become [z]. It is [z] that actually deletes when it appears before a consonant.

Table IX.13

dis + tend	dis + gest	eks + tend	eks + merge	
"	diz + gest	"	egz + merge	Voicing Assimilation
"	"	"	ez + merge	g C C → C C
"	di + gest	"	e + merge	z C → C
distend	digest	extend	emerge	Remove "+"

The rule

$[g\ C\ C \to C\ C]_{Latin}$

has apparent counter-examples. These are words with the sequence [gCC] and include *aggravate* and *aggregation*. One possible explanation for these is that, in Latin and Indo-European languages generally, many rules treat the sequence of stop + liquid as a single sound. For example, an English word can begin with *s* followed by a consonant or *s* followed by two consonants as long as those two consonants are a stop and a liquid in that order. An example from Latin is itsstress rule. A Latin word was stressed on the second last syllable if the vowel of that syllable was followed by two consonants. However, words like *integrum* were stressed on the third last syllable although the vowel in the second last syllable is followed by two consonants. The key is that these two consonants are [gr], a stop followed by a liquid.

There is a last allomorph of *ex-* that we will note without a full, satisfying explanation (Table IX.14).

Table IX.14: Simplification of *ex-*

effort	ex + fort	√fort	strong	fort
effect	ex + fac + e+ t	√fac	make, do	fact
efferent	ex + fer + e + nt	√fer	bear	infer
effete	ex + fet	√fet	bring forth	fetus
effigy	ex + fig +y	√fig	mold	figure
effluent	ex + flu + e + nt	√flu	flow	fluid
effusive	ex + fud + e + t + ive	√fud	pour	fusion

If we expressed the rule as an orthographic rule, the solution would be simple. The rule would be

$$ex + f \rightarrow eff$$

But this is not what is really happening. First, we know that the prefix *ex-* is phonetically e[ks]. So the actual change is:

$$eks + f > ef + f$$

We know that there is a rule already demonstrated in Table IX.6:

$$s + f \rightarrow f + f$$

so part of the change of *eks + f > ef + f* is explicable by a rule we need for other reasons. But this leaves us with a problem that won't be solved here, but can be explored. Our established rule will accomplish the following:

$$eks + f > ekf + f$$

The problem is explaining what happened to [k]. Two possibilities suggest themselves. One is that there is a rule:

$$kff \rightarrow ff$$

That is, [k] deletes before the sequence [ff].

This isn't particularly satisfying because there is no obvious reason for [k] to delete.

A second possibility is that [k] assimilates to a following [f]:

$$kf \rightarrow ff$$

Together, this rule with the rule that assimilates [s] to [f] will convert *eks+fort* to *efffort*. The new rule necessary to get the right result is

$$fff \rightarrow ff$$

This looks like a likely rule. It makes a kind of sense that the sequence [fff] would simplify to [ff]. But we don't have other examples of [k] assimilating to a following [f] nor does this look like a likely rule.

We will leave this problem at this stage, with possible solutions but without the necessary data to choose among them.

abs- (away)

This prefix is usually analysed in dictionaries as *ab-* which occasionally but inexplicably appears as *abs-*. If we scan the terms in Table IX.15, we note that it appears as *abs-* before *c* (originally [k]) and *t*, but as *ab-* before *d*, *n*, *j*, *l*, *r*, and *s* (*abhor* requires another explanation).

Table IX.15: *abs-*

abscess	abs + ced + e + t	√ced	go	secede
abstention	abs + ten + e + t + ion	√ten	hold	tenant
abstract	abs + trag + e + t	√trag	drag	tractor
abscond	abs + cond	√cond	hide	recondite
abduct	abs + duc + e + t	√duc	lead	deduce
abnormal	abs + norm + al	√norm	rule	normative
abdicate	abs + dic + a + t	√dic	say	dictation
abject	abs + jac + e + t	√jac	throw	adjective
ablution	abs + lav + e + t + ion	√lav	wash	lavatory
abrupt	abs + rup + e + t	√rup	break	rupture

absolve	abs + solu	√solu	free	resolve
avert	abs + vert	√vert	turn	verse
abhor	abs + hor	√hor	bristle	horror

We have already created a rule that will account for *absolve*. If the prefix is actually *abs-* then the rule

$$[C\ s + s \rightarrow C\ s +]_{Latin}$$

that was created to account for some of the reflexes in past participles correctly predicts that only *s* will remain. This leaves loss of *s* before *d, n, l, j, v,* and *r*. If we look to see what they have in common, we note that they are all voiced, whereas *c* [k] and *t*, the consonants before which *s* is retained, are voiceless. Once again, we already have a set of rules that correctly predict that the *s* will delete:

$$[\text{Voicing Assimilation}]_{Latin}$$

$$[z\ C \rightarrow C]_{Latin}$$

We are left with *avert* where the *b* is lost as well. Without other data, no good solution is possible. One might speculate that the fact that both [b] and [v] are labials is important, but there is no other data that indicates why.

The last form *abhor* presents an interesting problem: Since the sound [h] is voiceless, so the *s* should not delete. In many phonological systems, the sound represented by the character *h* is ambiguously a consonant or transparent. For example, English has the following rule governing the alternation of the indefinite article between *an* and *a*:

$$[an\ \#\ C \rightarrow a\ \#\ C]_{English}$$

Sometimes, *h* counts as a consonant for this rule: *a history, a handle*. But, sometimes it does not: *an historical novel*. A possible explanation of *abhor* is that the *h* counts as a consonant for the *s* deletion rule but is transparent to voicing and so inherits its voicing from the vowel (which is voiced). As with *avert*, we don't have enough data to resolve this issue and leave it as a problem to be explored.

re- (back, again)
At noted in the introduction, the prefix *re-* is a clear example of a naturalized morpheme. It can be added to virtually any verb to indicate that the action indicated by the verb is repeated. Aside from the fact that it can be added to

English as well as Latin verbs, further evidence that it has been naturalized is that it has also be reanalyzed: its etymological form is not *re-* but *red-*.

The etymological form is not readily apparent in English. It appears in only a few forms, the roots of which always begin with a vowel.

Table IX.16

redact	red + ag + t	√ag	drive, act	agent
redolent	red + ol + e + nt	√ol	smell	olfactory
redundant	red + und + a + nt	√und	wave	undulate
redemption	red + em + e + t + ion	√em	buy	preemptive

In Latin, a rule such as

$$[d + C \rightarrow + C]_{Latin}$$

deleted the [d] before a consonant. Since more roots begin with a consonant than with a vowel, there will be more instances of *re-* than *red-*. As a consequence, English speakers reanalyzed the prefix as *re-* and use this form everywhere, including before vowels, as in *reopen*.

Notice that the rule above is not quite right. Previously, we have proposed for the prefix *ad-* that [d] will assimilate to a following consonant. Now, we have contradictory rules. One rule states that [d] will assimilate:

$$d+t \rightarrow tt$$

The other, expressed above, states that [d] will delete.

A solution is to restrict the deletion rule to situations where the preceding vowel is *e* and apply it first.

$$[e\ d + C \rightarrow e + C]_{Latin}$$

This rule will delete [d] when it appears after [e] but not after [a]. The [d] in *ad-* will not delete and consequently can assimilate to other consonants.

prod- (before, forth)

Another prefix that has been reanalyzed along the same pattern as *red-* is *prod-* (Table IX.17). In English, we know it as *pro-*, meaning "before".

Table IX.17

produce	prod + duc	√duc	lead	induce
progress	prod + grad + e + t	√grad	step	grade
promiscuous	prod + misc + uous	√misc	mix	miscellaneous
promise	prod + mit + e + t	√mit	send	permit

One could question why the prefix is proposed as *prod-* and not as *pro-*. To see what has happened, notice that all examples of original Latin *pro-* appear before consonants. The analysis of *red-* in the preceding section shows that there was a rule that deleted [d] before consonants in Latin. This rule will not apply before vowels, so we should look for a root that begins with a vowel. There are that roots that begin with a vowel and take *prod-*. They have identical forms but different meanings and show that the prefix must have been originally *prod-* because the final [d] is present in both.

Table IX.18

prodigal	prod + ag + al	√ag	drive	agent
prodigy	prod + ag +y	√ag	say	adage

The argument here is the same as that used for *red-* since the prefix appears as *prod-* before vowels and as *pro-* before consonants, the etymological form must be *prod-*, and there is a rule:

$$[od + C \rightarrow o + C]_{Latin}$$

Of course, the prefix has been reanalyzed as *pro-* and that is the form that is used in English to create new words, as in *proactive*.

sed- (apart)

Continuing in the same vein, we examine the prefix *sed-* (Table IX.18). This prefix is no longer productive in any form. However, what is salient is that it shows the same pattern as *red-* and *prod-*.

Table IX.18

sedition	sed + i + t + ion	√i	go	transition
seduce	sed + duc	√duc	lead	duct

segregate	sed + greg + a + t	√greg	flock	gregarious
select	sed + leg + e + t	√leg	read	legible
separate	sed + par + a + t	√par	arrange	prepare

There is an interesting configuration of rules applying to the final [d] of a prefix. Earlier, the behaviour of *ad-* and *red-* were contrasted. The [d] of *ad* will assimilate to a following consonant but the [d] of *red-* deletes before a consonant. This contrast seems to persist with every prefix that ends with [d]. Table IX.19 summarizes how the rules apply to the prefixes that terminate with [d].

Table IX.19

ad-	Assimilation	ad + tend > attend
red-	Deletion	red + duc + e + t + ion > reduction
prod-	Deletion	prod + duc + e + t + ion > production
sed-	Deletion	sed + duc > seduce

What sort of rule set will ensure that [d] assimilates to [g] in *aggression* but deletes in *regression* and *progression*? As It appears that [d] deletes after vowels other than [a] and the rule set could be:

$$ad + C_1 \rightarrow aC_1C_1 \text{ (Assimilation)}$$
$$d + C \rightarrow C \text{ (Deletion)}$$

Notice that this gets the results right, although does not explain why assimilation is preferred after [a].

sub- (under)

Consider the data in Table IX.20.

Table IX.20

substantial	sub + sta + nt + ial	√sta	stand	statue
subtract	sub + trag + e + t	√trag	drag	tractor
subduct	sub + duc + e + t	√duc	lead	reduce

subsistence	sub + sta + e + nt + ia	√sta	stand	statue
suborn	sub + orn	√orn	wear	ornament
submit	sub + mit	√mit	send	mission
submerge	sub + merg	√merg	plunge	merge
subjugate	sub + jug + a + t	√jug	join	junction
subject	sub + jac + e + t	√jac	throw	adjective
support	sub + port	√port	carry	important
supplicate	sub + plic + a + t	√plic	fold	applicant
suppose	sub + pos	√pos	place	position
suggest	sub + ges + e + t	√ges	carry/bear	gestation
success	sub + ced + e + t	√ced	go	intercede
suffer	sub + fer	√fer	carry/bear	fertile
suffuse	sub + fud + e + t	√fūd	bottom	fundamental
sufficient	sub + fac + ie + nt	√fac	make	factory

The first few words illustrate the prefix *sub-*. This prefix is still productive in English. One demonstration that it is still used in English is the creation of new lexemes like *subfloor* and *subheading*. These are hybrids, built from the English lexemes *floor* and *heading*.

The next group demonstrates that the *b* of the prefix will assimilate completely to a following *c* [k], *p, f,* and *g*. Curiously, although it assimilates to following labials (*p* and *f*) and velars (*c* and *g*), it does not assimilate to dentals in *substantial, subsistence, subtract* and *subduct*.

Finally, there is a small group of words where none of these rules apply (Table IX.21); instead it appears that *b* is reduced to *s*.

Table IX.21

sustenance	sub + ten + e + nt + ia	√ten	hold	continent
susceptible	sub + cap + e + t + ible	√cap	have	captive
suspend	sub + pend	√pend	hang	pendant
suspect	sub + spec + e + t	√spec	see	spectacle

These are rare exceptions to the rules that we have considered above.

ambi- (both)

This prefix is, in fact, cognate with the English word *both*, although all they now share in common is the labial stop [b].

Table IX.22

ambidextrous	ambi + dextr + ous	√dextr	*right*	dexterity
ambition	ambi + i + t + ion	√i	*go*	initial
ambiguous	ambi + ag + uous	√ag	*drive*	agent
ambivalent	ambi + val + e + nt	√val	*be strong*	value

Ambition illustrates the rule of contraction, where two (often identical) vowels will contract to a single vowel. Notice that there are two instances of [i] in the etymological form. These two instances contract to a single (often long) vowel.

trans- (across)

This prefix exhibits an alternation between *trans-* and *tra-* in Latin. English did not inherit the rule responsible for this alternation and, consequently, the prefix is now productively *trans-*. To determine what the rule responsible for the alteration is, consider the examples in Table IX.23.

Table IX.23

transition	trans + i + t + ion	√i	*go*	exit
transfusion	trans + fūd + e + t + ion	√fūd	*pour*	profuse
transfer	trans + fer	√fer	*carry*	refer
transaction	trans + ag + e + t + ion	√ag	*act, drive*	agent
transport	trans + port	√port	*carry*	export
tradition	trans + da + t + ion	√da	*give*	data
traduce	trans + duc	√duc	*lead*	duct
trajectory	trans + jac + ory	√jac	*throw*	adjective

By now, it should be evident that Latin was sensitive to the juxtaposition of voiceless and voiced sounds. As we examine the forms below, we note that when the root begins with a vowel or voiceless consonant, the prefix appears as *trans-*. However, if the root begins with a voiced consonant, the prefix is transformed to *tra-*. Thus there are appears to be a rule:

$[\text{ns + voiced consonant} \rightarrow \text{voiced consonant}]_{\text{Latin}}$

As was the case in the discussion of the alternation between *ex-* and *e-*, a solution like this is not particularly satisfying. Instead, we can try to break it down into more specific rules. First, we note that we already have rules that assimilate [s] to [z] before a voiced consonant and delete [z] before a consonant. This will do most of the job. We complete the job by proposing the rule:

$[\text{nz} \rightarrow \text{z}]_{\text{Latin}}$

Although we have no explanation for this rule, we know that the others are otherwise necessary. With the proper ordering of rules we get the derivation in Table IX.24.

Table IX.24 Simplification: of *trans-*

trans + duce	
tranz + duce	[Voicing Assimilation]$_{\text{Latin}}$
traz + duce	$[\text{n z} \rightarrow \text{z}]_{\text{Latin}}$
tra + duce	$[\text{z C} \rightarrow \text{C}]_{\text{Latin}}$
traduce	Remove "+"

The voicing assimilation rule applied selectively and erratically. Table IX.25 shows a variety of forms that do not correspond to the analysis given above.

Table IX.25: *trans-* II

transmontane	trans + mont + ane	√mont	hill	Montana
tramontane	trans + mont + ane	√mont	hill	Montana
transverse	trans + vert + e + t	√vert	turn	revert
traverse	trans + vert + e + t	√vert	turn	advertise
transduce	trans + duc	√duc	lead	duct
traduce	trans + duc	√duc	lead	induce
transmit	trans + mit	√mit	send	mission
translate	trans + lat		carry	
transmute	trans + mut	√mut	change	mutate

Forms such as *traverse* and *tramontane* are borrowed from French and Italian respectively and show reduction of *trans-* by Romance rules. Words such as *transverse, translate, transduce,* and *transliterate* appear to be later creations and so escaped reduction.

Other Prefixes

The list of prefixes considered in this chapter is not exhaustive. It includes only those with interesting phonological alternations. Others that can be mentioned (Table IX.26) are easily perceived once the principle of prefixation has been established because they do not have alternations and, in many cases, their semantics is transparent.

Table IX.26

post-	*after*	posthumous
pre-	*before*	prevent
circum-	*around*	circumnavigate
de-	*down*	decline
super-	*above*	superficial
per-	*thoroughly*	perfect

Extensions

We have previously noted that prefixation was a structure developed later in Latin than, for example, the past participle. Latin prefixes are derived from what were once independent prepositions.[5] We saw earlier that, in English, some prepositions can inflect like adjectives. Table IX.27 gives a few examples.

Table IX.27

near	nearer	nearest
close	closer	closest
far	farther	farthest
in	inner	

---

5 A quick examination of common English prefixes reveals the same origin: *input < in + put, outcome < out + come, downtown < down + town, upset < up + set.*

Similarly, some Latin prepositions could also inflect like adjectives. When the preposition was converted to a prefix, these inflections could be retained. Although formed from the inflectional morphology, in the derivational morphology, we will simply consider these to be extensions to the original prefixes, marking those prefixes with slightly different meanings than the originals.

The prefixes in which we are interested are the locative *in-*, the collective *con-*, the aggressive *ex-*, the subordinate *sub-* and, *pre-* "before". There are three extensions that can be added to these, although not all are added to each prefix. These extensions are *-ter-*, *-tra-*, *-tro-*. The starting point for each of these extensions is the comparative inflection. Just as the comparative of the English *in* is *inner*, the comparative of the Latin *in* was *inter*. And from *inter-*, the other possible prefixes *intra-* and *intro-* were created. Table IX.28 gives a brief summary of the possible combinations.

Table IX.28

Prefix	-ter-		-tra-		-tro-	
in-	inter-	interject	intra-	intravenous	intro-	introduction
con-			contra-	contradiction		
ex-	exter-	external	extra-	extradition	extro-	extrovert
sub-	subter-	subterfuge				
pre-	preter-	preternatural				
re(d)-					retro-	retrospective

The differences among these extensions can be important. Imagine the difference between being asked to create an *internet* or an *intranet*. An *intranet* is a network of computers inside a company or local installation. An *internet* is a possibly very large set of interconnected intranets. Of course, the Internet is the largest of them all.

Further Reading

Ayers, Donald M. *English Words from Latin and Greek Elements*. Tucson: University of Arizona Press, 1965.

Moore, Bob, and Maxine Moore. *NTC's Dictionary of Latin and Greek Origins: A Comprehensive Guide to the Classical Origins of English Words*. Chicago: NTC Publishing Group, 1997.

10 Other Operations in Latin

Introduction
To this point, we have examined some phonological rules whose application obscures the original structure of lexemes derived from Latin roots. For the most part, these rules have been straightforward, usually involving assimilation of some sort. In this chapter, we examine phonological rules and morphological structures that are somewhat more exotic.

The Nasal Increment
A small group of roots have a nasal inside the root in some forms but not in others (Table X.1).[1]

Table X.1: Nasal Roots

√tag	touch	tangent	tactile
√frag	break	frangible	fracture
√pos	place	component	composition
√met	measure	dimension	meter
√fūd	pour	fundamental	fusion
√cub	lie	incumbent	concubine
√strig	compress	stringent	strict
√vic	conquer	invincible	victory

---

1 To this group, we could add the root √fig, "mold". It appears in *figment* and *fiction*. The infinitive was *fingere*, showing the nasal increment; the infinitive will be cited in dictionaries in the entries of lexemes with this root. This root is not listed in Table X.1 because it does not appear in English lexemes with the nasal increment.

√pag	strike	impinge	impact
√pug	pierce	punctual	pugilist
√sac	holy	sanction	sacerdotal

This extra consonant has been called the *nasal increment*. Its exact purpose has been lost. However, many other Indo-European languages retain remnants of this ancient structure. For example, the English pair *stand/stood* shows it as well.

Given its antiquity, we cannot reconstruct what the function of the nasal increment once was. However, we can reconstruct the processes by which it is inserted. At first glance, it may appear that the nasal increment is inserted inside the root. For example, if we compare *tactile* and *tangent*, both with the root √tag, it appears that the latter is derived by inserting *n* inside *tag*. This would be a strange rule, unlike the others that we have examined, although much like the rules of Arabic that we briefly examined in Chapter 4. In fact, we don't have a way of expressing this in our morphological rules.

Our morphological rules are designed to add prefixes and suffixes. They are not designed to insert material inside other morphemes. Note that morphological rules have the form

X => Y + af
X => af + Y

We have no mechanism for inserting *af* inside "Y" to create "X". This demonstrates the power of a representation system. The representation that we are using to describe morphology prohibits us from thinking of the nasal increment as an infix; that is, as a morpheme that is inserted morphologically. We will return to this point below.

However, there is good evidence to show that there is a better analysis available. To see it, it is best to examine derivatives of the root √pos (Table X.2).

Table X.2: √pos

compose	component
propose	proponent
expose	exponent
depose	deponent

The thing to notice about these data is that when the nasal is present, the final [s] of the root has disappeared. We should recall that [s] will always disappear in Latin phonology when it is followed by a voiced consonant.[2] This observation was made when we examined the prefix *dis-*.

Recall that, in Latin, consonants will usually assimilate in voicing to a following consonant. Since [n] is voiced, [s] will assimilate to [z]. This [z] will then delete:

[Voicing Assimilation]$_{\text{Latin}}$
[z C → C]$_{\text{Latin}}$

Thus, if the structure of the root and nasal increment is

pos + n

then Latin phonology will create the correct forms. For example, Table X.3 shows how *exponent* and *proponent* are derived by these rules.

Table X.3: *exponent* and *proponent*

ex + pos + n + e + nt	pro + pos + n + e + nt	
ex + poz + n + e +nt	pro + poz + n + e +nt	[Voicing Assimilation]$_{\text{Latin}}$
ex + po + n + e + nt	pro + po + n + e + nt	[z C → C]$_{\text{Latin}}$
exponent	proponent	Remove "+"

This tidy result is not available with the alternative analysis that the nasal increment is somehow inserted inside the root. That analysis predicts the following forms:

con + pons + e + nt
pro + pons + e + nt
ex + pons + e + nt

From these forms, there is no good way to get rid of the *s*.[3] Lexemes like *sense* and *pension* show that the *s* does not normally delete in this position.

---

2   Recall that [n] is voiced.
3   In fact, the sequence *ns* often triggered lengthening of the preceding vowel in Latin: compare *dēns* (< *dent* + *s*). "tooth", in the nominative singular with *dentis* in the genitive singular. That the vowel is not long in *component* is further evidence that the *n* is not inserted inside the root.

These considerations suggests that in the early years, Latin (and other Indo-European languages) had the rule

$$\text{Root}_{nasal} \Rightarrow \text{Root} + n$$

Adding this rule to the set that we have created gives the tree diagram for *exponent*, as in Figure X.1.

Figure X.1: exponent

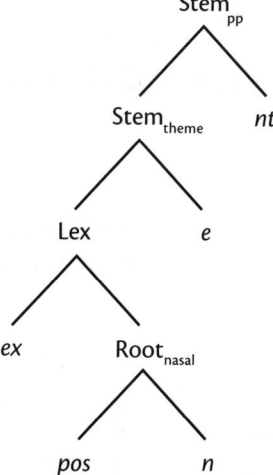

Given that the etymological structure of the forms in Table X.1 with the nasal increment is *root + n*; the structure of *tangent*, etc. must be as in Table X.4.

Table X.4

tangent	tag + n + e + nt
frangible	frag + n + e + ble
dimension	dis + met + n + e + t + ion
incumbent	in + cub + n + e + nt
stringent	strig + n + e + nt
invincible	in + vic + n + e + ble
impinge	in + pag + n
punctual	pug + n + e + t + ual
sanction	sac + n + e + t + ion

To get the correct forms, we must first move the nasal inside the root: e.g., *tag + n > tang*. Processes of this sort are called metathesis.[4] A metathesis rule is a phonological rule that switches the positions of two sounds. Formally, we write the rule as:

$$[C + n \rightarrow nC]_{Latin}$$

The effect of this rule is to insert the nasal increment into the root.

Notice that, whereas it was not possible to create a morphological rule that inserted the nasal increment into the root, it is easy to create a phonological rule that generically switches positions of two sounds. This demonstrates how a formalism can determine an analysis. Sometimes, this is a good thing. In fact, if the formalism is useful it will restrict the kinds of analyses that are possible. If the formalism is the correct one, it will restrict us to just the correct analyses. In the case we are considering, the formalism for morphological rules does not permit us to insert morphemes. We can evaluate the formalism by determining whether this is a good feature or not. To do so, we would have to examine all the languages of the world to determine if in fact any language needs a morphological rule of this sort. If we can find such a language, then we have determined that the formalism that we are using for morphological rules is not optimal for human languages.

In fact, many argue that there are languages that require a more sophisticated way of talking about morphology than what we have been using. Among these languages are the Semitic languages, which were illustrated earlier by Egyptian Arabic, whose morphology includes templates for both derivation and inflection, and morphemes that are arrayed on these templates. This type of morphology is very different from the type that is considered in this book and cannot be described as simple prefixation and suffixation.

There are occasional examples of metathesis in English. For example, some people pronounce the verb *ask* as *aks*, sometimes to be humorous, sometimes as part of their dialect.

We have two forms left to explain: *dimension* and *incumbent*. Taking the latter first, we note that after metathesis, the resulting form is *in + cunb + e + nt*. The question we must answer is why the [n] has changed to [m]. This should be obvious when we recall the discussion from Chapter 6. There we examined the negative prefix of Latin *in-* and noted that [n] assimilated to a following labial. This is what has happened in *incumbent*. The nasal increment has partially assimilated to the following [b].

---

4 *Metathesis*: from the Greek *meta*, "over", and *tithenai*, "place". Metathesis is placing something over something else.

When we examine *dimension*, it should be clear that we already have mapped out all the rules necessary to explain its form. The derivation in Table X.5 makes explicit how the phonology that we have created will generate the appropriate form. The derivation of *proponent* is included to emphasize that the phonological rule responsible for deleting the *s* of the prefix in *dimension* also deletes the *s* of the root √*pos*.

Table X.5: *proponent* and *dimension*

pro + pos + n + e + nt	dis + met + n + e + t + ion	
pro + poz + n + e + nt	diz + met + n + e + t + ion	Voicing Assimilation
pro + po + n + e + nt	di + met + n + e + t + ion	zC → C
"	di + ment + e + t + ion	Metathesis
"	di + ment + t + ion	e + t → + t
"	di + menss + ion	t + t → ss
"	di + mens + ion	Css → Cs
proponent	dimension	Remove "+"

These words demonstrate the power that a phonology can have. Although we proposed each of the rules in Table X.5 to solve separate problems, they act in concert in dramatic ways to explain alternations in the morphemes that comprise lexemes.

An example of the nasal increment that is not as transparent as those above is found in *profane*. This consists of the prefix *pro-*, "before", and the lexeme *fan*, "temple". Related to this is the root √*fes*, "religious observance", found in *festival*. Ignoring the vowel change of *e* to *a*, we note that the alternation we see in *compose* and *component* is the same as that in *festival* and *profane*. That is, it appears that the structure of *profane* is *pro + fes + n* and that the *s* deletes by the same rules noted above.

If we look up the words in Table X.6 in the dictionary, it will indicate that they have the same root, exemplified in the Latin verb infinitive *cernere* "sift". If we remove the infinitive morpheme *-re* and the thematic vowel *-e-*, we are left with the apparent root √*cern*. It is easy enough to find the root in *discern* and *concern*. But how can the others possibly have the same root?

Table X.6

discern	dis + cern
concern	con + cern
indiscrete	in + dis + ?
excrete	ex + ?
secrete	sed + ?

One of the interesting things to note about the unexplained words is that if we were to guess the root, our first guess might be √cret. Notice that this ends in t. This is suspicious because it could be the past participle morpheme. This suspicion is reinforced when we noticed that all three will take the morpheme -ion (Table X.7). Recall that -ion is typically added to past participles.

Table X.7

indiscrete	indiscretion
excrete	excretion
secrete	secretion

If this is correct, then the etymological structure of *excrete* is *ex + cr + e + t*. That is, the root is √cr. The structure of *excrete* is the same as we have proposed for other past participles: a root, followed by a thematic vowel, followed by -t.

Of course, a first concern with this analysis is that we normally expect the thematic *e* to delete. This is the point at which we must consider whether it is useful to think of these forms as exceptions to the rule that deletes thematic *e*. The choice is between an analysis that shows that these forms are morphologically regular but are exceptions to a phonological rule, and a shoulder shrug, an admission that we can't explain why *discern* and *discrete* have the same root. The analysis that proposes a substantive hypothesis is superior to conceding defeat, so we will accept that the root is √cr and that it does not obey the deletion rule.

Although the forms in Table X.7 first looked odd, in fact they are quite regular. One might be bothered that the root √cr has no vowel, but liquids ([l] and [r]) often play the role of vowels. Consider a word like *bird*. When you say it aloud, is there actually a vowel represented by *i* or is the word actually [br̥d]?[5] It happens that English spelling rules reflect a requirement that every syllable contain a vowel,

---

5   When a sound that is usually a consonant functions as a vowel, it is usual to indicate its vocalic function with the subscript circle under it.

but the orthographic rules only recognize *a, e, i, o,* and *u* (and sometimes *y*) as vowels and do not recognize other sounds that can function similarly. Consequently, when a sound like [r] plays the role of a vowel, the spelling rules require that a vowel letter nonetheless be present.

Whether [r] is a vowel or a consonant depends on the context in which it appears. In *bird* [br̥d], it is between consonants and functions like a vowel. In *secrete*, it is between a consonant and a vowel, and functions like a consonant.

In the history of English, this ability of liquids to function as vowels has occasionally meant that a vowel is no longer necessary and we find that the vowel is deleted, only to be replaced orthographically, although not phonetically. For example, the word *bird* that was discussed previously was in Old English *bridd*, and the contemporary English *third* was originally in Old English *thridda* (compare with *three*). In each, the liquid [r] assumed the role of the vowel. But, since English orthography requires a vowel letter, one was inserted before the *r*.

Another example of the alternation between *Vr* and *rV* from Latin is found in *consternation* and *strenuous*. These each developed from the Indo-European root √*ster*, "rigid"; the English cognate is *stare*. Although they each apparently have the nasal increment, one developed as *ster + n*, the other as *stre + n*.

To return to the original data, the real problem is explaining the words that looked easy: *discern* and *concern*. To begin, notice that the root originally proposed (√*cern*) ends with *n*. This *n* looks like it could be the nasal increment. If so and the root is √*cr*, then the etymological structure of *concern* is *con + cr + n*.

Notice that metathesis fails here. One way of explaining this is to note that the metathesis rule is:

$$[C + n \rightarrow nC]_{Latin}$$

This rule switches a consonant and *n*. But we have just noted that *r* functions like a vowel between consonants. Consequently, the rule cannot apply to *cr + n* because *r* is a vowel here.

Another possible explanation is that the rule applies only when the consonant is a stop and fails to apply when the consonant is a liquid (or a sibilant, recall *component < con + pos + n + e + nt*).

Finally, we can ask why, if *r* functions like a vowel, *concern* is not *concrn*. The answer is the same we gave for *bird*. Recall that the English spelling system was inherited from Latin (Chapter 4). The requirement that the spelling of a syllable contain a vowel is one inherited from the Latin spelling system. Since the second syllable of *concrn* does not have a vowel letter (although it does have vocalic [r]), one must be inserted.

For another example of how the spelling system wrestles with pronunciation, notice how a liquid ([r] or [l]) is represented at the ends of words when it is functioning as a vowel. For example, the Canadian spelling is *centre*, but the American spelling is *center*. There is no difference in pronunciation. So, the same sound is represented sometimes as *re*, sometimes as *er*. Of course, this kind of alternation is infrequent, but it illustrates that orthography is not necessary phonetically accurate. Another example of orthographic idiosyncrasy is that although vocalic [r̩] is most frequently represented as *er*, vocalic [l̩], as in *bottle, kindle, throttle*, is always represented as *le*.[6]

It is interesting to note that all the examples that we have considered to this point are verbal roots. What happens if the nasal is added to a nominal root? Table X.8 gives some examples of nominal roots with a following nasal.

Examining the data, it appears that when the last consonant is a dental or labial, it assimilates to a nasal. So *sop + n* becomes *somn*, and *pet + n* becomes *penn*. However, when the last stop is a velar, the outcome is a bit more difficult to see. It appears that the velar stop assimilates in voicing to the nasal. So, *dec + n* becomes *dign*,[7] and *mag + n* becomes *magn*. However, this analysis is a result of a misinterpretation of the orthography. The digraph *gn* was likely used to signify the sound [ŋ], the velar nasal. In other words, the velars also assimilate to a nasal.

Table X.8: Nouns with Nasal

insomnia	sop + n	√sop	sleep	soporific
pennate	pet + n	√pet	feather	(helicopter < Greek)
animal	at + n	√at	spirit	(Mahatma *great spirit* < Sanskrit maha + atma)
magnify	mag + n	√mag	great	magistrate
dignity	dec + n	√dec	befit	decent
sign	sec + n	√sec	cut	secant

The problem that these examples pose is the explanation for why the nasal should metathesize in verbs but not in nouns. We cannot completely solve this problem, but two explanations suggest themselves. One is that the nasal increment of verbs is a different construction from that of the nouns and that somehow this makes

---

6 The liquids are not the only consonants that switch roles and function as vowels. Consider words like *bottom* and *bacon*. Does the *o* in the last syllable represent a vowel sound or is it orthographic support of the rule that every syllable must have a vowel letter? It seems here that [m̩] and [n̩] are functioning as vowels.

7 See the discussion about the words in the section *Medial Vowel Weakening and the Nasal Increment* for the explanation of the change in vowel.

the difference. The other is that the noun construction was created later than the verb construction and the metathesis rule no longer applied.

The latter explanation connects up with other facts about Latin. Previously, we noted that in the later periods of Latin, when new verbs were created, they were created with the *ā* theme. For example, *sensation* is an obvious past participle, *sens + ā + t + ion*. But the putative root is *sens*, which is also a past participle, *sent + ī + t*. What has happened is that the structure of the past participle *sens* became obscured and so was perceived as an atomic root from which new verbs could be created. Significantly, the thematic vowel that the new verb takes is *ā*. This is the vowel that is always used to form new verbs.

With this in mind, we can compare the infinitives *pungere*, with root √*pug*, and *pugnare*, also with the root √*pug*. Since they are both verbs, one would expect that metathesis would apply in both. That it doesn't in *pugnāre* indicates that the difference between nouns and verbs is not the significant feature. Instead, metathesis applies in the old verb *pungere* (with the correct thematic vowel) but not in the new verb *pugnāre* (with the thematic vowel *ā*).

Table X.9 gives examples that show both metathesis in an old verb with thematic vowel *e* and the failure of metathesis in a new verb with the same root but with the thematic vowel *ā*.

Table X.9

| puncture | pug + n + e + t + ure | √pug | pierce | pugilist |
| pugnacious | pug + n + ā (+ c + ious) | √pug | pierce | pugilist |

These forms give some credence to the notion that the metathesis rule is an older one and doesn't apply to newer formations. In this case, metathesis applies to the older *pungere* < *pug + n + e + re* but does not apply to the newer *pugnāre* < *pug + n + ā + re*. If this explanation works, then it suggests that the construction adding a nasal to a noun without metathesis is newer than that adding a nasal to a verb.

Medial Vowel Weakening

One of the dramatic changes that occurs to Latin vowels is a raising (for example, from [a] to [e] to [i]) when they appear in the middle of words. Consider the alternations Table X.10:

Table X.10

√spec	see	species	inspection	suspicion
√reg	rule	regal	correction	incorrigible
√sed	sit	sediment	session	insidious

When the vowel of the root is *e*, it will raise to i[8] if it is in the middle of the word and there is only one consonant following.[9] The vowel does not raise if it is the first vowel in the word (as in *spectacles*), or the last vowel in the word (as in *suspect*) or if it is followed by more that 1 consonant (as in *inspection*). To get this right, we propose the following rule:

$$[V\ C^n\ e\ C\ V \to V\ C\ i\ C\ V]_{Latin}$$

It is not a very attractive rule and perhaps in a more fully formed linguistic theory than what we are proposing here it would have a more succinct description. It says that the vowel *e* will change to *i* if it is preceded by a vowel and any number of consonants[10] and followed by just one consonant and a vowel.

Now consider the forms in Table X.11.

Table X.11

√fac	make, do	fact	effect	efficient
			defect	deficient
			infect	
√cap	have	capture	receptive	recipient
			deceptive	
			inception	incipient
√sta	stand	statue	obstetric	constituent
				restitution
√tag	touch	tact	integral	contiguous
			integrate	
√da	give	data		tradition

These roots illustrate that medial *a* will also change. In some cases, it will change to *e*, in others to *i*. As always, our intent is to determine when it changes to *e* and when to *i*, and how best to represent these changes.

---

[8] Note that here we are not being phonetically accurate and so the vowels are not placed inside squared brackets.

[9] In fact, it was only short *e* which raised. A long *e* did not.

[10] That is what "C^n" means. The superscript *n* means "any number of X" where X is the unit to which it is superscripted.

When we examine lexemes such as *deficient, recipient,* and *constituent,* which have the underlying structures

>   de + fac + ie + nt
>   re + cap + ie + nt
>   con + sta + t + ue + nt

we note that the *a* has changed to *i* in the same places that *e* will change to *i*, namely, when preceded by a vowel and some consonants and followed by one single consonant and a vowel. We could propose a rule such as:

$$[V\ C^n\ a\ C\ V \rightarrow V\ C\ i\ C\ V]_{Latin}$$

Notice that this has the same result in the same environment as the medial vowel weakening rule for *e*. This suggests that we may be able to use the *e* medial vowel weakening rule.

If we examine the other change, we note that *a* will change to *e* when a prefix has been added. Thus, we can propose the rule:[11]

$$[V\ C^n\ a \rightarrow V\ C^n\ e]_{Latin}$$

Now, we can ask how these various rules fit together and whether we need all of them. The first thing to notice is that the rule that converts *a* to *e* will apply to structures like

>   de + fac + ie + nt > de + fec + ie + nt (*deficient*)
>   re + cap + ie + nt > re + cep + ie + nt (*recipient*)
>   con + sta + t + ue + nt > con + ste + t + ue + nt (*constituent*)

Next, we note that the result of this rule creates *e* that can be raised to *i* by the first rule that we created. That is, if we have the two rules

$$[V\ C^n\ a \rightarrow V\ C^n\ e]_{Latin}$$
$$[V\ C^n\ e\ C\ V \rightarrow V\ C^n\ i\ C\ V]_{Latin}$$

we do not need a third to convert *a* to *i*. The first rule converts *a* to *e*. The second converts *e* to *i*. Under the right circumstances and applied in the right order,

---

11 This isn't really quite right. In actual Latin, the rule was $[V\ Cn\ a\ Cn\ V \rightarrow V\ Cn\ e\ Cn\ V]_{Latin.}$ That is, the [a] must be in the middle of the word just as [e] must be in the middle of a word to change to [i]. Once borrowed into English, the syllable following the [a] is often just a case marker (marking *nominative, accusative,* etc.) and so is deleted. For example, the Latin form of *infect* with the root √fac is *infectus*. The *-us* ending is ignored when the lexeme is borrowed into English.

these two rules will together convert *a* to *i*. Examine the derivations of *defect* and *deficient* to see how this works.

Table X.12

de + fac + t	de + fac + ie + nt	
de + fec + t	de + fec + ie + nt	$[V\ C^n\ a \rightarrow V\ C^n\ e]_{Latin}$
"	de + fic + ie + nt	$[V\ C^n\ e\ C\ V \rightarrow V\ C^n\ i\ C\ V]_{Latin}$
defect	deficient	Remove "+"

In situations like this, one rule, $a \rightarrow e$, creates an opportunity for another rule, $e \rightarrow i$, to apply. Together, the two rules do the work of a rule like $a \rightarrow i$. Since the rules $a \rightarrow e$ and $e \rightarrow i$ are needed anyway, the rule $a \rightarrow i$ is unnecessary.

This kind of argument is quite common in linguistics. Faced with two different analyses (Table X.13), it is usually argued that the first is preferred because it is, in some sense, simpler. At the least, it contains fewer rules than the alternative.

Table X.13

$a \rightarrow e$
$e \rightarrow i$

$a \rightarrow e$
$a \rightarrow i$
$e \rightarrow i$

Although linguists have traditionally relied on this argument, it does not always provide the correct analysis.

To see this, first consider the compounds in Table X.14.

Table X.14

manu + fac + e + t + ure	manufacture
satis + fac + e + t + ion	satisfaction
bene + fac + e + t + ion	benefaction

These compounds consist of two roots, the second of which is √fac in each case. The first question that arises is why the medial vowel weakening rule fails to apply. The answer we can create is that compounding is a relatively late morphological process in Latin. If medial vowel weakening is an early process, then it may have died out before the compounding process entered the language. Whatever explanation we offer, it is clear that medial vowel weakening does not apply to these compounds.

Now consider the compounds in Table X.15. Again the second root in these compounds is √fac. However, in these, the medial vowel weakening rule has applied. Furthermore, we have a good argument that these compounds are more recent than simple lexemes with the same root: the last two lexemes have the wrong thematic vowel, indicating that they were formed later, outside the older regular morphology of the language. The first shows the thematic vowel *e*, although the root √fac regularly shows *ie* in the present participle; see *deficient* and *efficient*. The others show the thematic vowel *a*, which we have argued can be an indication of recent creation.

Table X.15

mag + n + i + fac + e + nt	magnificent
sec + n + i + fac + a + nt	significant
quanti + fac + a + t + ion	quantification

Paradoxically, although they are formed outside the regular morphology, they are subject to the regular phonology, particularly the medial vowel weakening rule.

The problem we have identified is that medial vowel weakening applies in Table X.15 but not in Table X.14. To get at the answer, notice that the change that has occurred in Table X.15 is

$$a \rightarrow i$$

while the change that *has not* occurred in Table X.14 is

$$a \rightarrow e$$

Notice that if our rule set is

$$a \rightarrow e$$
$$e \rightarrow i$$

and $a \rightarrow e$ does not apply to compounds (as we argued for *manufacture*), then *magnificent* is impossible because no *e* is created for the rule $e \rightarrow i$.

Since the rule $a \rightarrow e$ fails to apply in compounds, the only way to explain the data in Table X.15 is to assume that the rule

$$[V\ C^n\ a\ C\ V \rightarrow V\ C^n\ i\ C\ V]_{Latin}$$

really exists and that it applies to compounds. This makes it appear that the second set of rules in Table X.13 is the correct analysis. This is, of course, contrary to the idea that the analysis with the fewest rules is best.

Another root with similar behaviour is √ag "drive". The data in Table X.16 show that in the past participle, the rule $a \rightarrow e$ does not apply, although it is expected: cf. *infection* < *in + fac + e + t + ion* but *inaction* < *in + ag + e + t + ion* although we expect *ᶜinection*. There seems to be no explanation for this; this root is simply an exception to this rule. However, since $a \rightarrow e$ fails, the vowel of the root √ag cannot convert to *e* and so the rule $e \rightarrow i$ cannot apply and, consequently, the root √ag should never convert to *ig*. But *prodigious*, etc. show that, in fact, it does. Since the rule $a \rightarrow e$ does not apply to this root, there must be a rule $a \rightarrow i$ to create *prodigious*.

Table X.16: √ag

inaction	in + ag + e + t + ion
redaction	red + ag + e + t + ion
interaction	inter + ag + e + t + ion
transaction	trans + ag + e + t + ion
prodigious	prod + ag + ious
navigation	nau + ag + a + t + ion
fumigation	fum + ag + a + t + ion

Medial Vowel Weakening and the Nasal Increment

Consider the words in Table X.17.

Table X.17

√frag	break	infringe
√tag	touch	contingent
√pag	strike	impinge

Given the rules to this point, we expect that these words will have the vowel *e* because the root vowel is followed by two consonants. Instead, each word has the vowel *i*. How can this be explained?

The first step in explanation is to note that the sequence of consonants in both these words is *ng*. To solve the problem, we have to ignore contemporary pronunciation and refer to how these words were pronounced in Latin. We know from previous discussion that in Latin the character *g* corresponds to the sound [g]. We also know that a nasal will assimilate in place of articulation to a following consonant. So, in Latin, the character sequence *ng* is equivalent to [ŋg].

Thus, a possible solution is that *a* raises to *e* by Medial Vowel Weakening, and *e* raises to *i* before [ŋ]. The rule is apparent in Table X.8 which includes *dignity* < *dec + n + ity* and *sign* < *sec + n*. In both cases, we noted that the sequence *gn* was used to represent [ŋ]. In both words, *e* raises to *i* before [ŋ]. This provides further evidence that such a rule is necessary. Table X.18 gives a sample derivation.

Table X.18: *infringe* and *contingent*

sec + n	in + frag + n	con + tag + n + e + nt	
seg + n	"	"	Assimilation
"	in + freg + n	con + teg + n + e + nt	$[V\ C^n\ a \rightarrow V\ C^n\ e]_{Latin}$
"	in + freng	con + teng + e + nt	$[C + n \rightarrow nC]_{Latin}$
"	in + freŋg	con + teŋg + e + nt	$[Assimilation]_{Latin}$
sign	in + friŋg	con + tiŋg + e + nt	$[eŋ \rightarrow iŋ]_{Latin}$
"	infringe	contingent	Remove "+"

There are three roots that we have said do not take a thematic vowel: √*i* "go", √*sta* "stand" and √*da* "give". It is obvious why we would say √*i* is athematic: Given a word like *exit*, if the *i* is a thematic vowel then the etymological structure would be *ex + ∅ + i + t*; that is, there would be no root at all. Instead, we say that the root is √*i* and it does not take a thematic vowel.

But, why say that √*sta* and √*da* are athematic? Why not say that the roots are √*st* and √*d*, and that their thematic vowel is *a*? The Medial Vowel Weakening Rule gives us an argument for athematic roots. This rule applies only to short vowels, and the thematic *a* was always long. Thus, we have a prediction:

If the *a* of *sta* and *da* is the thematic vowel, Medial Vowel Weakening will not apply to it. However, if the roots are √sta and √da with short vowels, then Medial Vowel Weakening could apply to them.

In fact, Medial Vowel Weakening does apply to both, verifying that the *a* cannot be a thematic vowel and must be part of the root: note *constituent* < con + sta + tu[12] + e + nt and *tradition* < trans + da + t + ion.

Other Alternations

In the preceding sections, the focus has been on roots from which Latin verbs were created. In the following sections, we widen the range and examine roots that were used to form nouns and adjectives as well.

Rhotacising Roots

There is a curious relationship between [s] and [r]. Often, when [s] appears between vowels it will rhotacise[13] to [r]. Table X.19 gives examples.

Table X.19: Rhotacism

		Unrhotacized	Rhotacized
√corpus	body	corpse	corporeal
√honus	honor	honest	honorable
√os	mouth	osculate	oral
√rus	country	rustic	rural
√jus	law	justice	jury
√venus	love	Venus	venereal
√opus	work	opus	operate
√genus	kind	genus	generate
√onus	burden	onus	exonerate
√ques	ask	question	query
√ges	carry	suggest	gerund

---

12 Latin has a causative construction that takes a verb like *sta*, "stand", and creates from it *statu*, "cause to stand".
13 Rhotacize: from the Greek rho, the letter ρ, pronounced [r].

As long as the [s] is followed by a consonant, it appears as such. However, whenever it appears between vowels, it transforms to [r].

$$[VsV \rightarrow VrV]_{Latin}$$

It is worth noting that the data in Table X.19 is presented is a slightly different way than previously. To clarify what is represented here, note that the column labelled *Unrhotacized* contains roots with an *s*. In the next column, the same root appears with an *r*. The rule

$$[VsV \rightarrow VrV]_{Latin}$$

has applied to the lexemes in the column labelled *Rhotacized*. That is, a lexeme like *rural* is derived from **rusal*, and *oral* is derived from **osal*.

Why doesn't rhotacism apply to a word like *rustic* or *osculate*? Because the *s* in each does not appear immediately between vowels.

Data is presented in this way to show that the roots in question actually have *s* (as in *rustic*) but that the *s* rhotacizes between vowels (as in *rural*).

An oddity about Latin rhotacism is that sometimes, though not always, a high vowel before the rhotacising [s] will lower and front to *e* and other times it will lower to *o*. So, for example, we have *genus* and *generate*, *venus* and *venerate*, and *opus* and *operate* with *e* and *corpus* and *corporation* with *o*. The odd thing about this rule, whatever it is, is that it does not apply before [s] nor before [r]; it only applies before either an [s] that is about to rhotacize or an [r] that was originally an [s].

If we keep the rhotacism rule in mind, we can note a correspondence between Latin and English cognates. The rhotacized form appears in Latin in Table X.20 but as [s] in English.

Table X.20

Latin	English
Aurora	Easter
sorority	sister

Notice that English had a rule that inserted [t] between [s] and [r].

$$[sr \rightarrow str]_{English}$$

That these are cognates may be easier to see if we undo the rhotacism and insertion rules (Table X.21). Examining the result, it should be clear that the major difference is that the vowels have changed and that Latin has a vowel between *s* and *r*, thereby providing the environment for rhotacism.

Table X.21

Latin	English
*Ausora	*Easr
*sosority	*sisr

English shows some signs of an ancient rhotacising rule: see Table X.22.

Table X.22: English Rhotacism

was	were
is	are

Alternations between u/v

In the discussion on the history of the alphabet, it was noted that the character *v* was created from the character *u*. The alphabetic innovation is analogous to an historical change by which [w] became [v], thus giving rise to an alternation between the character *u*, which originally represented both [u] and [w], and *v*, which now represents [v].

Table X.23: Alternation between u/v

		u	v
√nau	ship	nautical	naval
√solu	loosen	solution	solve
√salu	health	salute	salvation
√cau	be on guard	caution	caveat
√volu	roll	revolution	revolve
√diu	god	diurnal	divine

222 OTHER OPERATIONS IN LATIN

This is an instance where the orthography does not reveal the actual process. It appears that a rule of the sort

$$u + V \rightarrow v + V$$

has applied. In fact, the actual process was subtler and consisted of two steps. In Latin, whenever [u] appeared before a vowel, it converted to [w]. Recall that this regularity permitted the Romans to use a single character *u* to represent both.

$$[u\ V \rightarrow w\ V]_{Latin}$$

During the early Romance period, [w] converted to [v], a change which necessitated the creation of a new character.

$$[w \rightarrow v]_{Romance}$$

Vowel Raising

English has two versions of *l* depending on where in the syllable it is located. When it appears at the beginning of a syllable, it is produced relatively forward in the mouth and is called a "light *l*". When it appears at the end of a syllable it is produced farther back and is called a "dark *l*". The difference can be felt (by native English speakers) when producing *light* (with the light *l*) and *full* (with the dark *l*).

Latin also had these different forms of [l]. When a vowel appeared before the dark *l*, it assimilated by moving back and high. Thus, roots that ended in *l* will often show *u* when the root is followed by a consonant, as in the past participle stem (Table X.24).

Table X.24: Vowel

		Etymological Vowel	Raised Vowel
√col	cultivate	colony	cult
√sal	leap	salient	desultory
√stol	stupid	stolid	stultify
√ol	old	adolescent	adult
√pell	drive	compel	compulsion
√fac	make, do	difficile	difficult

The rule responsible for this alternation is given below. The rule states that any vowel will change to *u* if followed by *l* and another consonant.

$$VlC \rightarrow ulC$$

The "s" Increment

At the beginning of this chapter, we discussed a group of verbs that occasionally contain a nasal increment. We cannot determine what the function of this increment was and so we cannot predict when it will occur or what contribution it makes to the meaning of a word. However, if it does occur, we can predict where it will occur: There is, apparently, a slot after the root for this increment. Table X.25 shows verb roots that take a different increment. These verbs have been augmented with *s* in the words in the right-hand column. Again, the function of this increment is unknown. The primary point of interest is the effect that the increment has on the root.

Table X.25: The "s" Increment

√fig	attach		infix
√pell	drive	compel	compulsion
√noc	injure	innocent	noxious
√vegh	bring, way	vehicle	convex
√misc	mix	miscellaneous	mix
√fluc	flow	fluctuate	flux
√tag	touch	intact	tax
√sec	cut	sectarian	sex
√fall	deception	fallacy	false
√vell	pluck	vellicate	convulse

The easiest roots to analyze are those that end in a velar stop (Table X.26).

Table X.26: Velar roots

√fig	attach	infix	in + fig + s
√noc	injure	noxious	nok + s + ious

√vegh	bring, way	convex	con + vegh + s
√misc	mix	mix	misk + s
√fluc	flow	flux	fluk + s
√tag	touch	tax	tag + s
√sec	cut	sex	sec + s

When the final stop is [k] (the character *c*) as in the root *noc*, the result is the sequence [ks], which is represented by the character *x*. In the root *misc* the resulting sequence [sks] reduces to just [ks]. When the final stop is [g], the resulting sequence [gs] converts to [ks]. This should be a familiar change because it is the assimilation of [g] to the voiceless stop [k] when followed by the voiceless fricative [s]. All of these show the character *x* representing the sequence [ks].

The root *vegh* is subject to several changes whose order must be considered. We have already seen that Latin contained the rule

$[gh \rightarrow h]_{Latin}$

This rule has applied in the lexeme *vehicle*. However, in the lexeme *vex* we know that the [g] has remained because the character *x* represents [ks] and the [k] must be a reflex of original [g]. It appears that when the [s] increment is added, the [h] is lost. Thus, the derivations of *vehicle* and *vex* will be as in Table X.27. The [h] of [gh] must be lost in *vex* before the rule that deletes [g] from [gh].

Table X.27

veghicle	vegh+s	
"	veg+s	gh+s → g+s
"	vek+s	g+s → k+s
vehicle	"	gh → h
"	vex	Remove "+"

The second group comprises those roots that end in [l], or more properly [ll] (Table X.28). The first thing to note is that although the roots end in a geminate [ll], there is only one [l] after the [s] is added. We might propose a rule such as:

$[ll+s \rightarrow l+s]_{Latin}$

Table X.28: Roots ending in [ll]

√pell	drive	pulse	pell + s
√fall	deception	false	fall + s
√vell	pluck	convulse	con + vell + s

This will work, but it doesn't integrate with the other rules that we have seen in Latin. Instead of proposing a new rule, it is useful to explore the rules that we have already proposed. For example, we have proposed rules that assimilate one consonant to another. In particular, we have seen that a consonant will assimilate to a following [s]. So, the following is possible:

$[l+s \rightarrow s+s]_{Latin}$

This sort of rule will feed into the rule that we have already proposed that converts [ss] to [s] if preceded by a consonant

$[C\ s\ s \rightarrow C\ s]_{Latin}$

Given this set of rules, the sequence of changes would be:

ll + s → lss
lss → ls

What is the difference between the two proposals? The data do not let us choose between them because they have the same consequences. Wherever one works, the other will as well. Wherever one fails, the other will also fail. However, we might prefer the second analysis because it makes use of rules that have been previously proposed for Latin. Because it fits with those rules, we have greater confidence in them and the analysis makes these lexemes coherent with the rest of the Latin partition. The first analysis, in contrast, proposes a new rule that doesn't seem to have any other motivation.

Examining the roots that have the vowel *e*, we note that the vowel converts to *u* when followed by *ls*. This is predicted by the rule that we created in the preceding section.

The word *false* seems to be an exception to this rule. The rules we have proposed predict *°fulse*. There are a number of possible explanations. Perhaps *false* is a relatively new word and is not susceptible to the rule that raises vowels before dark [l]. Or, possibly, the difference between the root *fall* which has the geminate [ll] rather than a single [l] and *sal* (in *result*) is important. Unfortunately, there is very little data on which to base an analysis and so we will simply note that our rule doesn't apply to this word.

Epenthesis

Occasionally, a particular cluster of consonants will be broken up by the insertion of another consonant. We saw earlier, that in English the sequence *sr* was interrupted with an intrusive *t*. For example, one difference between Latin *soror* and English *sister* is the insertion of *t* in the latter. This process is called *epenthesis*.[14]

Latin had an epenthesis rule as well. The common root to which this rule applied is √em, "buy", and the rule applied in the past participle. This rule inserted *p* between the *m* of the root and the past participle *t* (Table X.29). There is no borrowing from Latin that has only the root form. Another very rare root is √temn, "scorn", which appears in the archaic word *contemn*. Much more familiar is the epenthetic form, *contempt*.

The Latin epenthesis rule is:

$$m + t \rightarrow mpt$$

Table X.29

exempt	ex + em + e + t
pre-empt	pre+em+e +t
redemption	red + em + e + t + ion

Notice that there is a certain predictability to this rule. Given that something is inserted, it makes sense that it is labial because [m] is also labial. This is pertinent because when we examine French, we will note a similar rule which inserts a stop after a nasal, either [b] or [d], depending on whether the nasal is [m] or [n].

Another form of the root √em is created by adding the prefix *sub*. After numerous rules that do not concern us, the structure *sub+em* reduces to *sum*. The lexemes in which this form participates clearly show the epenthesis rule. With *sum*, we can compare verbal forms with forms nominalized with *-ion* (Table X.30).

---

14 *Epenthesis*: from the Greek *epi-*, "in addition", *en-*, "in", and *tithenai*, "to place".

Table X.30

consume	consumption	con + [sub + em] + e + t + ion
resume	resumption	red + [sub + em] + e + t + ion
presume	presumption	pre + [sub + em] + e + t + ion

Reduplication

Reduplication is, in the simplest case, the repetition of some part or all of a linguistic unit. This unit could be a morpheme, lexeme, syllable or sound. Reduplication occurs rarely and unsystematically in English. It is very common in the Phillipine languages, and in Fijian and Mandarin among many others. An English example is the lexeme *chitchat*. Beginning with the lexeme *chat*, reduplication applies to the entire lexeme to create *chatchat*. The first vowel is then altered to create *chitchat*. Altering some part of the reduplicated section is common: cf. *seesaw* and *geegaw*.

The way we understand the derivation of *chitchat* is to first reduplicate the root:

    chat $\Rightarrow$ chatchat

Then a phonological rule changes the vowel:

    chatchat $\rightarrow$ chitchat

An ancient formation that required that the root be reduplicated was preserved in Latin in only a few forms. One root √*sta*, "stand", was borrowed into English in both its reduplicated and unreduplicated forms. An example of the nonreduplicated form is *statue*. An example of the reduplicated form is *resistant* < re + sta + nt.

To generate the reduplicated form, a standard analysis is that which we applied to *chitchat*, with an extra rule applied at the end. First, the entire root is reduplicated:

    sta $\Rightarrow$ stasta

Then the vowel is changed as it was in *chitchat*:

    stasta $\rightarrow$ stista

Finally, a dissimilation rule applies to delete the first *t*. The rule will delete a portion of a consonant cluster whenever the cluster is repeated in the lexeme:

stista → sista

To see how this gives *resistant* from *re + sta + nt*, it is helpful to follow the steps. First, the root reduplicates:

re + sta + nt ⇒ re + stasta + nt

Then the first vowel changes

re + stasta + nt → re + stista + nt

Then dissimilation removes the first [t]:

re + stista + nt → re + sista + nt

When the morpheme boundary marker "+" is removed, the result is *resistant*. Other examples of reduplication are those in Table X.31.

Table X.31

Reduplicated Root	Reduplicated Present Participle	Unreduplicated Present Participle
assist	assistance	
consist	consistent	constant
desist		
insist	insistence	instant
persist	persistent	
resist	resistant	
subsist	subsistent	substance

The verb *to be*

It appears that Proto-Indo-European had two forms that function like the English *be*. It is possible that they originally made an important semantic distinction. For example, it is common for languages to distinguish between states and actions and to mark this distinction with different forms of auxiliary verbs when they appear with a verb. Whatever the reason for the distinction, by the time records of the various Indo-European languages become available, the two verbs have fused into a single paradigm. This is evident in English where we find *be*, *been*, *was*, and *were*, but also *is* and *are*. We can call the first set, remnants of a labial verb, and the second, remnants of a sibilant verb.[15]

Latin also had both the labial and sibilant forms. The labial form is found in *fui* ,"I have been"; the sibilant form in *sum* "I am", and *es* "you (sg.) are". The labial root is borrowed into English in *future* from *futurus*, "about to be".

The sibilant root is a bit more productive but is difficult to find. It appears in *essence*. This is clearly a present participle. It is formed exceptionally off the infinitive *esse* < *es* + *se*, "to be". Notice that the infinitive morpheme appears as *-se* instead of *-re* as usual. This is because the usual *-re* is in fact a rhotacized form of the original infinitive *-se*. Other sibilant borrowings with just *s* are *absence/absent* and *presence/present*.

Further Reading

Allen, W. S. *Vox Latina: A Guide to the Pronunciation of Classical Latin.* Cambridge: University Press, 1965.

Ayers, Donald M. *English Words from Latin and Greek Elements.* Tucson: University of Arizona Press, 1986.

Buck, Carl Darling. *Comparative Grammar of Greek and Latin.* Chicago: University of Chicago Press, 1933.

Moore, Bob, and Maxine Moore. *NTC's Dictionary of Latin and Greek Origins: A Comprehensive Guide to the Classical Origins of English Words.* Chicago: NTC Publishing Group, 1997.

---

15 Recall that the *r* of *are* is a rhotacized *s*.

11 Latin Suffixes

We have observed previously that affixes can be added both to the beginning and ends of lexemes. The type of affix added to the end is called a *suffix*. It should be apparent by now that this term is composed of the prefix *sub-*, "under", and the Latin root *fig*, "fix". Latin used both suffixes and prefixes to modify the meaning of the base lexeme. Unlike prefixes, Latin suffixes also created forms with grammatical categories different from the original. This chapter examines some of the more frequently appearing Latinate suffixes.

Basic Suffixes
-al (pertaining to)
Examine the following table to determine which grammatical category *-al* creates. As always, other lexemes created from the roots are provided for illustration.

Table XI.1: -al

√leg	read, select	legal	collect
√voc	voice	vocal	vocation
√reg	rule	regal	correct
√equ	equal	equal	equivalent
√manu	hand	manual	manufacture
√semen	seed	seminal	seminary
√norm	rule	normal	normative
√annu	year	annual	annuity
√anima	life	animal	animate
√nav	sailor	naval	nautical

It should be apparent that the lexemes formed from *-al* are adjectives. Thus, the morphological rule is:

$$[\text{Lex}_{adj} \Rightarrow \text{Lex} + al]_{\text{Latin}}$$

There is a second suffix that glosses as "pertaining to" but has the shape *-ar*.

Table XI.2: *-ar*

√sim	same	similar	simulate
√popul	people	popular	population
√famili	household	familiar	family
√jug	join	jugular	junction
√schol	school	scholar	scholastic
√sol	sun	solar	solstice
√stell	star	stellar	Stella

That this suffix has the same meaning as *-al* and a similar shape—both are made up of *a* and a liquid—suggests that they are allomorphs. When we scan Table XI.2, we note that in every instance the suffix *-ar* is immediately preceded by *l* (with the exception of *familiar*, which has an extra vowel). We could propose two different suffixes with the same semantics:

$$[\text{Lex}_{adj} \Rightarrow \text{Lex} + al]_{\text{Latin}}$$
$$[\text{Lex}_{adj} \Rightarrow \text{Lex} + ar]_{\text{Latin}}$$

This should be suspicious: the suffixes have the same meaning and are remarkably similar in shape: They both consist of the vowel *a* followed by a liquid. Rather than proposing two suffixes, *-al* and *-ar*, in the lexicon, there should be just one: *-al*. The *-ar* reflex can be predicted by a rule:

$$[l + (i) \, a \, l \rightarrow l + (i) \, a \, r]_{\text{Latin}}$$

A rule of this sort is called *dissimilation*. We have already seen assimilation rules, by which different sounds come to resemble each other. The opposite can also occur: similar sounds can change to maximize the difference between them. In this case, the liquid *l* changes to the liquid *r* when it is preceded by *l*.

One can ask whether dissimilation can apply over longer distances. The rule as written suggests that the root must end with *l* and that the two segments must be close together. In fact, there is evidence that rule applies over longer distances (Table XI.3).

Table XI.3

√plant	plant	plantar	plant
√plan	flat	planar	plane
√line	line	linear	line
√lun	moon	lunar	lunatic
√lumb	loin	lumbar	lumbago

These examples suggest that dissimilation can apply over long distances. However, there are other quite similar examples where dissimilation fails (Table XI.5).

Table XI.4

√leg	read	legal	legislate
√loc	place	local	location
√glob	ball	global	globe
√claud	close	clausal	include

What seems to distinguish the forms in Table XI.3 where dissimilation applies over a long distance from those in Table XI.4, where it does not, is that the roots in Table XI.3 contain a nasal while those in Table XI.4 do not. Compare *lunar* < **lun + al*, with *local* < **loc + al*. It seems that nasals facilitate dissimilation.

Another class of exceptions to long distance dissimilation are those in Table XI.5. The difference here, particularly with *plural* and *floral*, is the presence of *r*, a liquid like *l*.

Table XI.5

| √plus | plus | plural | plus |
| √flos | flower | floral | florist |

√col	cultivate	cultural	colony
√litter	letter	literal	literate
√liber	free	liberal	liberty
√lat	side	lateral	latitude

-ic (pertaining to)

The suffix -ic also creates adjectives (Table XI.6).

Table XI.6: -ic

√civ	home	civic	civilian
√acid	sour	acidic	acidity
√class	rank	classic	classify
√met	measure	metric	meter
√giga	huge being	gigantic	gigabyte
√lact	milk	lactic	lactate
√canon	rule	canonic	canonize

Occasionally, this suffix is augmented as -tic (Table XI.7).

Table XI.7: -tic

√rus	country	rustic	rural
√aqua	water	aquatic	aquifer
√err	wander	erratic	error
√here	choose	heretic	heresy
√luna	moon	lunatic	lunar

$$[\text{Lex}_{Adj} \Rightarrow \text{Lex} + (t)ic]_{Latin}$$

It is often possible to add more than one suffix. In fact, the borrowing patterns of Latin words into English have established preferred sequences of suffixes. The sequence -ic + al is one of these. Some examples are given in Table XI.8.

Table XI.8

metric	metrical
classic	classical
heretic	heretical
canonic	canonical

-ity (quality of)

This is another noun forming suffix (Table XI.9).

Table XI.9: -ity

Root	Gloss		
√grav	heavy	gravity	grave
√san	healthy	sanity	sane
√am	love	amity	amateur
√annu	year	annuity	annual
√brev	brief	brevity	breviary
√cav	hollow	cavity	cave
√lumen	light	luminosity	luminous

One of the curious properties of this suffix is that it attracts stress. Recall that stress is the relative force with which a syllable is produced. Table XI.10 gives examples of the stress alternation that *-ity* induces.

Table XI.10: Stress

c'ausal	caus'ality
c'omplex	compl'exity
cont'inue	contig'uity
c'ordial	cordi'ality
h'uman	hum'anity
imp'etuous	impetu'osity

The reason the *-ity* attracts stress is that the Latin stress rule counted syllables from the end of the word. Unless the second last syllable from the end either contained a long vowel or ended in a consonant, the third syllable from the end of the word was stressed. Since *-ity* meets neither of those conditions, when it is added to created a new lexeme, the syllable immediately preceding it will always carry the main stress.

-bil- (able to)

One of the vexing problems for those learning English spelling is whether a word such as *invincible* should not be ⁶*invincable*. There appear to be two suffixes, *-able* and *-ible*, and it is not always clear which to use. The problem is furthered by the naturalization of the suffix as *-able*. Notice that new words such as *workable* and *openable* can be created with this new suffix. As a consequence, the *-ible* form seems foreign.

If we recall that Latin forms new words off both the past participle stem and the thematic stem, a partial solution to the problem becomes evident.

Table XI.11: Thematic Stem + *ble*

Root	Gloss	Thematic Stem	
√prob	test	prob + a	probable
√port	carry	port + a	portable
√aud	hear	aud + i	audible
√vic	conquor	vic + n + e	invincible
√reg	rule	reg + e	corrigible
√cred	believe	cred + e	credible

It should be apparent that, when the new lexeme is formed from the thematic stem, it is the thematic vowel that is alternating, not the suffix itself, and that the suffix is *-ble*, not either *-able* or *-ible*. That is, the structure of the lexemes in Table XI.11 is:

> prob + a + ble
> aud + i + ble
> cred + e + ble

When the thematic vowel is *-e-*, it is raised to *-i-*. Thus, one way to determine which vowel to use is to determine the thematic stem.

The situation is complicated by another structure that also uses this suffix. Table XI.12 gives examples of words that appear to formed off the past participle.

Table XI.12: Past Participle Stem + *ble*

Root	Gloss		
√rup	break	corrupt	corruptible
√duc	lead	deduct	deductible
√ges	carry	digest	digestible
√fac	do	perfect	perfectible
√leg	read, select	collect	collectible

When examined carefully, these examples turn out to be odd words. Since they are formed from the past participle, they will have the structure shown in Table XI.13. Notice that the past participle already has a thematic vowel, and so the vowel of *-ible* cannot be the thematic vowel as it is in *credible*.

Table XI.13

Prefix	Root	Thematic Vowel	Past Participle	Suffix
con	rup	e	t	ible
de	duc	e	t	ible
dis	ges	e	t	ible
per	fac	e	t	ible
con	leg	e	t	ible

Instead, this is a newer formation than the original, which was formed by adding *-ble* to the thematic stem. What seems to have happened is that the past participle became opaque and was for many verbs perceived as a separate word, isolated from the other members of its paradigm. As a consequence, other words could be formed from it.

Examples of this process with a different morphological formation are the words in Table XI.14. Each is recognizably a present participle formation with the thematic vowel *-a-*. However, when the roots are examined, it is also clear that each normally takes the thematic vowel *-e-* and that in each case the present participle has been created by adding *-ant* to the past participle. Since this is not the normal rule, we must conclude that these are new constructions. In some instances, the new construction had a regular semantic function. In particular, forming new *a* theme verbs from the past participle often marked the new verbs as frequentatives, verbs that are marked for frequent and repeated action. *Expectant* is such a verb. The root is √*spec* meaning "see". The past participle is *spec + e + t > spect*. *Expectant* is formed by adding the thematic vowel *-a-* and the present participle *-nt* to this stem. To be expectant is to frequently look for the person or event that one is expecting. That these verbs are formed from the past participle provides further evidence for the idea that some past participles become viewed as words isolated from the original paradigm.

Table XI.14

attractant
consultant
digestant
disinfectant
expectant
inhabitant
reactant

The last complication in the investigation of the vowel of this suffix is to note that the productive form in English is *-able*, so that when new words are created in English this is the form that is used. Note *workable, doable, openable*, and so on, which clearly have English roots.

In summary, there are three rules that control how the *able/ible* suffix is used.

1. In original Latin words, the suffix was *-bil-*, and the vowel that precedes it was the thematic vowel of the verb. If thematic vowel was *e/ē/ī* then the suffix appeared as *ible*. Otherwise, the thematic vowel of the verb was *ā* so the suffix appeared as *able*.
2. In new Latin words where the thematic vowel was no longer apparent, the suffix was reanalyzed as *-ible*.
3. Words that are formed in English use *-able*.

Further examination of this suffix demonstrates another alternation (Table XI.15).

Table XI.15

probable	probability
credible	credibility
deducible	deducibility
collectible	collectibility
portable	portability

As mentioned previously, there are preferences for sequences of suffixes. The string *-bility* looks like it is composed of *bil + ity*. The latter was illustrated previously. The former is obviously related to *-ble*. The problem posed is whether an *i* has been inserted in *portability*

$$[bl + ity \rightarrow bil + ity]_{Latin}$$

or deleted in *portable*

$$[bil \rightarrow bl]_{Latin}$$

Neither of these is particularly elegant, but they are the only choices. As a general rule, insertion rules are to be avoided because they raise the awkward question of why in this case an *i* inserted and not some other vowel. On the other hand, if the suffix was originally *-bil-*, then the deletion of the vowel is relatively straightforward.

Our approach is to question why the vowel deletes in *portable*, but not in *portability*. Recall that *-ity* always attracts stress. As a consequence, when it is added, the vowel of *-bil-* will be stressed:

p^1ortabile > portable
p^2ortab^{1}ility

The difference in stress assignment provides the answer for why the vowel deletes in one but not the other. Since stressed vowels are produced with more force than unstressed vowels, they are less likely to delete. The vowel of *-bil-* is unstressed in **portabile > portable* and so deletes. It is stressed in *portability* and so does not delete. The rule for the alternation *-bil- ~ -bl* is

$$[i^{\circ} \rightarrow \emptyset]_{Latin}$$

The symbol "°" is used to indicate that the vowel is unstressed. Deletion of unstressed vowels is a fairly common rule in languages, so this rule is not unexpected.

-ous (characterized by)

The -*ous* suffix is used to create adjectives which attribute the quality referred to by the root to the noun that the adjective modifies.

Table XI.16: -ous

Root	Gloss		
√fam	*fame*	famous	fame
√popul	*people*	populous	populate
√vari	*change*	various	vary
√fabul	*story*	fabulous	confabulate
√decor	*beauty*	decorous	decorate
√norm	*rule*	enormous	normal

Many words have a "connecting" vowel which is apparently unpredictable. It will be either *i*, *e*, or *u* (Table XI.17).

Table XI.17

Root	Gloss		
√cur	*care*	curious	cure
√tag	*touch*	contagious	contact
√spec	*see*	suspicious	spectacle
√aqu	*water*	aqueous	aquatic
√ign	*fire*	igneous	ignite
√nau	*ship*	nauseous	nautical
√spec	*see*	conspicuous	suspicious
√noc	*harm*	innocuous	innocent
√ag	*do, act*	ambiguous	act

Past Participial Suffixes

A number of suffixes are restricted to the past participle stem of the verb.

-or (Agentive)

The *-or* suffix is one that is often added to the past participle to create a new nominal lexeme referring to the person or object that performs the action that is indicated by the verb. It is cognate with the English suffix *-er*, which performs the same function. The latter suffix appears in terms like *reader, worker, opener* and *driver*.

The Latin *-or* suffix functions similarly, though not productively, in English.

Table XI.18: -or

Root	Gloss	Past Participle	Nominal
√ag	drive	act	actor
√dic	say	indicate	indicator
√teg	cover	detect	detector
√cīd	cut	incisive	incisor
√fac	make, do	defect	defector
√grad	step	aggressive	aggressor

The *-or* suffix is classically derivational as opposed to inflectional. Not only does it create a lexeme of a different grammatical category from the original lexeme, but it also introduces a new semantics, one that is usually predictable. To see this consider that

- an *actor* is one who *acts*
- an *indicator* is one that *indicates*
- a *detector* is one that *detects*
- a *defector* is one who *defects*

So, the morphological rule is

$$[\text{Lex}_N \Rightarrow \text{Lex}_{V[\text{ppp}]} + or]_{\text{Latin}}$$

but, if we wanted to talk about the semantics of this rule, we would include that the individual indicated by the *-or* word is the individual who performs the action of the original verb.

-ion (act of)

The *-ion* suffix was also used to nominalize verbs (Table X.19).

Table XI.19: *-ion*

Root	Gloss	Past Participle	Nominal
√ag	drive	act	action
√dic	speak	indicate	indication
√grad	step	aggressive	aggression
√fac	do	defect	defection
√cīd	cut	incisive	incision

$$[\text{Lex}_N \Rightarrow \text{Lex}_{V[ppp]} + ion]_{\text{Latin}}$$

Comparing this rule with the previous, it is apparent that if we intend to fully develop the grammar to distinguish between the different suffixes, it will be necessary to include a way of representing semantics. Although both *-or* and *-ion* create nouns from verbs, they create different kinds of nouns. The noun created by the *-or* suffix refers to the agent who performs the action of the verb. The noun created by the *-ion* suffix refers to the action itself. We would like to be able to express this in a fully developed grammar.

There are lexemes that are formed with this suffix that are not formed from the past participle (Table XI.20). These seem to be exceptions to the more general rule that a past participle stem is required.

Table XI.20: *-ion*

Root	Gloss	Past Participle	Nominal
√leg	read	collection	legion
√reg	rule	correction	region
√leg	choose	election	religion
√spec	see	inspection	suspicion
√op	choose	option	opinion
√tag	touch	contact	contagion

-ure (result of)

This suffix is typically added to the past participle stem, although there are frequent exceptions (Table XI.21). As with the preceding suffixes, this one creates nouns from the past participle.

Table XI.21: -ure

Root	Gloss		
√cap	have	capture	incipient
√pug	pierce	puncture	pugilist
√fid	cleave	fissure	fission
√frag	break	fracture	fragment
√rup	break	rupture	corrupt
√gn	born	nature	pregnant
√leg	read, select	lecture	legend

$$[Lex_N \Rightarrow Lex_{V[ppp]} + ure]_{Latin}$$

-ive (nature or quality of)

A final suffix that is attached to past participle stems is -ive (Table XI.22). This suffix creates adjectives:

Table XI.22: -ive

Root	Gloss	Past Participle	Nominal
√jac	throw	ejection	adjective
√scrib	write	description	descriptive
√ag	drive	action	active
√pend	hang	pension	pensive
√pos	place	position	positive
√dic	say	prediction	predictive

$$[Lex_A \Rightarrow Lex_{V[ppp]} + ive]_{Latin}$$

Extensions

In this section, we consider other suffixes which typically do not create a lexeme (although they may sporadically), but instead create a stem which requires a further suffix to create a new lexeme.

Diminutive -ul-

The diminutive expresses smallness in size or function. The English suffix *-let* is a diminutive; cf. *book/booklet*, *pig/piglet* and *play/playlet*. Sometimes diminutives are used as forms of endearment. The conversion of proper names such as *Bill* and *Jack* to *Billy* and *Jacky* is an example of this.

The suffix *-ul-* was used to this effect in Latin. Although it is not always possible to discern this meaning, it is nonetheless useful to be able to pick out this suffix when it occurs. Table XI.23 illustrates this suffix with roots that should be familiar.

Table XI.23-*ul*-

√spec	see	species	speculate
√calc	chalk	calcium	calculate
√jac	throw	adjective	ejaculate
√circ	ring	circus	circulate
√und	wave	inundate	undulate
√reg	rule	regal	regulate
√sim	same	assimilate	simulate
√capit	head	capital	capitulate

In the examples shown, the past participle of the new root is given. In every case, the thematic vowel in the past participle is *a*. This is noteworthy because the correct thematic vowel of √spec, √jac, and √reg is *e*. The change of thematic vowel is evidence a truly new root has been created. We can further argue that this is a newer structure than the original past participle because it uses *a* for the thematic vowel, rather than the vowel that is correct for the root. We have previously seen that newer words use the *a* theme vowel.

A common landing site for this suffix is on forms which end with the suffix *-ic* (Table XI.24).

Table XI.24: *-icul-*

√mater	mother	maternal	matriculate
√art	art	art	articulate
√ges	carry	gesture	gesticulate
√curr	run	current	curriculum
√pend	hang	pendulum	perpendicular
√ret	net	retina	reticular
√rid	laugh	risible	ridicule
√vegh	way	vex	vehicular
√met	fear		meticulous
√rid	laugh	risible	ridicule
√part	part	partition	particular

This suffix is also itself a popular landing site for the suffix *-al*. Since the diminutive ends in *l*, the expectation is that it will trigger dissimilation of the *l* of *-al*, and, in fact, this is what occurs (Table XI.25).

Table XI.25: *-ulal*

√joc	joke	jocosity	jocular
√circ	ring	circus	circular
√glob	ball	globe	globular
√nod	knot	node	nodular
√reg	rule	regal	regular
√jug	bind	junction	jugular
gran	grain	granite	granular
cell	room	cell	cellular

Adjectival *-il-*

In Latin, it was possible to create an adjective from a root with the suffix *-il-*. Frequently, the suffix *-ity* is now with this extension used to create a nominal lexeme.

Table XI.26: -il-

√frag	break	fragile	fragility
√ag	drive	agile	agility
√doc	teach	docile	docility
√hum	low		humility
√civ	home	civil	civility
√fac	make, do	facile	facility
√fer	bear	fertile	fertility
√gn	born	gentile	gentility
√puer	boy	puerile	
√sen	be old	senile	senior
√vir	man	virile	virtue

The Inchoative

If we were to create a language, the first things that we would look at would be ways to talk about objects, actions, and events. So, we would need nouns and verbs. But, if we examine actions closely, they get complicated. For example,

- they take place in time: the past, the present, the future
- they can have different aspects: completed, uncompleted, habitual, repetitive, frequent, etc
- they can be observed directly, reported or inferred

These and other aspects of actions are often marked on verbs in many languages.

One of the particulars of actions is that they start and stop. Languages usually have a method of expressing the start of an action, and this method is called the *inchoative*. An example of the inchoative from English is the difference between *Let's go* and *Let's get going*. The first is a direction to action, the second a direction to begin an action (which presumably will continue).

Latin had the inchoative morpheme *-esc-*, which was added to a root (before the thematic vowel). This morpheme takes a lexeme X and creates a new lexeme meaning something like "begin to do X or become X" (see Table XI.27).

Table XI.27

√qui	rest	quiescent	qui + esc + e + nt	quiet
√ol	old	adolescent	ad + ol + esc + e + nt	adult
√ferv	boil	effervescent	ex + ferv + esc + e + nt	fervent
√cre	create	crescent	cre + esc + e + nt	create
√val	be strong	convalescent	con + val + esc + e + nt	valor
√tum	swell	tumescent	tum + esc + e + nt	tumor
√sen	be old	senescent	sen + esc + e + nt	senate
√putr	be rotten	putrescent	putr + esc + e + nt	putrid
√flos	flower	florescent	flos + esc + e + nt	floral
√lumen	light	luminesent	lumen + esc + e + nt	luminous
√pub	old	pubescent	pub + esc + e +nt	puberty

An interesting observation that can be made about this suffix is that it creates new verbs that always take the *e* theme vowel. Notice that the roots √cre and √sen are *ā* theme verbs as in *create* and *senate*. However, the inchoative of each takes the *e* theme as in *crescent* and *senescent*. Recall that the rule that creates thematic stems is:

$$[Stem_{theme} \Rightarrow Root + V_{theme}]_{Latin}$$

This means that the rule that creates inchoatives actually creates new roots which then take the thematic *e*:

$$[Root_{Inchoative} \Rightarrow Root + esc]_{Latin}$$

One additional phonological rule is needed. The morphological rule for the inchoative by itself predicts that *crescent* should in fact be *creescent* (< *cre + esc + e + nt*). It should be evident that a phonological rule reducing a sequence of two identical vowels to one is necessary.

Further Reading

Ayers, Donald M. *English Words from Latin and Greek Elements*. Tucson: University of Arizona Press, 1986.

Buck, Carl Darling. *Comparative Grammar of Greek and Latin*. Chicago: University of Chicago Press, 1933.

Fabb, Nigel. "English Suffixation is Constrained Only by Selectional Restrictions." *Natural Language & Linguistic Theory*, 1988. pp. 527–539.

Moore, Bob, and Maxine Moore. *NTC's Dictionary of Latin and Greek Origins: A Comprehensive Guide to the Classical Origins of English Words*. Chicago: NTC Publishing Group, 1997.

The Greek Partition

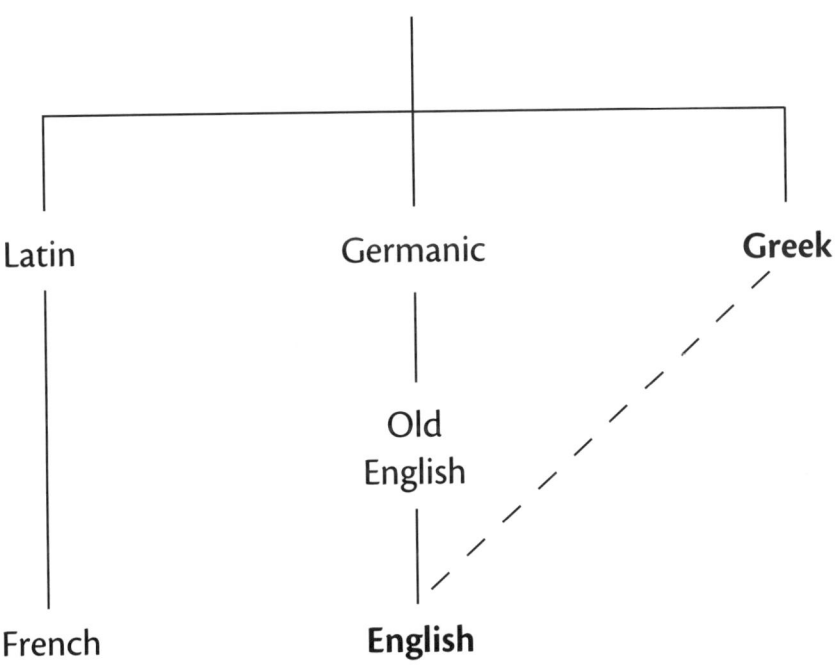

12 Greek Borrowings

Introduction

In this chapter, we will review some useful Greek prefixes and roots that are often resurrected when new concepts require a name. English borrowed so much of Latin that it inherited much of Latin morphology. The same is not quite true of Greek. There are a considerable number of borrowings from Greek, but not so many that the morphology of Greek can be teased out in the same way as we did for Latin. That said, there are suggestions of Greek rules among the borrowings that are considered below. In particular, there are suggestions of rules that resemble the rules that were discovered among the Latin borrowings. For example, there are suggestions of the past participle -*t* and the rules that converted it to *s*. To be able to see these similarities is to simultaneously verify one's understanding of the previous chapters and to experience the same insights that Sir William Jones experienced 200 years ago, namely, that Greek and Latin are intimately related.

This insight extends to the morphemes themselves. Latin and Greek are so closely related that it is quite easy to see that various morphemes are cognate. In some cases, it is more than easy, it is drop-dead obvious: the morphemes are identical. For example, Latin and Greek both have roots $\sqrt{i}$, "go", and $\sqrt{met}$, "measure" and the prefix *ex*, "out".

However, the languages are not identical, and when we search for the reason for the difference, we find that while they may have similar structure and cognate morphemes, they have different phonologies. It is the difference in phonological rules that accounts for the divergences that we will observe in these languages, although, as we saw when comparing Old English with Contemporary English, there are other reasons as well. This is most obvious with cognate morphemes. You should notice, for example, that both Latin and Greek have a prefix *ex*-, but these prefixes behave quite differently phonologically.

Prefixes

syn- (together, with)

The prefix shows a patterning similar to that of Latin *con-*. Coincidentally, they are cognates. Table XII.1 provides examples of the prefix and introduces new Greek roots. A second example of each root is also provided.

Table XII.1: *syn-*

syntax	syn + tax	√tax	arrange	taxi
synagogue	syn + ag	√ag	do	demagogue
synchronize	syn + chron + ize	√chrono	time	chronometer
synergy	syn + erg + y	√erg	work	energy
synonym	syn + onym	√onym	name	homonym
synthetic	syn + the + t + ic	√the	place	thesis
syllable	syn + lab	√lab	hold	astrolabe
syllogism	syn + log + ism	√log	word	logic
symbiotic	syn + bio + tic	√bio	life	biology
symbol	syn + ball	√ball	throw	embolism
symmetry	syn + metr + y	√metr	measure	metric
sympathy	syn + path + y	√path	feel	pathetic
symphony	syn + phon + y	√phon	sound	telephone
symptom	syn + pt + om	√pt	fall/feather	helicopter

Just as in Latin, the [n] of the prefix assimilates to a following [l] or a labial consonant.

$[n + l \rightarrow l + l]_{Greek}$
$[n + labial \rightarrow m + labial]_{Greek}$

This rule set creates a problem that needs to be addressed before we can move on. When we considered the negative prefix *an-* we proposed a rule that deleted [n] before other consonants. Now, unfortunately, we require a rule that assimilates [n] to following consonants. How will a computer program know which one to apply? If they apply in the order that we have created them

$$[n + C \rightarrow C]_{Greek}$$
$$[\text{Assimilation}]_{Greek}$$

the second will never have an opportunity to apply because the [n] will have deleted. On the other hand, if they apply in the opposite order

$$[\text{Assimilation}]_{Greek}$$
$$[n + C \rightarrow C]_{Greek}$$

then a structure such as *an + biotic* will incorrectly generate *ambiotic* instead of *abiotic*.

The solution to this problem is to constrain the deletion rule more tightly so that it applies only after [a]:

$$[a\ n + C \rightarrow a + C]_{Greek}$$

When it is expressed this way, the rules can apply in the first order (deletion/assimilation) and only instances in [n] after [a] will be deleted.

One might argue that it is just as easy to restrict the assimilation rule so that it applies only to the *syn-* prefix. However, this won't do because the Greek locative *en-* is also susceptible to assimilation. Previously, the locative prefix was presented, and the assimilation rule was noted without comment on the problem that it created. That both *syn-* and *en-* will assimilate is evidence that it is the deletion rule that must be constrained.

Notice that a similar problem was examined in Latin although there the rules behaved in opposite fashion. There, the prefix *ad-* showed assimilation, but all other prefixes that ended in [d] showed deletion before consonants.

There is one environment where the story of the *n* of *syn-* is not so straightforward. This environment is illustrated in Table XII.2.

Table XII.2: *syn-*

system	syn + st + em	√(hi)st	stand	histamine
syssarcosis	syn + sarc + osis	√sarc	flesh	sarcasm
systolic	syn + stel + ic	√stel	order	systaltic
syzygy	syn + zyg + y	√zyg	yoke	zygote

One might be tempted to propose a rule that deletes *n* before *s*:

$$n + s \rightarrow + s$$

However, *syssarcosis* shows that this is not likely correct. This word has *ss* instead of just *s*. Let us suppose that the assimilation rule proposed above holds for *s* as well. Then the following will apply:

$$n + s \rightarrow s + s$$

This will correctly produce *syssarcosis*. In a lexeme like *syn* + *stem*, this rule will produce ᵉ*sysstem*. But we have previously seen during the examination of Latin prefixes that rules such as

$$[s + s \text{ consonant} \rightarrow + s \text{ consonant}]_{\text{Latin}}$$

are necessary to explain words such as *aspire* < *ad* + *spire*. After *d* assimilates to *s*, it deletes if there is a following consonant. A similar rule for Greek will explain *system* and *systolic*. In these lexemes, the forms *syn* + *stem* and *syn* + *stolic* convert to *sys* + *stem* and *sys* + *stolic*. These forms then convert to *system* and *systolic* by this new rule:

$$[s + s \text{ consonant} \rightarrow + s \text{ consonant}]_{\text{Greek}}$$

We are left with *syzygy*. The rules that we have proposed to this point predict ᵉ*syzzygy*. To derive the correct Greek form, we require the rule

$$z\,z \rightarrow z$$

This is a degemination[1] rule. It is interesting to note that the sequence of *zz* will degeminate in Greek, but the sequence of *ss* does not, even though the sequences differ only in voicing.

ana- (up, throughout)

We have already examined the negative prefix *an-* in Greek. The prefix *ana-* (Table XII.3) undergoes a change that can result in confusion with the negative prefix.

Table XII.3: ana-

analysis	ana + lys + is	√lys	loosen	dialysis
anadromous	ana + drom + ous	√drom	run	hippodrome

---

1 *Degemination*: from the Latin *de-*, "undo", and *gemina* "twin".

analogy	ana + log + y	√log	word	logic
anatomy	ana + tom + y	√tom	cut	appendectomy
anabolic	ana + ball + ic	√ball	throw	symbolic
anachronism	ana + chron + ism	√chron	time	chronometer
anagram	ana + gram	√gram	letter	grammar
anaphor	ana + phor	√phor	carry	phosphorus
Anabaptist	ana + bapt + ist	√bapt	dip	baptism
anode	ana + hode	√hod	way	odometer
aneurism	ana + eur + ism	√eur	broad	eurythmics
anion	ana + i + on	√i	go	cation

Before consonants, the prefix appears as *ana-*. However, before vowels, the final [a] deletes so that the prefix appears to be *an-*.

$$[a + V \rightarrow + V]_{Greek}$$

Notice that, because of this change, this prefix can at times be homophonous with the negative prefix *an-*. For example, how can we tell whether the prefix of *anabiotic* is *ana-* or *an-*? The key is to pay attention to the root. In *anabiotic*, we should recognize the root √bio from terms like *biology* and *antibiotic*. The negative formed from this root is *abiotic*.

dia- (through, across)

To correctly generate the forms in Table XII.3, we require a rule that deletes [a] before other vowels. As always, our confidence in this rule increases if we can find other instances of it. To discover other instances, we examine other prefixes that end in [a])Table XII.4).

Table XII.4: *dia-*

dialogue	dia + log	√log	word	logic
dialysis	dia + lys + is	√lys	loosen	catalyst
diameter	dia + metr	√metr	measure	metric
diagnosis	dia + gno + sis	√gno	know	agnostic
diaphanous	dia + phan + ous	√phan	appear	phenomenon

dieresis	dia + her + sis	√her	take	heresy
diachronic	dia + chron + ic	√chron	time	chronometer
diabolic	dia + bol + ic	√ball	throw	symbol
dialect	dia + log + t	√log	word	logic
diarrhea	dia + rhea	√rhea	flow	logorrhea
diatom	dia + tom	√tom	cut	anatomy
diopter	dia + opt + er	√opt	eye	optic
diuresis	dia + ure + sis	√ure	urine	urea

As was the case with *ana-*, the final [a] in *dia* will delete when followed by another vowel, as in *diopter*.

cata- (down)

Not unexpectedly, this prefix behaves regularly with respect to the deletion rule. It appears as *cata-* before consonants, and *cat-* before vowels (Table XII.5).

Table XII.5: cata-

catabolic	cata + bol + ic	√ball	throw	anabolic
catastrophe	cata + strophe	√stroph	turn	boustrophodon
catalyst	cata + lys + t	√lys	loose	dialysis
cation	cata + i + on	√i	go	anion
catoptric	cata + opt + ric	√opt	eye	optical

para- (beside)

Once again, *para-* provides further evidence for the deletion rule. It appears as *para-* before consonants as in *parabolic*, but as *par-* before vowels, as in *parody* (Table XII.6).

Table XII.6: para-

parasite	para + sit	√sit	food	
parabolic	para + bol + ic	√ball	throw	symbol
paraphernalia	para + pher + nalia	√phor	carry	anaphor
paralysis	para + lys + is	√lys	loose	dialysis

paradox	para + dox	√dox	*opinion*	orthodox
parallel	para + all + el	√all	*other*	allomorph
parameter	para + metr	√metr	*measure*	metric
paraplegic	para + pleg + ic	√pleg	*stroke*	quadriplegic
parody	para + od + y	√od	*song*	ode
paronym	para + onym	√onym	*name*	homonym

meta- (after, change)

The final prefix demonstrating the vowel deletion rule is *meta-*. As usual, it appears as *meta-* before consonants but as *met-* before roots that begin with a vowel (Table XII.7).

Table XII.7: *meta-*

metaphor	meta + phor	√phor	*carry*	anaphor
metabolic	meta + bol + ic	√ball	*throw*	symbol
metaphysics	meta + phys + ic	√phys	*nature*	physics
metathesis	meta + the + sis	√the	*place*	prothesis
meteor	meta + eor	√eor	*air*	
method	meta + hod	√hod	*way*	anode
metonymy	meta + onym + y	√onym	*name*	synonymy
metestrus	meta + estrus	√estr	*frenzy*	estrogen

Meta- is still used productively in English. Evidence for productivity is a term like *metafiction*, which has a Greek prefix and the Latin root √*fig*.

anti- (against)

This prefix has become naturalized in English and is used productively. We can apply it to any noun to indicate a position critical of the object or idea referenced by the noun. For example, one can be *anti-cat*. Likely, one of the reasons that this prefix became productive in English is that, although the Latin form of this prefix is *ante-*, Medial Vowel Weakening often converts it to *anti-*, so that English was inheriting words from both languages with prefixes that are superficially similar. Note that if a word contains the prefix *ante-*, as in *antebellum* or *antecede*, it cannot be a Greek word, but must be Latin.

Table XII.8: *anti-*

antidote	anti + dot	√dot	give	
antibiotic	anti + bio + t + ic	√bio	life	biology
antipathy	anti + path + y	√path	feel	sympathy
antipode	anti + pod	√pod	foot	podiatrist
antithesis	anti + the + sis	√the	place	thesis
antonym	anti + onym	√onym	name	synonym

As it appears in Greek words, this prefix alternates between *anti-* and *ant-* (note *antonym*) (Table XII.8). The truncated form appears before a vowel; the longer form appears before consonants. This suggests that the rule that deletes [a] before vowels is not quite right. Instead of just deleting [a], perhaps all vowels should delete before other vowels. That is, the rule should be:

$$[V_1 + V_2 \rightarrow V_2]_{Greek}$$

The vowels are subscripted so that it is clear that they need not be identical and so that it is possible to specify which vowel is retained.

Is this a legitimate move? That is, can we correctly say that all vowels deleted before other vowels, or is it necessary to create a separate rule for each vowel, perhaps for each prefix? Our preference would be to have a single general rule. To consider the question further, we consider other prefixes that end in a vowel.

epi- (upon, in addition)

This prefix demonstrates that the deletion of [i] before vowels as observed in the case of *anti-*, is not restricted to that prefix. The same deletion applies to *epi-* as well (Table XII.9).

Table XII.9: *epi-*

epidermis	epi + derm + is	√derm	skin	hypodermic
epidemic	epi + dem + ic	√dem	people	democracy
epiphany	epi + phan + y	√phan	appear	phantom
epicanthic	epi + canth + ic	√canth	corner of eye	
eponym	epi + onym	√onym	name	antonym

eparch	epi + arch	√arch	*ruler*	monarch
epenthesis	epi + en + the + sis	√the	*place*	synthesis

endo- (within)

This prefix demonstrates that the deletion rule applies to vowels other than just [a] and [i] (Table XII.10). Note that the [o] deletes in *endergonic* from *endo + erg*. This provides further evidence that a general deletion rule is appropriate: it appears that [a], [i], and [o] all delete before other vowels.

Table XII.10: *endo-*

endoderm	endo + derm + ic	√derm	*skin*	hypodermic
endogamy	endo + gam + y	√gam	*marry*	bigamy
endomorph	endo + morph	√morph	*shape*	morpheme
endophagic	endo + phag + ic	√phag	*eat*	ichthyophagous
endoplasm	endo + plasm	√plasm	*form*	plasma
endameba	endo + amoeb + a	√amoeb	*change*	amoeba
endergonic	endo + erg + on + ic	√erg	*work*	synergy

This prefix itself has some structure. Recall that, in Latin, some prefixes had some structure themselves. Similarly, *endo-* is clearly formed from the Greek locative *en-* with an extension *-do-*. The source of this extension is not clear.

apo- (from, off)

If we are correct that the deletion rule is a general one, applying to all prefixes that end with a vowel, then we should find it confirmed with other prefixes. The argument for the prefix *apo-* is a bit difficult because it does not seem to appear before roots that begin with a vowel (Table XII.11).

Table XII.11: *apo-*

apology	apo + log + y	√log	*word*	dialogue
apocalypse	apo + calypt + s	√calypt	*cover*	eucalyptus
apocope	apo + cop	√cop	*cut*	syncope
apostrophe	apo + stroph	√stroph	*turn*	catastrophe
aphelion	apo + heli + on	√heli	*sun*	heliotropic
apheresis	apo + her + esis	√her	*take*	heresy

However, it does line up with the other prefixes that we have examined. To see this, it is necessary to remember that the Greek orthography did not have a character *h*. This character was added later to the spelling system to indicate words that began with aspiration. In effect, the aspiration was transparent, so that, if a root began with *h* it was as though it began with a vowel. Consequently, a form like *aphelion* is a instance of the deletion rule.

We have been developing a rule that deletes a vowel when it comes in contact with a following vowel. A wrinkle to this rule is how *h* is interpreted by the rule. Table XII.12 collects some examples.

Table XII.12: The Greek *h*

anode	ana + hod	√hod	way	odometer
method	meta + hod	√hod	way	anode
aphelion	apo + heli + on	√heli	sun	heliotropic
apheresis	apo + her + esis	√her	take	heresy
parhelion	para + heli + on	√heli	sun	heliotropic

There are two points to notice, two problems to solve. First, the *h* is transparent to the rule that deletes vowels. It doesn't seem to be treated like a consonant. In fact, the rule seems to ignore it and just assumes that there is only a vowel following the prefix. Second, sometimes the *h* remains and sometimes it does not.

To get at the solution to these problems, we have to review Greek phonetics and how Greek sounds were represented. The description of the Greek alphabet in Chapter 4 did not include a character for the sound [h]; the Roman alphabet used the Greek letter H *eta* to represent this sound. The Greek alphabet represented [h] as a diacritic over the following segment, often a vowel but sometimes ρ ([r]). There was no separate symbol in the Greek alphabet because the sound was perceived only as aspiration that accompanied another sound, not as a separate sound.

These observations help to explain why the character *h* is ignored by the vowel deletion rule: Greek phonology treated aspiration as a property of other sounds, not as sound by itself. Latin treated aspiration as a separate sound and the Romans adopted the character H to represent it. So, the *h* is invisible because it is a Roman character for a sound that Greek treats as part of the following vowel.

Why does the *h* remain in *method* but not in *anode*? After the deletion of the vowel of the prefix, the aspiration must attach to something. The rules governing what sounds can combine with other sounds in Greek govern what happens. After the vowel deletes, the *h* must attach to the consonant of the prefix. Whether the *h* remains depends on whether it can attach to this consonant.

Table XII.13

anode	ana + hod	an + hod
method	meta + hod	met + hod
aphelion	apo + heli + on	ap + heli + on
apheresis	apo + her + esis	ap + her + esis
parhelion	para + heli + on	par + heli + on

In the discussion of the Germanic Consonant Shift, we saw that Greek had voiceless aspirated consonants: [ph], [th], [kh]. Thus, the aspiration in a root like *hod* will attach to a preceding [p], [t] or [k]. This explains *method* and *aphelion*.

The explanation of *parhelion* is only slightly more complicated. Table XII.17 on gives examples showing that a word initial [s] would convert to [h] in Greek. The sequence [sr] will convert to [hr]. When this sequence was transliterated into Roman orthography, it was written as *rh*. So, we find *rheum* in *rheumatism* (note cognate English *stream* < *sream*) and, consequently, *parhelion*.

But, there is no [nh] in Greek, and, consequently, the *h* does not appear in *anode*.

hypo- (below)

Continuing the theme, we note that *hypo-* loses the vowel when the root to which it is added begins with a vowel (Table XII.14).

Table XII.14: *hypo-*

hypodermic	hypo + derm + ic	√derm	skin	dermatitis
hypothesis	hypo + the + sis	√the	place	metathesis
hypochondria	hypo + chondr + ia	√chondr	cartilage	chondroma
hypotenuse	hypo + ten + use	√ten	stretch	tenotomy
hypaethral	hypo + aethr + al	√aethr	sky, burn	ether
hypanthial	hypo + anth + ial	√anth	flower	anthology

Given that *hypo-* apparently behaves in line with the vowel deletion rule, what can we say about a term like *hypoallergenic*? We would like to keep the Greek rule, but in this term [o] did not delete.

Our final note on *hypo-* is to observe that it is cognate with Latin *sub-*.

eu- (good)

We have previously noted that the characters *u* and *v* have the same origin. In this prefix (shown in Table XII.15), there is an alternation between these two characters, indicating that the sounds that they represent are also related. The prefix appears as *eu-* before consonants, but before vowels it converts to *ev-*:

Table XII.15: eu-

eugenic	eu + gen + ic	√gen	seed, birth, kind	genetic
euphonic	eu + phon + ic	√phon	sound	phonetics
eudaemonia	eu + daemon + ia	√daemon	god	daemon
eulogy	eu + log + y	√log	word	dialogue
euphemism	eu + phem + ism	√phem	voice	blaspheme
euphoria	eu + phor + ia	√phor	carry	anaphor
eurhythmic	eu + rhythm + ic	√rhythm	rhythm	rhythm
euthanize	eu + than + ize	√than	death	thanatophobia
eucalyptus	eu + calypt + us	√calypt	cover	apocalyptic
evangelical	eu + angel + ic + al	√angel	messenger	angel

$$[u + V \rightarrow v + V]_{Greek}$$

The form *evangelical* looks like a counter-example to the general rule that all vowels delete before a root that begins with a vowel. Can these two rules be ordered with respect to each other so that [u] converts to [v], but other vowels delete?

hyper- (over)

Hyper- is another Greek prefix that is productive in English and is now combined with forms that are not Greek. The first group in Table XII.16 are native Greek. The second group are hybrids.

Table XII.16: hyper-

hyperbole	hyper + bol	√ball	throw	symbol
hyperbaric	hyper + bar + ic	√bar	pressure	barometer
hyperemia	hyper + hem + ia	√hem	blood	hemoglobin

hypergamy	hyper + gam + y	√gam	*marry*	bigamy
hyperkinetic	hyper + kin + et + ic	√kin	*motion*	kinesiology
hypermnesia	hyper + mn + es + ia	√mnes	*mind*	amnesia
hyperpneic	hyper + pne + ic	√pne	*breathe*	pneumonia
hypertension	hyper + tend + e + t + ion	√tend (Latin)	*stretch*	pretend
hypertext	hyper + tex + e + t	√tex (Latin)	*weave*	textile
hypercorrection	hyper + con + reg + e + t + ion	√reg (Latin)	*rule*	regular

A note on Latin and Greek Cognates

Many of the prefixes that we have examined from Latin and Greek are cognates. We have commented already that Greek *syn-* and Latin *con-* are related.

The pair of *super-* (from Latin) and *hyper-* (from Greek) illustrates a common rule from Ancient Greek: a word initial [s] disappeared, leaving only aspiration *h* behind. Thus, when an unfamiliar Greek form has an initial *h*, it is sometimes possible to find the potentially familiar Latin form by substituting *s* for *h* (Table XII.17).

Table XII.17: $s \rightarrow h$

Latin	Greek	Gloss
subnormal	hypodermic	under
serpent	herpes	snake
superman	hypercorrect	over
semiliterate	hemisphere	half
sexagenarian	hexagon	six
September	heptameter	seven
solar	heliocentric	sun
similar	homogenous	same
salvation	holocaust	safe, whole
persuade	hedonism	sweet
sagacious	hegemony	lead

Latin	Greek	Gloss
sa<u>line</u>	<u>hal</u>ogen	salt
so<u>po</u>rific	<u>hyp</u>notic	sleep

ex- (out)

Cognate with the Latin prefix *ex-* is The Greek *ex-* (Table XII.18). Although cognate, they are susceptible to different rules. Whereas Latin *ex-* had an allomorph *e-*, the Greek prefix alternates with *ec-*.

Table XII.18: ex-

exodus	ex + hod + us	√hod	way	odometer
exarch	ex + arch	√arch	rule	monarchy
exegesis	ex + heg + e + sis	√heg	lead	hegemony
eccentric	ex + centr + ic	√centr	centre	centre
eclectic	ex + log + t + ic	√log	word	logic
eclipse	ex + leip + s	√leip	leave	
ectopic	ex + top + ic	√top	place	topology
eczema	ex + zem + a	√zem	boil	

To understand the rule underlying this alternation, we have to remember that the character *x* represents the sequence [ks]. Thus, the actual etymon of *eclipse* is [eks + lips]. The consonant in the allomorph *ec-* is phonetically [k]. Thus the rule converts [eks] to [ek]. This rule applies only before consonants. Before vowels, the prefix remains [eks]. So the rule is:

$$[ks + C \rightarrow k + C]_{Greek}$$

This rule is a form of cluster simplification, by which the cluster [ksC] is reduced to [kC].

exo-, ecto- (outside, external)

Clearly related to *ex-* are *exo-* and *ecto-*. The latter is an extension of *ex-* with the addition of *-to-*. As expected, the resulting cluster simplifies so that the new prefix is *ecto-*, not *exto*. *Exo-* is an extension by adding *-o-* (Table XII.19).

Table XII.19: exo-, ecto-

exogamy	exo + gam + y	√gam	*marry*	bigamy
exocentric	exo + centr + ic	√centr	*center*	central
exosphere	exo + sphere	√sphere	*sphere*	hemisphere
exothermic	exo + therm + ic	√therm	*warm*	thermometer
ectoderm	ecto + derm	√derm	*skin*	dermatitis
ectomorph	ecto + morph	√morph	*shape*	morphology
ectoplasm	ecto + plasm	√plasm	*fluid*	plasma

dys- (bad, difficult)

Cognate with Latin *dis-* is Greek *dys-* (Table XII.20). As expected, they do not behave quite the same way. Whereas Latin *dis-* lost the *s* before voiced consonants, Greek *dys-* has no other allomorphs.

Table XII.20: *dys-*

dyslectic	dys + log + t + ic	√log	*word*	logic
dysphagia	dys + phag + ia	√phag	*eat*	ichthyophagous
dysphonia	dys + phon + ia	√phon	*sound*	phonology
dysphoria	dys + phor + ia	√phor	*carry*	phosphorescence
dyspnea	dys + pne + a	√pne	*breathe*	apnea
dysuria	dys + ur + ia	√ur	*urine*	urethra
dyspeptic	dys + pep + tic	√pep	*cook*	pepsin
dystrophy	dys + troph + y	√troph	*nutrition*	atrophy
dysentery	dys + enter + y	√enter	*bowels*	enteritis
dystopia	dys + top + ia	√top	*place*	topic

Suffixes

As the language of science and medicine, Greek morphology plays a significant role in the naming of new chemical compounds, diseases, medicines, and medical procedures. Few of these structures make it into everyday discourse and so a complete examination of them is not useful in the context of this book.

Some are deserving of mention because they do appear in words of everyday discourse and because they are productive.

Some of the scientific forms are worthy of mention because they do appear with some frequency, so it is useful to be aware of them, and because their etymology is interesting. The suffix *-ose*, appearing in *glucose, fructose, sucrose, lactose,* and so on. is used to form nouns referring to sugars. Its origin is from the French *glucose*, which was itself borrowed from Greek *glykys*, meaning "sweet". The French term was used to refer to various naturally occurring sugars. Eventually, the last syllable *-ose* was reanalyzed as a suffix and came to be used to create other nouns referring to sugars.

Another common suffix with a definite semantic field is *-ene*. This refers to hydrocarbons of a particular structure. It appears in words like *benzene, propylene, butylene, kerosene,* and many others.

-oid (resembling)

This suffix is productive in English. Evidence for its productivity are hybrid words such as *factoid, hominoid* and *polaroid* which are formed off Latin roots. Since *-oid* begins with a vowel, it triggers vowel deletion on roots that terminate in a vowel (Table XII.21).

Table XII.21: -oid

asteroid	astero + oid	√astero	star	astrology
deltoid	delta + oid	√delta	triangle	delta
hypnoid	hypno + oid	√hypno	sleep	hypnosis
schizoid	schizo + oid	√schizo	cut	schizophrenia
thyroid	thyra + oid	√thyra	door	
hemorrhoid	hemo + rhe + oid	√hemo √rhe	blood flow	hemoglobin logorrhea

-tomy (cut)

Naturally enough, this suffix is used in conjunction with terms for body parts to name medical procedures. This suffix is, in fact, formed from the root √tom meaning "cut". Its first appearance in this book was in the word *atom*, literally "not cut". It also appears in *anatomy*, "cut up" (Table XII.22).

Table XII.22: *-tomy*

lobotomy	lobo + tomy	√lobo	lobe	lobed
craniotomy	cranio + tomy	√cranio	skull	cranium
mastotomy	masto + tomy	√masto	breast	mastitis
necrotomy	necro + tomy	√necro	dead	necrophilia
neurotomy	neuro + tomy	√neuro	nerve	neuron
tracheotomy	tracheo + tomy	√tracheo	windpipe	trachea

Medical procedures referred to by the *-tomy* suffix are ones in which something is cut. For example, in a *neurotomy*, a nerve is cut to alleviate pain. However, in many cases, the named procedure results in the removal of an organ or body part. Terms referring to such procedures are coined by first creating a new suffix by combining the prefix *ex-* with *-tomy* to create *-ectomy*, "cut out". Compare the difference between a *lobotomy*, where a lobe is cut, and a *lobectomy*, where a lobe is removed (Table XII.23).

Table XII.23: *-ectomy*

mastectomy	masto + ectomy	√masto	breast	mastitis
cystectomy	cysto + ectomy	√cysto	cyst	cystoid
embryectomy	embryo + ectomy	√embryo	fetus	embryological
laryngectomy	laryngo + ectomy	√laryngo	larynx	larynx
lobectomy	lobo + ectomy	√lobo	lobe	lobotomy
pneumectomy	pneumo + ectomy	√pneumo	breathe	pneumonia

Ablaut

One of the mysteries of the Indo-European languages is a set of vowel alternations that do not seem to have any explanation. Examples of these alternations are the lexemes formed from the root √*ball* "throw". The vowel *a*, which we hypothesize for the root, appears in the lexeme *ballistic*. However, *symbol* contains the same root with the vowel *o*. In *emblem*, the root has no vowel at all. This phenomenon is called *ablaut*.[2]

These inexplicable changes are common in Indo-European languages. Sometimes, the vowel change signals inflectional categories. For example, the

---

2 *Ablaut* from the German *ab-*, "from", and *laut*, "sound".

so-called strong verbs of English are inflected for the past tense and the past participle by changing the vowel, rather than the regular way of adding morphemes. Table XII.24 gives a few examples. Anyone who has learned English as a second language has no doubt spent many hours memorizing these.

Table XII.24: Ablaut English Verbs

sing	sang	sung
drink	drank	drunk
ring	rang	rung
sink	sank	sunk

There does not seem to be any general rule that governs these changes. It is not possible to predict when they will occur. For example, one might think that this change depends on the following velar nasal consonant. But this can't be right because the past tense of *bring* is *brought*, not *ᵉbrang*. Similarly, whatever rule we might propose, it would not be a natural one: unlike many of the rules that we have considered, it would not relate the change of the vowel to any of the other sounds in the word. The assimilation rules that we have looked at are classic examples of natural rules: the change is obviously consequent to the other sounds.

The phenomenon of ablaut demonstrates the inadequacy of the representation that we have been using to describe morphology. If there are underlying regularities to the ablaut system (for example, the verbs in Table XII.24 all contain a velar nasal), we cannot express these in morphological rules of the form

$$X \Rightarrow Y + af$$

Instead, the ablaut forms look like a little bit of Arabic morphology has sneaked into English.

The 19th century philologists[3] were able to map out the vowel changes and isolate the basic patterns of ablaut. These alternations were described as different degrees or grades of the vowels. For example, we might describe the English verbs in Table XII.24 as having *i*, *a*, and *u* grades. This is a typical case of ablaut, where the vowel signals an inflectional category instead of the usual suffix.

---

3 *Philologist*: from the Greek *philo*, "love", and *log* "word".

In the case of Greek borrowings, we can distinguish among four grades. If we compare *dialog* and *dialect*, we can see the *o* and *e* grades of the root √log, "word".[4] Similarly, if we compare *symbol*, *ballistic*, and *emblem*, we can see the *o*, *a* and *0* "zero" grades of the root √ball, respectively. That is, *symbol* < *syn* + *ball*, *ballistic* < *ball* + *istic*, and *emblem* < *en* + *ball* + *em*.[5] So, the four grades are: *a*, *e*, *o* and *0*. Table XII.25 gives some examples of ablaut in Greek.

Table XII.25: Ablaut

		o grade	e grade	a grade	0 grade
√pher	carry	anaphor phos<u>phor</u>escence semaphore	Christopher periphery paraphernalia		
√log	word	dialogue analogue	dialect		
√gen	seed, birth, kind	gonad	genesis gene genocide		pregnant (Latin)
√phan	appear		phenomenon	epiphany cellophane phantasy sycophant diaphanous	
√erg	work	organ	energy		
√ball	throw	symbol		ballistic	emblem
√astero	star		asteroid		astronomy astrology
√pha	speak		prophet prophecy	dysphasia	
√stel	order	systolic		systaltic	
√mn	mind		mental (Latin)		amnesia

How does something like this happen? This is a question for historical linguistics, since an examination of a slice of the language at particular points in time does not reveal the source of the alternation. We have an example from the history of

---

4 Notice that in a system like this, it is somewhat arbitrary which vowel we take to be the basic vowel of the root.
5 There is another change that passes without comment: the change of *ll* to *l*.

English that suggests one possible mechanism. In this example, the original change that created the vowel alternation was completely explicable. However, later changes removed the environment in which the change occurred, so that there is no longer a natural rule to which one can appeal. To see this change, consider the nouns in Table XII.26.

Table XII.26

mouse	mice
louse	lice
foot	feet
tooth	teeth
woman	women
man	men

This could be a classic case of ablaut: the difference between the singular and plural is found in the vowel.[6] As before, there is no way to write a simple morphological rule that will build these words, followed by a phonological rule that adjusts the pronunciation. However, a little detective work reveals that there is an explanation.

Ignoring much phonetic detail, notice that the difference between the singular and the plural is that the singular has a back vowel (or a back diphthong) and the plural has a front vowel (or a front diphthong) and that this is completely regular among these nouns. This suggests that there could be a rule

$$[V_{bk}X \rightarrow V_{ft}X]$$

where V_{bk} means "back vowel", V_{ft} means "front vowel", and X is the cause of the change.

If we research farther back into the history of the Germanic language family, we discover that the original forms were probably something like those in Table XII.27. Notice that these words formed the plural by adding -iz. This was, in fact, one of the regular mechanisms for forming the plural. This -iz has been lost, but not before it provided the motivation for the fronting of the root vowel.

---

6 David Crystal, in *The Cambridge Encyclopedia of Language*, cites this plural formation as an example of ablaut.

Table XII.27

mouse	mūs	mīsiz
louse	lūs	līsiz
foot	fōt	fētiz
tooth	tōθ	tēθiz
man	man	meniz

Notice that now there is a very good reason for the vowel in the root to move to the front in the plural. In the plural, the next vowel in the word after the root vowel is a front vowel and this causes the vowel of the root to become a front vowel as well. This is quite common in the Germanic languages. For example, the suffix *-jan* ([yan]) was used to create verbs. The [y] caused the vowel of the root to front. Thus we find *dēm* (modern *deem*) < **dōmjan*, compared with the modern noun *doom*, and *fill* < **filljan*, compared with *fill*.

This is often called *i-mutation* or *umlaut* in Germanic linguistics; it can be seen as a variant of assimilation:

$$[VCV_{ft} \rightarrow V_{ft}CV_{ft}]$$

Notice that we have been able to coerce these irregular plurals into a form that is handled by the mechanisms that we have been using through this text: first, a morphological rule adds an affix—in this case the plural morpheme *-iz*—then phonological rules adjust how the word is pronounced. After the vowel of the root has been fronted, the plural morpheme is progressively lost.

Of course, this is not how anyone would argue that people now learn these irregular plurals. But, it does seem to be the historical process. One reason why we do not think that people actually learn a rule like that above for these plurals is that the cause of the change—the final vowel *i*—is no longer present. As a consequence, the cause of the change cannot be discerned except as an historical exercise.

Compounding
One of the productive uses of Greek borrowings is compounding. A compound is a lexeme that has been created from two or more lexemes. Unlike affixation, in which an affix is added to a base, in compounding both forms can function as bases. For example, *grandmother* is clearly constructed from the lexemes *grand* and *mother*.

This word formation process is used extensively in science and medicine with Greek formatives. The following tables offer without comment a selection of Greek roots that are useful to have under one's command.

When the concept of *morpheme* was first introduced in this text, it was noted that the definition "smallest meaningful unit" probably wasn't quite right because some material that is left after analysis doesn't seem to mean anything at all. The example offered then was *speedometer*, which is composed of *speed* + *o* + *meter*. This word seems to have been formed on analogy with the Greek *odometer*. From the preceding examination of various prefixes, we have seen that the first lexeme in this word is √od, the second √metr. So, what is the source of the medial *o*? In some analyses, it is seen as a kind of "linking vowel" inserted to preserve meter, as is the *o* of *speedometer*. On the other hand, if we wanted to pursue Greek word formation further, we could look to the vowel deletion rule discussed above to provide the solution. Instead of proposing a "linking vowel", we would suppose that the vowel was part of the first root and was deleted before vowels.

The root √mono, "one", from Table XII.28 provides a good example. It appears as *mono* in *monorail*, but as *mon* in *monarchy*. The structure of *monarchy* is *mono* + *arch* + *y*. The second [o] of *mono* is in exactly the position that vowels of prefixes are deleted. We have not created a way of distinguishing prefixes from roots in our phonological rules, so it is not unexpected that the rule will apply to both.

Table XII.28: Quantity

√mono	one	monarchy monorail monotone	√octa	eight	octopus
√di(pl)	two	diploma diploid dipolar	√ennea	nine	ennead
√tri	three	tricycle	√dec	ten	decathlon
√tetra	four	tetrahedron	√kilo	one thousand	kilobyte kilometer
√penta	five	Pentagon Pentecost	√mega	one million (hence, *large*)	megabyte megalomania megatheatre
√hexa	six	hexadecimal	√poly	many	polyglot polygamy
√hepta	seven	heptathlon	√proto	first	protohuman proton

Table XII.29: Humanity

√anthropo	human	anthropology misanthrope philanthropy	√philo	love	Philadelphia Anglophile philosophy
√gyn	woman	gynecology misogynist androgynous	√er(ot)	love	erotic erogenous
√andro	man	philander android	√miso	hate	misogynist misanthrope misoneism
√paed/ped	child	pediatrician encyclopedia	√pha	speak	prophet dysphasia
√aut	self	automatic autistic	√glott	tongue	glottal glossolalia glossary
√dem	people	democracy endemic	√ethno	race	ethnic ethnocentric
√gen	kind	genetics genocide	√metro	mother	metropolis
√necr	dead	necrophilia necropolis necrosis	√xeno	stranger	xenophobia
√gam	marriage	bigamy polygamy exogamous monogamy			

Table XII.30: The Universe

√cosmo	universe	cosmology	√hydro	water	hydrology
√astero	star	astrology	√angel	messenger	evangelist
√chron(o)	time	chronometer	√da(e)mon	divine power, god	demonic
√geo	earth	geology	√dyn(am)	power	dynamic
√heli	sun	heliocentric	√bio	life	biology symbiosis

Table XII.31: Logic and Philosophy

√pseudo	false	pseudonym	√gno	know	agnostic, Gnosticism
√tauto	same	tautology	√homo	same	homology, homogenous
√soph	wise	philosophy, sophisticate	√log	word	biology, dialogue, logic

Further Reading

Ayers, Donald M. *English Words from Latin and Greek Elements*. Tucson: University of Arizona Press, 1986.

Crystal, David. *The Cambridge Encyclopedia of Language*. Cambridge: Cambridge University Press, 1987.

Moore, Bob, and Maxine Moore. *NTC's Dictionary of Latin and Greek Origins: A Comprehensive Guide to the Classical Origins of English Words*. Chicago: NTC Publishing Group, 1997.

Pyles, Thomas. *The Origins and Development of the English Language*. 2nd ed. New York: Harcourt Brace Javonovich, 1964.

Smith, Robert W. L. *Dictionary of English Word-Roots*. Totowa, NJ: Littlefield, Adams and Co., 1972.

The French Partition

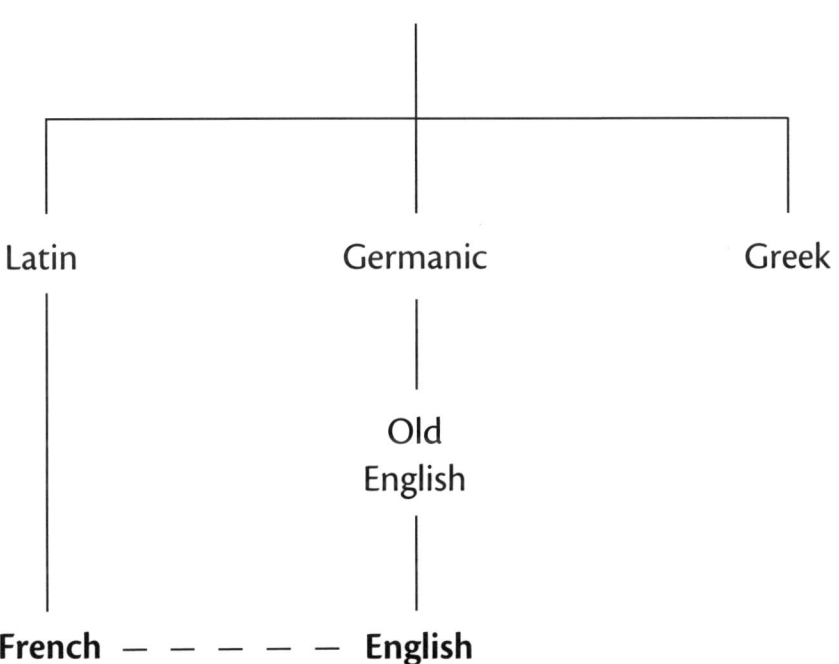

13 After the French Invasion

Introduction

In 1066 CE, at the Battle of Hastings, the Norman French led by William the Conqueror began their invasion of England and established French as the language of England. The Normans were originally Vikings (*Norman = North man*) who had settled in Seine valley beginning in the middle of the 9th century. In 864, a pirate named Rollon, banished from Scandinavia, joined this group of Normans in their attacks up the Seine river, eventually attacking Paris. The French king, Charles the Simple, was persuaded to enter into an peace treaty with Rollon. In exchange for the land which is now Normandy, Rollon was to cease attacks on the French and even protect Paris from further attack.

Part of the execution of this treaty was that the Viking lord was to kiss the feet of Charles the Simple as proof of his fealty to the French king. There are several versions of how Rollon kissed Charles' feet, an act considered demeaning by the Normans. In one version, Rollon or one of his lieutenants grabbed Charles by the ankle and lifted Charles' foot to his lips and, in the course of doing so, dumped the king to the floor. In another slightly more dignified version, the king's attendants hoisted him upside down so that the Norman lord could kiss his foot. Either way, Rollon was invested as the Duke of Normandy.

Rollon was successful at developing a feudal system and the economy of Normandy. The Normans intermarried with the local French and become a French community, albeit one with a unique dialect. It was a century after the establishment of this community that William became its fourth duke after Rollon. At this time, William was known as William the Bastard, indicating the doubt in the community about his lineage and right to the title. This doubt seemed to hone William's political skills because, having become at least as powerful as the king of France, he was able to raise a fleet and army to invade England and conquer the army of the new king there, King Harold, in 1066.

After William installed himself as King William I, he redistributed the lands of England among his supporters. As a consequence, Norman French became the prestige language of England, the language of government, justice, and education.

The effect of this social situation had significant consequences for the English language that penetrated the lexicon and even the grammar of English. English lost the inflectional morphology characteristic of the Germanic languages, and the word order of English came to resemble the French more than the Germanic.

The social stratification of this period can sometimes be observed when comparing native words and French borrowings from the same semantic domain. For example, Table XIII.1 demonstrates that the name for the animal is English, but the name for the food is French, illustrating who was tending the animals and who was eating them.

Table XIII.1

English	French
pig	pork
chicken	poultry
cow	beef
sheep	mutton
deer	venison
calf	veal

In Chapter 3, we discussed briefly how English has borrowed continuously from Latin and, beginning in the Middle English period, from French. This pattern of borrowing establishes the opportunity for English to borrow the same word at different points in its history. For example, English borrowed *humility* from Latin. This word developed in French and was borrowed again into English as *humble*. Note that two changes have occurred:

The *i* of *humil* is has been deleted;
A *b* has been inserted between *m* and *l*.

These are French rules, and this example illustrates how by examining the same word borrowed at different times, we can determine how the language from which these words were borrowed (in this case, French) has changed.

Not only has English borrowed the same words from Latin and French, but it has borrowed Germanic words from French as well. This has happened when French has borrowed words from the Germanic languages which English, some centuries later, then borrowed back. The tree illustrating this pattern of borrowing is given in Figure XIII.1. This diagram shows the history of *ward* and *guard*. The first is a native English word. The second began its history in the Germanic languages and was borrowed into French. Subsequently, it was borrowed from French into English.

Figure XIII.1: *ward* and *guard*

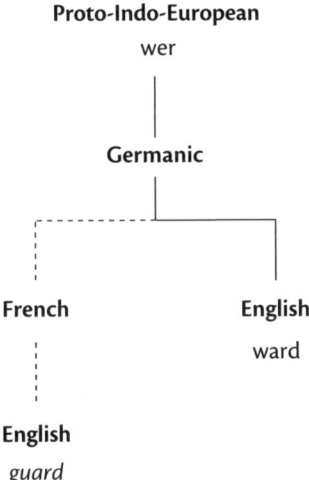

These words will have been naturalized in French. That is, they have become to look like French words because they have become susceptible to French rules. As a consequence, they betray some French phonological rules. The words in Table XIII.2 compare native English words with the same words borrowed French and then back into English. Notice that, consistently, whenever a word began with *w*, French added *g* to it.

Table XIII.2

English	French
ward	guard
war	guerrilla (< Spanish)
wise	guise
wile	guile

$$[w \rightarrow gw]_{French} (\rightarrow g)$$

Oddly, Latin seems to have undergone the opposite process. For example, the Latin word *vivus*, "life", was originally pronounced [wiwus]. The root has been borrowed in words like *vivid* and *vivacious*. The English cognate is *quick*, indicating that the original Proto-Indo-European word began with [gw]. The Greek cognate is *bios*,[1] showing a compression of [gw] to [b]. Consequently, in Latin, the [gw] must have converted to [w]. Although *quick* now means "swift", its archaic meaning is "life". It appears with this meaning in the phrase *the quick and the dead*.

A knowledge of French phonology will help correlate Latin and French borrowings. In this chapter, we will examine several of the phonological rules that contributed to the transformation of Latin into French and that now relate the Latin and French partitions of the English lexicon. The extensive phonological changes that created French from Latin obscure the original structure of each word. So, the focus of this chapter is the set of rules that transformed Latin into French. We will not say much about structure.

Lenition[2]

The first rule to consider is illustrated by the words *probe* and *prove*. Note that the change that applied here was a change of labial stop to fricative:

$$V p V \rightarrow V v V$$

This was a general rule that applied to labial stops generally when they appeared between vowels.

Table XIII.3: Lenition of Labials

Latin Borrowing	Latin	French
pauper	paupertas	poverty
probe	probare	prove
deception	decipere	deceive
reception	recipere	receive
conception	concipere	conceive
capricorn		chevron

---

1 See *biology*, "the study of life".
2 *Lenition*: from the Latin *len-*, "soften", as in *lenient*.

Latin Borrowing	Latin	French
febrile	febris	fever
gubernatorial	gubernator	governor
super		sovereign

In Table XIII.3, we are contrasting Latin borrowings with French borrowings. But the French word is derived from a Latin word, not the borrowing as it appears in English. So, a third column is provided giving the actual Latin word from which the French borrowing is derived. While we are contrasting Latin and French borrowings, we need to keep in mind that, etymologically, they each represent slightly different forms.

The lenition rule is responsible for a series of alternations found in words that are built from the root √cap, "take". Words with this root have past participle derivatives with the labial stop. However, their verbal forms have *v*. Consider, as an example, *deception* and *deceive*. The explanation for this alternation is that the nominal form was borrowed from Latin, while the verbal form was borrowed from French (Table XIII.4).

One way of remembering this root is to consider its English cognate. Recall that one of the sub-rules of Grimm's Law is $k \rightarrow h$. The English cognate of √cap is *have*.

Table XIII.4: Reflexes of √cap

Latin	French
conception	conceive
deception	deceive
perception	perceive
reception	receive

This kind of rule is called *lenition*, literally a "softening". The idea is that a fricative, like [v], is somehow weaker or softer than stops, like [p] and [b]. While the phonetics behind this idea may be impressionistic, it is the case that a natural outcome of lenition is loss of the consonant altogether. Table XIII.3 includes a French reflex of *super* in *sovereign*. In this instance, lenition has converted [p] to [v]. However, the [p] of *super* can also be deleted completely in French:

super > sur

Complete lenition in *super* creates the prefix *sur-*. This prefix appears in a large number of familiar words that one may not appear to have internal structure nor to be borrowings (Table XIII.5).

Table XIII.5: The Prefix *sur-*

surcharge	surrender
surmount	surround
surname	surtax
surpass	surveillance
surplus	survey
surprise	survive
surreal	

Lenition also applied to dentals ([t] and [d]) between vowels, although these dentals always softened to the point that they disappeared (Table XIII.6).

Table XIII.6: Lenition of Dentals

Latin	French
native	naive
vital	viable
invidious	envy
cadence	chance
radius	ray
gaudy	joy

If both labial and dental stops lenite, then it is expected that velar stops will as well. Although the fate of intervocalic velars is ambiguous (see the section, "Vocalization", below), there are some examples of lenition of velars (Table XIII.7).

Table XIII.7: Lenition of Velars

Latin	French
secure	sure
regulate	rule
gigantic (< Gk)	giant

Vocalization

As mentioned above, intervocalic velars could develop in either of two directions. In addition to leniting, they could also become more vowel like. The rule for the latter process usually had the form:

$$V \{k,g\} V \rightarrow V y V$$

Sometimes the *y* appears as *i* as in *lieu* in Table XIII.8.

Table XIII.8: Vocalization of velars

Latin	French
regal	royal
legal	loyal
decenal	doyen/doyenne
locus	lieu (e.g. lieutenant)

One of the more important roots to which this rule applied is √*fac*, "make". The French version of this is *-fy*. This root has become a suffix that can be added to a noun or adjective to create a verb meaning "to make X". Table XIII.9 contains some examples. It should be apparent that this form has become productive in English. Lexemes such as *prettify* and *uglify* have English roots and demonstrate the suffix's productivity.

Table XIII.9: Compounds with *-fy*

amplify	fructify	ossify	signify
beatify	gasify	oversimplify	simplify

beautify	glorify	pacify	solidify
calcify	gratify	personify	specify
certify	horrify	petrify	speechify
clarify	humidify	preachify	stratify
classify	identify	prettify	stultify
codify	indemnify	purify	stupefy
declassify	intensify	putrefy	syllabify
deify	justify	qualify	terrify
dignify	liquefy	quantify	testify
disqualify	magnify	ramify	transmogrify
diversify	modify	rarefy	typify
edify	mollify	ratify	uglify
electrify	mortify	rectify	unify
emulsify	mummify	revivify	verify
exemplify	mystify	sanctify	versify
falsify	notify	satisfy	vilify
fortify	nullify	scarify	vitrify

These lexemes continue a pattern that began in Latin: using the root √fac, "make", in compounds. Recall that compounds are lexemes that are created from more than one root. Table XIII.10 gives some examples with glosses for the roots with which √fac has compounded. Borrowings with the first member of the compound are also provided. The frequent use of √fac as the second member of a compound established a trend which, although the root was changed in French to -fy continued in French and now in English.

Table XIII.10: Compounds with -fac

manufacture	√manu	hand	manual
magnificent	√mag	great	magnanimous
satisfaction	√satis	enough	satiate
benefaction	√bene	good	benediction

liquefaction	√lique	*liquid*	liquid
putrefaction	√putre	*rotten*	putrid
rarefaction	√rare	*rare*	rare
stupefaction	√stupe	*stun*	stupid
significant	√sign	*sign*	sign
quantification	√quant	*how much*	quantity
ramification	√ram	*branch*	ramose

The root √*fac* in table XIII.9 is just one example, albeit one that appears in numerous words, of the ultimate conversion of the sequence *Vc* in Latin to *y* in French. Another example is the root √*plic*, "fold", which is borrowed from the French as *ply*.

The velars also vocalized when they were followed by a consonant (Table XIII.11). Note that in this case, the character representing the reflex is *i*, rather than *y*. Again, this emphasizes the historical relationship between these two characters and the phonological relationship between the sounds [i] and [y].

Table XIII.11: Vocalization of Velars

conduct	conduit
biscotti (Italian < L. biscoct)	biscuit
fructose	fruit
ma<u>g</u>nificent	main
direct	adroit
tractor	trait

$$[\{k,g\}C \rightarrow y\ C]_{French}$$

Clusters of Rules

As we worked out the Latin past participle and nasal roots, we noted that often phonological rules are organized into clusters that obscure the morphological structure. While sometimes a morphological structure creates the opportunity for a single rule to apply, often a phonological rule will create opportunities for another phonological rule, which itself creates opportunities for further rules, and so on. It is useful to keep this in mind when trying to find relations among lexemes.

Consider the cognates in Table XIII.12.

Table XIII.12

Latin Borrowing	Latin	French
sanctify	sanctus	saint
punctual	punctum	point
junction	junctus	joint
stringent	√strig + n	strain
unction	unguimentum	ointment

In every case, we see that a velar has disappeared and that the preceding vowel has become a diphthong. For example, we know from previous discussions that *sanctify* is a compound composed of *sanct* and *fac*. The first of these has developed into *saint*. Our problem is to construct a reasonable explanation.

We know in advance that a velar will vocalize to [y]. Thus, from √*sanct*, we expect *sanyt*. Is there a reasonable method of converting this to *saint*?

In our examination of Latin nasal roots (Chapter 10), we observed a process called metathesis that switched the positions of different sounds. This process would do exactly what we need for *saint*. From *sanyt*, metathesis would create *saynt*. Given that the characters *i* and *y* are often used interchangeably, it is justifiable to equate *saynt* with *saint*.

But is metathesis justified for French?

To justify our explanation of *saint*, we must first show that the metathesis rule also occurs in French. We have already done this for the vocalization rule. To see metathesis in action, consider the forms in Table XIII.13. As before, the French borrowing is derived from the actual Latin word, not the Latin word as it appears in English. As we have noted previously, usually when Latin words are borrowed into English the inflectional endings are discarded. So, the *-us* of *cuneus*, the *-is* of *potionis*, and the *a* of *folia* are ultimately discarded, but not before they have affected the French words. In the comments that follow, we are comparing the French borrowing to the actual Latin word, not the Latin word as it appears in English.

Table XIII.13

Latin Borrowing	Latin	French Borrowing
cuneal (wedge)	cuneus	coin
potion	potionis	poison
foliage	folia	foil
memory	memoria	memoir
adjutant	adjutans	aid
solitary	solitarius	solitaire

A few comments are necessary to normalize the data. First, in the evolution of Latin into the Romance languages, both [i] and [e] convert to [y] when they were followed by other vowels:

$$[\{i,e\}\ V \rightarrow y\ V]_{\text{French}}$$

With the exception of *adjutant/aid*, all the Latin forms have either [i] or [e], followed by a vowel. So we can expect that these will convert to [y] in French.

Second, recall that the character *j* is a new one and was created by elongating *i*. In fact, in a word like *adjutant*, the character was originally an *i* in Latin. Thus, *adjutant* was originally *adiuntant* which will have converted to *adyutant* by the rule just proposed.

These observations normalize the data to that in Table XIII.14.

Table XIII.14

	French
cuny	coin
potyon	poison
foly	foil
memory	memoir
ady	aid
solitary	solitaire

The pairs *memory/memoir* and *foly/foil* show what happened next. When a word contained a consonant followed by [y], metathesis applied to reverse their order so that the [y] preceded the consonant and formed a diphthong with the preceding vowel:

$$[C\ y \rightarrow y\ C]_{French}$$

Once again, the orthographic *i* of *memoir, foil* and so on does not represent [i]. Instead, it appears to represent an historical [y].

We now have our explanation for *saint, point, joint,* and others (Table XIII.15). The velar vocalizes to *y* before a consonant and then metathesizes.

Table XIII.15: Derivations of *saint, point,* and *memoir*

sanct	punct	memory	
sanyt	punyt	"	Vocalization
saynt	puynt	memoyr	Metathesis
saint	point	memoir	[y] = *i*

The point of this exercise was to demonstrate how two rules that are required for independent reasons can interact with each other to produce more mysterious output.

Syncope

One of the common rules in the evolution of the Romance languages is the loss of an unstressed vowel. When the vowel is in the middle of a word, its loss is called *syncope*.[3] Table XIII.16 gives some examples.

Table XIII.16: Syncope

Latin Borrowing	Latin	French Borrowing
debit	debitus	debt
capital	capitaneus	captain
circulate	circulus	circle
minister	ministerialis	minstrel

---

3 *Syncope*: From the Greek *syn-*, "together", and *kop*, "cut".

Latin Borrowing	Latin	French Borrowing
tabular	tabula	table
copulate	copula	couple
capital	capitulum	chapter
general	generis	genre
populous	populus	people
circular	circulus	circle
angular	angulus	angle
singular	singulus	single
articulate	articulus	article
angular	angulus	angle
strangulation	strangulare	strangle
fabulous	fabula	fable

Syncope applied only to *unstressed* vowels. Recall from our discussion of compounds in Chapter 5 that stress is the relative force used when producing a vowel or syllable. Thus, we could write the rule as[4]

$$[V_1 C^n V_2° \, C^n V_3 \rightarrow V_1 CCV_3]_{French}$$

By bringing consonants into contact with each other, syncope provides the opportunity for other rules to apply. We will explore these possibilities in subsequent sections.

Epenthesis
One of the rules that syncope triggered was *epenthesis*.[5] Consider the data in Table XIII.17.

Table XIII.17: Epenthesis

Latin Borrowing	Latin	French Borrowing
camera	camera	chamber

---
4 The symbol "°" is used to indicate that the vowel is unstressed.
5 *Epenthesis*: from the Greek *epi-*, "upon", and *thesis*, "place".

Latin Borrowing	Latin	French Borrowing
numeral	numerus	number
memory	rememorare	remember
general	generis	gender
tenuous	tener	tender
humility	humilis	humble
tremulous	tremulus	tremble
similar	similis	resemble

In every case, the medial vowel has deleted to bring a nasal and r or l together. This sequence is then interrupted by the insertion of a stop. Notice that the type of stop that is inserted is determined by the nasal. When the nasal is labial—[m]—then a labial stop is inserted, when the nasal is dental—[n]—then a dental stop is inserted.[6]

$$[mr \rightarrow mbr]_{French}$$
$$[nr \rightarrow ndr]_{French}$$
$$[ml \rightarrow mbl]_{French}$$

If we wanted to think more about representation, we could ask how to write these three rules as a single rule. For example, these rules require that the first consonant be a nasal. The triggering feature is just that the consonant is a nasal, not any particular nasal. If we compare [r] and [l], we note that they are both liquids. So the rule could be rewritten as

$$[nasal, liquid \rightarrow nasal, voiced\ stop, liquid]_{French}$$

Unfortunately, the rudimentary representation system that we are using can't link up the inserted stop with the nasal so that the nasal controls whether [b] or [d] is inserted.

An advantage of this general rule (once we fix it so that the inserted stop connects up with the nasal) is that it makes a prediction: if we can find a word that undergoes epenthesis between a [n] and [l], the inserted consonant should be [d].

---

6 An example of this from Greek is *ambrosia* "the food of the gods". The prefix is, of course, the Greek negative *an-*. The root is √*mr*, "die", which shows the zero grade of vowel. English and Latin cognates *murder* and *mortal* show the *o* grade. Clearly, Greek contained the rule $mr \rightarrow mbr$.

Cluster Simplification

As noted, the deletion of a vowel will often bring together a cluster of consonants. Often, the resulting cluster will then be simplified by deleting one or more of the consonants in the cluster.

Table XIII.18: Cluster Simplification

Latin	Old French	French
hospital	hostel	hotel
masculine		male
blaspheme (< Gk)		blame
muscular	muscle	

The forms in Table XIII.18 present a number of interesting problems. First, the change of *hospital* to *hostel* requires explanation. We know that the medial vowel (*i*) will delete. It appears that, after syncope applies, the resulting cluster *spt* is simplified to *st*. A similar rule has applied in the other forms:

$$[C_1 C_2 C_3 \rightarrow C_1 C_3]_{\text{Old French}}$$

Finally, we note that in French *hotel*, the [s] delete. This demonstrates a more abstract type of change than the type that we have been considering: change to the rules themselves. Recall that in Latin we had proposed a rule:

$$[zC \rightarrow C]_{\text{Latin}}$$

This was proposed to account for deletion of [s] before voiced consonants. In French, we require a rule:

$$[sC \rightarrow C]_{\text{French}}$$

It appears that the original Latin rule has changed so that it applies to [s] as well as [z]:

$$[zC \rightarrow C]_{\text{Latin}} \rightarrow [sC \rightarrow C]_{\text{French}}$$

We can say that the original rule has generalized so that it applies to a larger class of sounds.

Prothesis[7]

A very common rule throughout the Romance languages is the addition of a vowel to the front of any word that began with [s], followed by a consonant.

Table XIII.19: Prothesis

Latin	Old French	French
scale	escalator	echelon
special	especial	
spouse	espouse	
spatula		epaulet
stable	establish	
state	estate	
stamen		etamine
study		etui
script	escritoire	
spectacle	espionage	

The forms in the Old French column of Table XIII.19 illustrate the Romance rule:

$$[\#sC \rightarrow \#esC]_{Romance}$$

In addition, the data from the French column provide further support for the rule deleting *s* which we proposed in the previous section. The derivation of *epaulet* combines a number of rules (Table XIII.20).

Table XIII.20

spatulet	stablish	
spaulet	"	$[Lenition]_{French}$
espaulet	establish	$[Prothesis]_{Old\ French}$
epaulet	"	$[sC \rightarrow C]_{Modern\ French}$

---

7 *Prothesis*: from the Greek *pro*, "before", and *thesis*, "place".

Assibilation[8]

We have already seen one aspect of French assibilation when we compared present participle derivatives such as *potent* and *potency*. At that time, we proposed the rule:

$$[t + iV \rightarrow s + iV]_{French}$$

It should be evident that we can change this analysis to bring it in line with what we have learned in this chapter. First, we already have a rule that converts *iV* to *yV*. Using this rule, we can rewrite the assibilation rule as:

$$[t\, y \rightarrow s\, y]_{French}$$

An example is the pair *vitiate/vice*. The Latin root is √*viti*, "fault", but it appears in French as *vice*.

We also find examples where the Latin past participle assibilates when the nominalizing suffix that triggered assibilation in the present participle is attached to it (Table XIII.21).

Table XIII.21

pirate	piracy
confederate	confederacy
delicate	delicacy
private	privacy
intimate	intimacy
accurate	accuracy
legitimate	legitimacy
literate	literacy

Assibilation of Velars

As it happens, [t] is not the only sound to undergo assibilation. In fact, it is not even the most likely. The velars very frequently assibilated. Earlier, we posed the following question: When does the character *c* represent the sound [k], and

---

8 *Assibilation*: from the Latin *ad-*, "to", and *sibil*, "hiss". To assibilate is to become a hissing sound.

when does it represent the sound [s]? It happens that this is one occasion when the English spelling system is quite regular.

Table XIII.22: The character *c*

[k]	[s]
cook	cease
cup	ceiling
create	celestial
capricorn	cell
clove	cicada
corner	recipient
carnival	cinema
claim	cistern
credible	circle
circle	city

A quick scan of Table XIII.22 shows that character *c* represents the sound [s] when it is followed by either *i* or *e*. In fact, this is no accident of English spelling. The character *c* always represented the sound [k] in Latin. However, in French (and most Romance languages) this [k] assibilated before [i] and [e]. This phonological rule is now reflected in the English spelling system. This is likely the most robust rule of English spelling.

$$[k\{i,e\} \rightarrow s\{i,e\}]_{\text{Old French}}$$

French took this process further that the other Romance languages. In addition to assibilating [k] before [i] and [e], French also assibilated [k] before [a], although here the reflex was [tʃ].

Table XIII.23: Assibilation of [k] before [a]

Latin	Old French [tʃ]	Latin	Old French [tʃ]
concatenate	chain	capital	chapter

Assibilation

Latin	Old French [tʃ]	Latin	Old French [tʃ]
calix	chalice	car	chariot
calcium	chalk	card	chart
calumny	challenge	caste	chaste
camera	chamber	castigate	chasten
cadence	chance	capital	chattel
canal	channel	cathedral (< Gk)	chair
mercantile	merchant		

$$[ka \rightarrow t\!\int\! a]_{\text{Old French}}$$

As it happens, the story did not stop there. In the history of French, the [tʃ] sound changed to [ʃ] in modern French. So, if a word was borrowed a second time, it would show this change, as well as the original assibilation. Table XIII.24 gives examples of triplets: words borrowed from Latin with [k], their cognates from Old French with [tʃ], and a second borrowing from French with the modern [ʃ].

Table XIII.24: Assibilated Borrowings from French

Latin	Old French [tʃ]	French [ʃ]
campus	champion	champagne
candle	chandler	chandelier
canto	chant	chanteuse
cape	chapel	chapeau
case	chase	chassis
castle		ch‰oteau
calefacient	chafe	chauffeur
cape	chape	chaperone

$$[t\!\int\! \rightarrow \int]_{\text{French}}$$

The relationship among the words in Table XIII.24 is illustrated with our usual method in Figure XIII.2.

Figure XIII.2: Multiple Borrowings

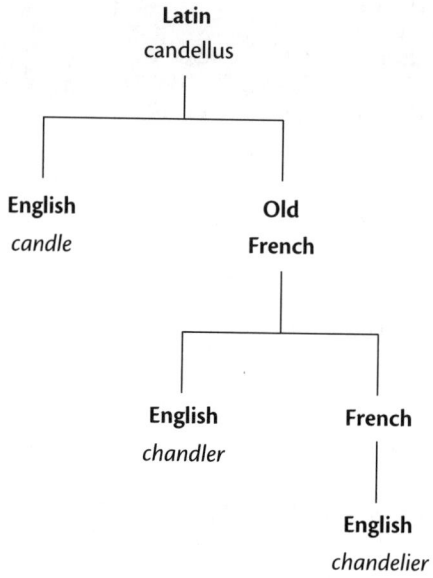

The voiced velar [g] also assibilated, although only before [i] and [e]. In addition, it shows the same progression from affricate to fricative in French (Table XIII.25).

Table XIII.25: Assibilation of [g]

Latin (original [g])	Old French [dž]	French [ž]
genus	gender	genre
gens	gentle	gendarme

There are, of course, numerous examples where the character *g* appears before either [i] or [e], but is pronounced [g]. For example, *geese*, *gild*, and *gill*. However, these are not French words. The spelling rule that the character *g* is pronounced [dž] or [ž] before *i* and *e* applies only to French and Latin borrowings because assibilation applies in those languages, but not in English or other languages from which it has borrowed.

Assibilation of Labials

Assibilation was so pervasive in French that labials also assibilated. To determine under what circumstances a labial will assibilate in French, it is first necessary to normalize the data in Table XIII.26.

Assibilation

Table XIII.26: Assibilation of Labials

Latin Borrowing	Latin	French Borrowing
cavity	cavea	cage
rabies	rabia	rage
ruby	rubeus	rouge
ante<u>delu</u>vian	dilivium	deluge
cambial	cambiare	change
sapient	sapius	sage

Recall that *i* and *e* will convert to [y] before another vowel. The original Latin words in Table XIII.26 all have this property: the labial [p], [b], or [v] is followed by either [i] or [e] which is itself followed by a vowel. In effect, the labial will at some point in the history of French be followed by [y]. Given this, the data in Table XIII.26 can be normalized, as in Table XIII.27.

Table XIII.27: Assibilation of Labials

	French
cavy	cage
raby	rage
ruby	rouge
deluvy	deluge
camby	change
sapy	sage

Finally, although all six of the examples are classified as French borrowings, there is a subtle difference. Whereas, the reflex of assibilation in *cage*, *rage* and *deluge* is [dž], in *rouge* it is [ž]. This is similar to the case of the assibilation of [k] before [a]. The affricate reflex is from Old French. *Rouge* is a more recent borrowing and shows the de-affrication of French.

[labial y → dž]$_{\text{Old French}}$
[dž → ž]$_{\text{French}}$

Assibilation of Nasals

Under the right conditions, nasals also assibilated in French (Table XIII.28). Either the nasal is immediately followed by [y], as in *extraneous*, or an intervocalic consonant has deleted, creating the conditions for converting [i] to [y]. Thus, the rule is that a nasal will assibilate in French if it is followed by [y].

Table XIII.28: Assibilation of Nasals

Latin Borrowing	Latin	French
dominate	dominare	danger
extraneous	extraneare	estrange
calumny	calumnia	challenge
granular	granica	grange

Contraction

The Latin diphthong *au* contracted to *o* in French (Table XIII.29).

Table XIII.29: Contraction

Latin	French
pause	pose
clause	close
nausea	noise
gaudy	joy
pauper	poverty

Notice that *noise* shows both contraction of *au* to *o* and metathesis to create a new diphthong.

Conclusion

Because English has borrowed so heavily from both Latin and French, and because French is a daughter language of Latin, English is a museum of the history of French. By comparing Latin and French cognates, it is possible to not only to chart the evolution of French, but also to compile a list of possible sound changes by which languages in general evolve.

The English Partition

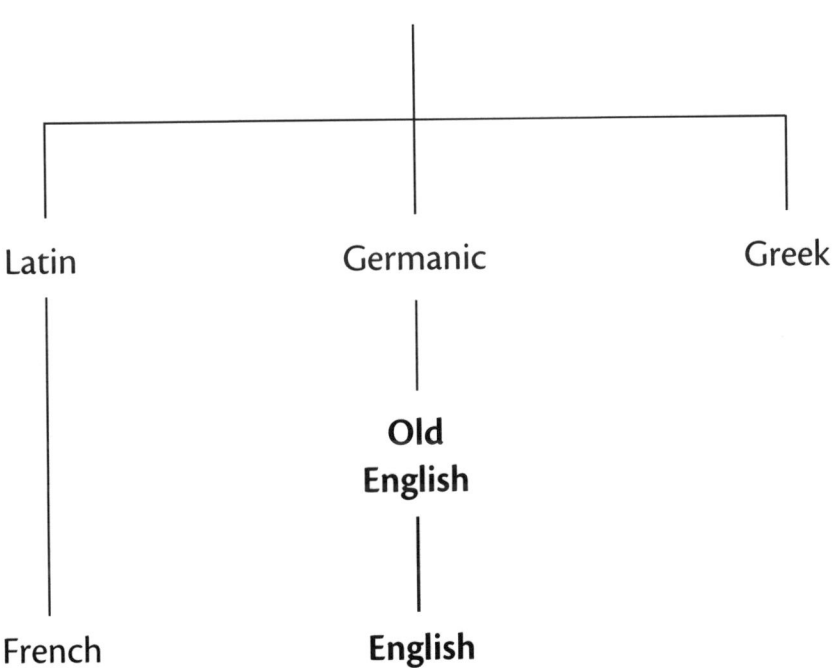

14 Word Formation Processes

Introduction

A morphological component that consists of a rich lexicon of morphemes and rules for their combination of the sort that were explored in the sections on Latin and Greek is one method that languages use to create new words. It is likely even the main method. This chapter explores other sorts of processes for word formation and even morpheme formation. Some of these, such as clipping and blending, are not as rule-governed as the affixation processes and depend more on the ingenuity of the speaker who creates them. Others, such as backformation, depend on there being a prior rule system that provides a structure for creating new words.

Shortening

Acronyms and Abbreviations

A common method of shortening a phrase is to select characters, usually the first, from each the words in the phrase to form a new term. The resulting word falls within one of two groups, depending on whether the new term is pronounced as a word or pronounced as a sequence of letters.

If the new term is pronounced as a word, it is an *acronym* (Table XIV.1) . Often the acronym is deliberately designed to look like a word of the language. Since an acronym can look like a normal word, its actual history can become increasingly opaque, as the word becomes common and its origin recedes in time.

Table XIV.1: Acronyms

Acquired Immune Deficiency Syndrome	AIDS
self-contained underwater breathing apparatus	scuba
radio detecting and ranging	radar

constable on patrol	cop
light amplification by simulated emission of radiation	laser
White Anglo-Saxon Protestant	wasp

Terms that are pronounced as sequences of letters are *abbreviations* (Table XIV.2). Their origins are more obvious than acronyms and it is evident that they abbreviate a longer phrase.

Table XIV.2: Abbreviations

television	TV
compact disk	CD
cash on delivery	COD
very important person	VIP
unidentified flying object	UFO
extrasensory perception	ESP

Backformation

Backformation is a process by which a new lexeme is formed by removing a morpheme or what could plausibly be analysed as a morpheme from a lexeme (Table XIV.3). For example, given the model of the agentive suffix *-er* presented by *teach/teacher, read/reader,* and *work/worker,* it is reasonable to assume that there must be a verb from which *swindler* is formed. In actual fact, the verb *swindle* was formed by removing *er* from *swindler,* there never was a verb *swindle*. A number of English verbs have been formed from nouns that look like they are agentives: for example, *edit* from *editor* and *peddle* from *peddler*.

Backformations are interesting because they are possible only because their creators must be aware of the morphological structure of words. One can create *swindle* from *swindler* only if one is aware of the agentive suffix. This suggests that the many of the rules that have been previously discussed are not abstractions but have some kind of psychological life among speakers of English.

Because backformations have a kind of morphological plausibility and fit in the morphological patterning of the language, they are difficult to recognize. In fact, typically they can be identified only by researching the etymology of a lexeme in a dictionary. Occasionally, there are clues. For example, the verb *self-destruct* must be backformed from *self-destruction* because the noun/verb pattern for the root is *destruction/destroy*. The verb should be ^e*self-destroy*. That it is not indicates that it was backformed from *self-destruction*.

Table XIV.3: Backformations

television	*televise*
beggar	*beg*
hamburger	*burger*
enthusiasm	*enthuse*
burglar	*burgle*

Swahili provides an interesting example of how backformation and naturalization can intersect. In one of the noun classes in Swahili, singular nouns are marked with a prefix *ki-*, and plural nouns are marked with the prefix *vi-*. Swahili has borrowed extensively from Arabic and so must incorporate borrowed nouns into this singular/plural system. When Swahili borrowed the Arabic noun *kitab*, "book", it fit it into the phonological system as *kitabu*. The Arabic plural is *kutub*. This does not look anything like a Swahili plural. Instead, Swahili speakers backformed a lexeme *tabu* from *kitabu* and, from it, created the plural *vitabu*.

Clipping

A new form can be created by removing arbitrary material from an existing word, in effect, clipping the word (Table XIV.4). A very recent example of this is the term *blog* which refers to an on-line journal. This word is formed from the compound *weblog*, the first two characters having been clipped. That this is truly a word is evident from the fact that it inflects like a verb: *blogs* and *blogging* are perfectly fine.

Table XIV.4: Clippings

professor	*prof*	disrespect	*diss*
laboratory	*lab*	gymnasium	*gym*
facsimile	*fax*	influenza	*flu*
mathematics	*math*	condominium	*condo*
submarine	*sub*	refrigerator	*fridge*
attitude	*'tude*	demonstration	*demo*
		memorandum	*memo*

Note that the critical difference between backformation and clipping is that the material removed by backformation is morphemic but that removed by clipping is not. In the *blog* example, the material that is removed is *we*, which is not a morpheme. An interesting example is the lexeme *helicopter*, which is a Greek compound formed from *helico*, "spiral", and *pter*, "flight". The informal term *copter* is clearly a clipping because the material that is removed–*heli*– was not a morpheme when *copter* was created. However, the clipping created the analysis *heli* + *copter*, and that analysis arguably created a new morpheme *heli-*, which allows words like *heliski*, *heliport*, and *helipad*.

Blends

Blends (Table XIV.5) resemble compounds in that both combine two objects to form a new lexeme. However, whereas a compound combines two lexemes to form a new one, the objects combined in a blend may not be linguistic units at all, but are simply sequences from two lexemes that are often chosen to fit the phonological constraints of the language. Typically, a blend consists of a sequence from the beginning of one lexeme and a sequence from the end of another.

A common example is *smog*, which is formed from *smoke* + *fog* → *sm* + *og* → *smog*. Notice that *smoke* + *fog* → *s* + *fog* → *ᵉsfog* is possible in principle, but was not selected, at least in part because English tends to avoid beginning words with the sequence *sf*.

Sometimes, blends are formed from a phrase: *sitcom* from *situation comedy* is an example. However, a blend can be a simple combination of two concepts, as in *smog* from *smoke* + *fog*, or *brunch* from *breakfast* + *lunch*. It is this opportunity to simply juxtapose two concepts without the complicated machinery of morphology or syntax that accounts for the popularity of blending: *brunch* is a simple descriptor of the meal that one wants after having slept in.

Table XIV.5: Blends

television	marathon	*telethon*	motor	hotel	*motel*
television	evangelist	*televangelist*	cranberry	martini	*crantini*
channel	tunnel	*chunnel*	frozen	cappucino	*frappucino*
smoke	fog	*smog*	situation	comedy	*sitcom*
information	commercial	*infomercial*	breath	analyzer	*Breathalyzer*
breakfast	lunch	*brunch*	parachute	troops	*paratroops*
			television	broadcast	*telecast*

Blends can become recognizable patterns so that their meaning is instantly discerned. For example, any style of language that has incorporated English elements can be designated with a blend of the name of that language and *English*: for example, *Franglais* < *Français* + *Anglais*, *Japlish*, *Spanglish* and *Swedlish*.

Sometimes, a blending pattern becomes so common that it may be argued that a new morpheme has been created. The frequent use of *-gate* to indicate a scandal is an example. After the Watergate scandal in the early 1970s, the American media began to blend *Watergate* with a descriptive term to name subsequent scandals. When it was discovered that Zoe Baird, a nominee for attorney general, had not paid Social Security taxes for an illegal immigrant who was working for her, the press dubbed the investigation *Nannygate*. Bill Clinton's famous indiscretion with an intern was called *Monicagate*. The British press coined the term *Camillagate* for the scandal that arose when Prince Charles secret relationship with Camilla Parker Bowles became public. It could be argued that this frequent pattern has created the suffix *-gate* which can be used to indicate a scandal.

Another potential new morpheme is *e-*. Its first appearance was in *e-mail*, a blend of *electronic* and *mail*. But, it soon appeared in *ebusiness*, *ecommerce* and *elearning* and is now part of the brand name *eBay*. One can easily imagine to what *emenu*, *eclass*, and *ebanking* could potentially refer.

Zero Derivation

In Chapter 11, we noted several suffixes whose job is to create new lexemes of a different grammatical category than the lexeme to which they are added. For example, the Latinate suffix *-ion* creates nouns from past participles.

It is often possible in English to create a new lexeme of a different category without adding a morpheme at all. For example, the verb *impact* is clearly from a past participle. However, although there is a noun *impaction* formed in the familiar way, this noun is not familiar. Instead, the familiar related noun is *impact*. Since *impact* is a past participle, and participles are formed from verbs, the verbal form must predate the nominal form. And the nominal form must be derived from the verbal form. That is, there must be a rule:

$$\text{Lex}_N \Rightarrow \text{Lex}_V + \emptyset$$

This phenomenon is sometimes called "zero derivation" because it is part of the derivational component of the morphology and it requires the addition of nothing to create a new lexeme. Rules like this cause some consternation because their effect makes it look like grammatical categories are fluid. At first, it seems that one can only classify particular uses of *impact* as nominal or verbal, but one cannot definitively categorize the lexeme *impact* as a noun or a verb. In fact, in languages like Thai, this is a considerable problem for those who would like to build a dictionary for computer use. Great numbers of lexemes can appear as words of a variety of grammatical categories. Even in English, computer understanding of a sentence is complicated by the large number of words whose grammatical category can only be determined by successfully parsing the sentence.

In the particular English case illustrated by *impact*, there is a subtle cue that nouns have been created by the zero derivation rule above. The evidence is not represented by English orthography and is only apparent when we compare how *impact* the noun is pronounced with how *impact* the verb is pronounced, particularly how the word is stressed. The verb form is stressed as *impa¹ct*, The noun form is stressed as *i¹mpa²ct*. These stress differences are part of a general pattern (Table XIV.6).

Table XIV.6

Verb	Noun
impa¹ct	i¹mpa²ct
permi¹t	pe¹rmi²t
addre¹ss	a¹ddre²ss

An explanation for these distinctive stress patterns begins with the observation that the primary stress falls on the last syllable in the verbs and the first syllable in the nouns. Why that is will be left unanswered; the details do not concern us. Notice also that the nouns are stressed twice, but the verbs only once. If we take the view of morphology developed in Chapter 6 and sketched in Figure VI.3, then the fact that nouns are stressed twice is explained because they were created as verbs and were converted to nouns. According to the architecture in Figure VI.3, after the verb is created, it is examined by the phonological component and given the stress pattern characteristic of verbs, in the case of *impact*, on the last syllable. The flow chart in Figure VI.3 indicates that further derivation is possible. The zero derivation rule given above converts the verb to a noun. Once again, the phonological component examines the lexeme and gives it the stress pattern characteristic of nouns, in this case, on the first syllable. The stress pattern in now *i¹mpa¹ct*. This is not just unusual, a lexeme without a stress contour is impossible in English (and likely other languages with stress). A word in English must have differently stressed syllables. Instead, the originally stressed vowel converts from primary to secondary stress. This phenomenon is called *downstepping*. It ensures that words that have two stressed syllables have a stress contour.

Brand Names

When a business creates a new product, considerable time and expense are spent creating a name for that product. That name should be unique and be quickly associated with the product. In the age of globalization, it should also travel well and not have unforeseen connotations in other languages.

Sometimes, the product is so successful that its name becomes the designator for all similar products. In effect, the name becomes *generic*. This often happens because the creator of the product has a patent which provides exclusive right to produce that product for a period of time. By the time that others are allowed to sell similar products, the name and product are closely associated.

Sometimes, it is the product's overwhelming success that makes it the model for all similar products. *Google* is a recent example of this: the verb *to google* has entered the language because of the success of the search engine product's of that name, although it was a late entry into the field of search engines. Others, such as Lycos and Yahoo, remain individualized.

Businesses are concerned about protecting their trademark and will take legal action to ensure that their brand name designates only their product. Sometimes, the methods they use are subtle. Johnson & Johnson changed the lyrics of an advertisement jingle from "I'm stuck on Band-Aid" to "I'm stuck on Band-Aid brand" to emphasize that *Band-Aid* was the name of a product, not the generic name for adhesive bandages.

A brand name can lose its protected trademark status if it can be shown that it has become the generic term for a range of products. When this happens, we can say a new word has been created, in the sense that previously these were proper nouns. Table XIV.7 gives some examples of what were once brand names but are now generic.

Table XIV.7: Generics

cellophane
dry ice
escalator
granola
heroin
linoleum
spandex
tarmac
yo-yo
zipper

One can speculate about which trademarked brand names are threatened. For example, the average football fan is unlikely aware of the various types of artificial turf and could use *Astroturf* as a generic. Others that are so much in the public domain that their trademark status could be challenged include *Kleenex* for all paper tissues, *Thermos* for any vacuum bottle used to keep things hot or cold, and *Teflon* for any non-stick coating.

An interesting case where a company argued that a morpheme had become generic is a proposal by Quality Inns International Inc. for a new chain of hotels to be called *McSleep*. They argued that the prefix *Mc-* had come to mean "thrifty and consistent" because it is usually used in Scottish names, and Scots are stereotyped as thrifty. These are the characteristics that this new chain would embody. Further, they argued that, although the fast food chain McDonalds Corporation uses the *Mc-* + noun structure as in *McNuggets* and *McMuffin*, this structure had become generic. McDonalds, on the other hand, sued to have Quality Inns stopped from using the name arguing that the *Mc-* + noun structure was part of their family of trademarks.

The prefix *Mc-* is of Celtic origin and means "son". Because of its prevalent use in McDonalds' array of food products and McDonalds considerable popularity, the prefix has entered the popular lexicon. During the trial between Quality Inns and McDonalds, the linguist Dr. Roger Shuy surveyed hundreds of uses of the *Mc-* + noun structure and distilled 27 definitions, including "inexpensive; high volume; lacks prestige, comfort, cost; everyday." From the 27 definitions, he distilled 4 terms: "basic, convenient, inexpensive, and standardized." Some examples are in Table XIV.8. The Oxford English Dictionary™ recognizes this new use of *Mc-* distinct from its original function and defines it as "something that is of mass appeal, a standardized or bland variety of or alternative to [the noun to which it is prefixed]".

Table XIV. 8 *Mc-* plus noun

McArt	low-cost mass produced art
McNews	digested news stories
McPaper	a newspaper higher emphasizing entertainment with short news stories
McSweater	a fashionable but affordable mass produced sweater
McGod	the god worshipped by TV evangelists
McJob	low paying, short term employment

A second linguist, Dr. David Lightfoot, argued that *Mc-* was not generic, and that it can not be assigned a single definition. He pointed out that Dr. Shuy's 4 term definition does not include all 27 of the definitions he had determined. Instead, Lightfoot argued that every use of *Mc-* + noun is a direct or indirect allusion to McDonalds, as everyone is aware of McDonalds' use of that structure for their food products.

In the end, the court found in McDonalds' favour, noting that, although the *Mc-* + noun structure is often used in the public domain, it is not generic and falls within the McDonalds' family of trade marks, that *McSleep* would create confusion about the hotel chain's connection with McDonalds, and, finally, that Quality Inns' use of *McSleep* was an attempt to benefit from McDonalds' reputation.

Fusion

It is not only possible to create new lexemes; new morphemes come into existence as well. The creation of *-gate* to designate scandals has already been mentioned. Similarly, the frequent blending with *cybernetics* (see *cybernaut, cyberspace, cyberpunk, cybersex*) may well create a new morpheme, *cyber-*.

Another process that can create a new morpheme is to fuse previously existing morphemes into a single morpheme. In the examination of Latin suffixes, it was noted that some suffixes attract others, so that combinations such as *-ical* are common. If these become frequent enough, they may be perceived as a single unit. In that case, a new morpheme is created.

An example of this process is the English morpheme *-ation*. That this is an English morpheme will be demonstrated later. First, we will examine the process by which it was created. Recall that when new words were created in later Latin, the thematic vowel was typically *a*. As an example, consider the ancient root √*leg*, "read". It is the base of the verb *legere*, "to read", and the noun *lex* "law", < *leg + s*. When a verb was created from the noun, it was created as *legare*, "to send as an ambassador" (see *legation, delegation*). Note that the original verb was an *e* theme verb, but the new verb is an *a* theme.

Since new verbs will have *a* as the thematic vowel rather than one of the others, *a* theme verbs predominate. Past participles with thematic *a* outnumber other types of past participles. The nominalizing suffix *-ion* is added to past participles to create nouns, and so nouns that end with *-ation* are more frequent than other nouns with *-ion*. As this process continues and more nouns end with *-ation*, this sequence comes to be perceived as an actual morpheme. So, even though *-ation* had internal structure, that structure is no longer apparent, and it is now perceived as an atomic morpheme that creates nouns from verbs.

That *-ation* has become a productive English suffix is apparent from the way the suffix *-ize* attracts it. The suffix *-ize* creates verbs. Just as the suffix *-ic* attracts *-al* (see *class, classic* and *classical*), the suffix *-ize* attracts *-ation*. Any verb created with *-ize* can be nominalized with *-ation* as in *demon/demonize/ demonization, organ/organize/organization, carbon/carbonize/carbonization*. The suffix *-ize* is borrowed from Greek. Consequently, the affinity between these two morphemes cannot be something that evolved in Latin. Instead, it is English speakers who re-analysed Latin nouns and created the nominalizing suffix *-ation* and began to create new nouns with it.

15 Representation and Sound Change

Introduction

As has been mentioned, a culture's journey into literacy requires that some method of representing the language be devised. In the case of English, it was possible to borrow and adapt the Roman alphabet, just as the Romans and Etruscans had borrowed the Greek alphabet. Although for literate speakers of English, the idea of the alphabet and the attendant notion of spelling are familiar, creating an alphabet or adapting one to a language means wrestling with various and often conflicting goals.

The goal of representing the sounds of a language is typically undermined by natural phonetic change over time, a natural and expected process. No matter how efficient and consistent an alphabetic system may be when initially devised, as change enters the language, the original system will break down. There are two responses to this process. Typically, the education system develops spelling rules that explain how a particular character should be mapped onto the system of sounds in a language. For example, a relatively easy case is the character *c*, which initially represented the sound [k] in the Romance languages. However, [k] assibilated in French before [i] and [e] and, as a consequence, when English borrowed French words, it also borrowed the spelling rule that the character *c* represents the sound [s] before the characters *i* and *e* and the sound [k] elsewhere. Notice that in this case, the spelling rule is a description of the actual phonological change.

Unfortunately, as the number of phonetic changes pile up, and, especially in the case of English, the language borrows large numbers of words from other languages, the system of symbols and rules of interpretation can become inconsistent and unwieldy. Most who have learned English and its spelling system have at some time thought that it has reached this point. It is often difficult to understand the logic behind the system, and, although some rules seem to be relatively stable, others have so many exceptions that one could question whether there is a rule at all. We have seen that, in many of these cases, the subset of words that the rule applies to are all borrowed from a particular language.

The second response to the inconsistency introduced by phonological and historical phonetic change has been the call for spelling reform. A complete spelling reform would realign the spelling system with the current pronunciation of the language. The argument for spelling reform is that it simplifies the education system. It is simply easier to teach spelling if it is consistent.

There is, however, a resistance to spelling reform. For one thing, in addition to representing how words are pronounced, representation can also highlight etymological or morphological relationships. For example, *create* and *creation* are clearly related items. However, the *t* of each represents different sounds. If the sounds were actually represented, the *t* of *creation* would be spelled differently from that of *create*, much as *division* is spelled differently from *divide*, although they are morphologically related. While it may be argued that a spelling system based on phonetic principles is easier to learn, it is at the expense of understanding the relationships among words.

A second, subtler, issue surrounding spelling reform is the selection of the dialect that will be the standard. While the initial spelling system for English arose haphazardly, a spelling reform must be a thoughtful and considered process. Since there are many dialects of English and they differ dramatically from one another, if any one of these is selected as the standard, the speakers of other dialects will be disadvantaged. Another possible method of spelling reform is that similar dialects cluster and each cluster designs its own system. This would acknowledge that there are different Englishes, but would also suggest that the English-speaking world is not unified and potentially inhibit communication among English speakers.

One of the successful spelling reforms of English actually took the latter course. When Noah Webster published *An American Dictionary of the English Language* in 1828, he introduced new spellings that he felt simplified spelling. Among these are *color* for *colour*, *humor* for *humour*, and *center* for *centre*. These new spellings helped to establish an identity for the American dialect of English and distinguished it from the British, which is likely a reason why these changes were accepted.

The notion of English spelling reform has been satirized many times. The typical format introduces new spelling rules into the text so that by the end of the text, the spelling appears to be regular but the text is indecipherable. One of the earliest and shortest is often attributed to Mark Twain (Samuel Clemens) but is actually an excerpt from a letter by M. J. Sheilds to the journal *The Economist*.

> For example, in Year 1 that useless letter "c" would be dropped to be replased either by "k" or "s", and likewise "x" would no longer be part of the alphabet. The only kase in which "c" would be retained would be the "ch" formation, which will be dealt with later. Year 2 might reform "w"

spelling, so that "which" and "one" would take the same konsonant, wile Year 3 might well abolish "y" replasing it with "i" and Iear 4 might fiks the "g/j" anomali wonse and for all.

Jenerally, then, the improvement would kontinue iear bai iear with Iear 5 doing awai with useless double konsonants, and Iears 6-12 or so modifaiing vowlz and the rimeining voist and unvoist konsonants. Bai Iear 15 or sou, it wud fainali bi posibl tu meik ius ov thi ridandant letez "c", "y" and "x" -- bai now jast a memori in the maindz ov ould doderez -- tu riplais "ch", "sh", and "th" rispektivli.

Fainali, xen, aafte sam 20 iers ov orxogrefkl riform, wi wud hev a lojikl, kohirnt speling in ius xrewawt xe Ingliy-spiking werld.

Interestingly, even this example illustrates the technical difficulty of revising spelling. Note that it is proposed that *useless* double consonants be eliminated. But, the spelling device of the double consonant has a purpose. For example, the present particular of *ride* is *riding*, while the present participle of *rid* is *ridding*, with a double consonant. With a single consonant, the vowel will be mispronounced; the function of the double consonant is to indicate how the vowel is pronounced.

It is not only the case that English spelling is complicated by its many borrowings. Recall that after the Norman French invaded England, French was the dominant language. One of the problems that the French had was that English used characters for sounds that were not in French and spelling rules for sounds that were in French. The French response was to introduce new spelling rules. For example, the digraph *th* was introduced to represent both [θ] and [ð].

One might ask why *th* was selected. A possibility is that the character *h* was already being used in digraphs to represent new sounds. For example, in the chapter on French, it can be noted that when [k] assibilated before [a], it was represented as *ch*. Thus, the character *h* is available for uses other than representing [h].

In Old English, the sound [tʃ] was represented by the character *c*. Thus, *chin* was spelled *cinn*. This was unacceptable to the French because the character *c* was already doing duty representing [k] and [s]. However, French was using the digraph *ch* to represent this sound and so substituted it for the original spelling.

This use of a consonant followed by *h* established a trend: consonantal sounds new to French could be represented in this way. Old English represented the sound [ʃ] with the digraph *sc*. See, for example, the Old English *scarp* and its contemporary spelling *sharp*. The *c* of this digraph presents the same problem as the *c* that represents [tʃ]: in French spelling, the sound that it represents is contingent on the following vowel. As a consequence, *sc* was substituted with *sh*.

Old English included the sound [x]. This is the sound that some English speakers use when attempting the correct pronunciation of *Bach* or *loch* and no longer exists in English (although its representation does). It was represented in Old English by *h*. Not only does this sound not exist in French, but *h* was already being used in a quite different way by participating in digraphs. Instead, the sound came to be represented with *gh*. See, for example, the Old English *riht*, which is now spelled as *right*. The answer to the question of why the digraph *gh* is not pronounced in *right, though, thought, slough*, and so forth is that the sound that it represnted elided in the history of English, but the spelling of these words was not changed to reflect this historical change.

This consistent use of a consonant symbol followed by *h* resulted in the re-spelling of the English digraph *hw* to align it with the others. In Old English, *what* and *while* were spelled *hwæt* and *hwil*. If you say these words carefully, it is apparent that the Old English spelling is closer to the phonetic reality.

There is some speculation about who introduced this last spelling change. The printing press was introduced into English in 1476 by William Caxton. Since it was a piece of new machinery, he needed to import workers to help set the press. The workers he selected were Dutch, and they did not necessarily speak English. They were setting the press for a text they likely did not understand by copying it letter by letter. It is thought that an observant worker (a budding linguist) noticed that the digraph *hw* did not follow the standard set by *th, sh, ch*, and *gh*, and concluding that it was in error, switched it to *wh*.

The introduction of the printing press is one of the reasons for the standardization of the spelling system. Because it made printed works available to a larger number of people, there was pressure for consistent presentation. Moreover, as in modern industry, a standardized product is cheaper to produce.

As important as the printing press is, the timing of its introduction to England is unfortunate. At the time of its introduction, English was undergoing a major sound change called the Great English Vowel Shift. The term *Great* is being used here in the sense of "large and encompassing", not in its more colloquial sense of "splendid or excellent". The English Vowel Shift is "Great" because it affected all of the long vowels of English. It is not "great" because it wreaked havoc on the spelling system of English.

We first illustrated part of the Vowel Shift when we began this book by considering how languages change over time. We will end where we began by briefly sketching the Vowel Shift and consider its effect on English spelling.

The Great Vowel Shift

Between the times of Chaucer in the 14th century and that of Shakespeare in the 16th century, the long vowels of English each underwent change. Incredibly, when the various changes were complete, all the vowels were affected and it was clear that they were organized into coherent shifts (and ones that were catastrophic to the English spelling system). The general rule was that all long vowels raised, so that low vowels became mid vowels, mid vowels became high vowels, and high vowels became diphthongs.

Short vowels also changed, but these changes were not as coherent as those for the long vowels. We will concentrate on the long vowels.

The main parts of the Vowel Shift can be sketched, as in Figure XV.1. There are many details that could be discussed but this will suffice to see the effect that this change had on the English spelling system. Since the spelling system was fixed before the completion of the Vowel Shift, it actually represents how words were pronounced in roughly the 14th century, rather than as they are now.

Figure XV.1: Great English Vowel Shift

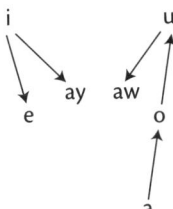

These changes can be illustrated by comparing Old English words that contained long vowels with their contemporary English reflexes. Table XV.1 contains examples showing the development of front and back high vowels. The Old English vowels are pronounced much like [ī] and [ū]. Their contemporary English equivalents have diphthongized to (approximately) [ay] and [aw] respectively.

Table XV.1: High vowels

Old English	English	Old English	English
rīdan	ride	mūs	mouse
bīdan	bide	fūnden	found
fīnden	find	brūn	brown

When introducing the distinction between orthography and phonetics, it was noted that, for pedagogical purposes, grammar-school teachers often refer to long and short vowels when teaching English spelling. The vowel of *wise*, for example, is said to be long. Of course, it is not a long vowel, but a diphthong. In contrast, the vowel of the *wisdom* is said to be short. These two words obviously contain the same root, so it is curious that they have different vowels.

The answer is in another spelling rule that is often taught, namely, that a vowel that is followed by two consonants is short. This spelling rule mimics an actual phonological rule that was discussed earlier: vowels are short when they appear in a closed syllable (with some caveats that we will ignore). This rule was introduced in the 10th century. Since the Vowel Shift affects only long vowels, the vowel of *wise* participated in the Vowel Shift, but the vowel of *wisdom*. did not. As a consequence, there will be alternations in vowels, contingent on these vowels appearing in open or closed syllables. Table XV.2 gives a few examples of the reflexes of what was originally a long [i]. Note that the reflex of the shortened version is [I].

When grammar-school teachers speak of long and short vowels, they are in a sense, correct. The vowels were once long or short, but, subsequent to the Vowel Shift, the difference is now a qualitative, rather than quantitative one.

Table XV.2

[ay]	[I]
five	fifth
wise	wisdom
ride	ridden
write	written

As indicated in Figure XV.1, the mid vowels raised to high vowels.

Table XV.3: Mid Vowels

Old English [ē]	English [i]	Old English [ō]	English [u]
sēkan	seek	rōt	root
mētan	meet	gōs	goose
kēpan	keep	dōm	doom
bēte	beet	tōth	tooth

Of interest is the spelling convention that was adopted to indicate long mid vowels. Whereas, vowel length is usually indicated by whether the orthographic syllable is open or closed, the convention of doubling the vowel to indicate a long mid vowel was adopted. Thus, when the vowel is represented with *ee* or *oo*, the Old English etymon was long.

Again, we find alternations in the vowel of a root when it can appear in both open and closed syllables. Table XV.4 gives examples of how the long [o] was affected. When shortened, it became [a], but when it remained long, the Vowel Shift raised it to [u].

Table XV.4

[u]	[a]
food	fodder
goose	gosling
lose	lost

These alternations can appear in inflectional paradigms. Consider these verbs which originally had a long [e] (Table XV.5).

Table XV.5

Present	Past
creep	crept
sleep	slept
keep	kept
weep	wept

These verbs differ from the majority of English verbs by forming the past tense with -t, instead of the regular -ed. But something else has happened as well: the spelling indicates that the vowel has shortened in the past tense. That is, whereas the present *keep* shows a double vowel character, indicating an original long vowel, the past *kept* has a single vowel character.

If we compare the actual sounds, we can see that the difference between present and past tenses has become greater than a simple difference in length. The vowel in the present tense of these verbs is [i], but that of the past tense is [ɛ]. Note that neither of these is the original vowel [ē], as indicated by the orthography.

In some respects, an inflectional paradigm like this, where the root has different forms, is unfortunate. Most would agree that the optimal situation is one in which inflection does not affect the form of a lexeme so that the lexeme is obvious in each inflected form. The past and present verb forms in Table

XV.5 seem to be moving away from each other in phonetic space, obscuring their relationship.

Finally, in the Vowel Shift, the low back vowel raised to [o].

Table XV.6: Low Vowels

Old English	English
stān	stone
hām	home
rāp	rope
tākn	token
dāl	dole
māl	mole
pāl	pole

When short, this vowel fronted to [æ]. Table XV.7 provides some examples where [o] and [æ] alternate. These vowels were all originally a long [a].

Table XV.7

[o]	[æ]
home	hamlet
holy	Halloween

There is considerably more that can be said of the Great Vowel Shift. For example, if a short vowel was lengthened, the long version would be susceptible to the Vowel Shift, while the original short version was not. An example would be the alternation in *signal* with the short vowel, and *sign*, with the long version. It is left to the reader to determine how the vowel lengthened.

Conclusion

By itself, the Great Vowel Shift created problems for the English spelling system. What once were similar vowels, differing in length only are now different vowels altogether. Yet, because spelling systems are by their nature conservative, these different vowels are still represented by the same characters. The problem that this presents to readers of English is that it is not always clear which sound a character represents.

There are some subtleties to the English spelling system that sometimes can help. The correlation of vowel length with syllable structure is usually a reliable guide for English rules, but not in all cases. For example, why is the vowel of *right* [ay], not [I]? Since it appears in a closed syllable, it seems that it should be the latter.[1]

Complicating matters are the various rules that lengthen and shorten vowels. Since the Great Vowel Shift applies only to long vowels, these rules distinguish lexemes and words with the same roots. The effect of this on the English lexicon is to obscure the relationships among these lexemes.

Further Reading

Freeborn, Dennis. *From Old English to Standard English: A Course Book in Language Variation across Time*. Ottawa: University of Ottawa Press, 1998.

---

1 The presence of *gh* in the spelling of *right* provides a hint to why this is so. Compare *right* with *sign*.

Index

A
ablaut, 267–269
affix, 114
　taxonomy, 114
agile, 172
alphabet, 73–99
　diacritics, 91, 97
　international phonetic alphabet, 8
　phonetic alphabet, 8, 9, 11, 33, 75, 96
alveolar, 34
Ancient Greek, 27, 28, 30, 38, 104, 263
articulatory points, 34
assibilation, 174
assimilation, 132–134, 136, 148, 149, 161, 162, 164, 181–186, 189, 196, 199, 203, 224, 232, 253, 254, 268, 271

B
binary rule, 107
borrowing, 38, 43, 44
boundary marker, 107, 228

C
Chaucer, 6, 7, 14, 87, 314
closed syllable, 93, 95, 316, 319
cluster simplification, 185, 291
complementary distribution, 86
compounds, 89, 103, 104, 215–217, 265, 284, 289, 304
conjugation, 88, 154, 155, 172
consonants, 33–34
contraction, 298

D
derivation, 108, 164, 199, 207, 208, 218, 227, 292, 305, 306
derivational morphology, 38, 110, 111, 154, 175, 201
derivational rule, 109, 110
diacritic macron, 11
digraph, 91
dissimilation, 232

E
epenthesis, 226, 289
etymon, 31, 42, 43, 67, 264, 316

F
French, 277–298

G
generality, 133–136, 144
Germanic consonant shift, 36
　Voiced Aspirates, 49
　Voiced Stops, 48
　Voiceless Stops, 46

H
hieroglyphics, 7, 78
hybrids, 125

I
infinitive, 14, 154, 155, 203, 208, 229
inflection, 14, 85, 86, 104, 153
inflectional rule, 105, 110

J
Jones, Sir William, 27

L

Latin, 27–29, 151–247
lenition, 280, 282, 283, 292
letter
  ash, 7
  edh, 7
  thorn, 7
lexeme, 105
lexical entry, 105
lexicon, 15, 19, 105
locative prefix, 149, 253

M

macron, 11, 12, 91, 153, 163, 164
medial vowel weakening, 212
metathesis, 207, 208, 288
Middle English, 6, 14, 15, 43, 56, 64, 66, 67, 68, 92, 93, 278
morpheme, 112–114
  affix, 113
  prefix, 113
  root, 113
  suffix, 113
  taxonomy, 113
morphological, 110
morphology, 14
  derivational morphology, 38, 110, 111, 154, 175, 201
  inflectional morphology, 16, 110, 157, 201, 278

N

naturalization, 40, 67, 122, 236, 303
nominative case, 6, 16, 84

O

Old English, 4–9, 11–18, 24, 30, 33, 43, 60, 64–67, 72, 92, 94, 121, 153, 164, 210, 251, 313–316, 318, 319
open syllable, 93, 94
orthography, 7
  ideographic, 74
  pictographic, 73, 74, 76
  syllabary, 7, 74, 76, 80
Orwell, George, 41, 69

P

page, 105
palate, 34, 91
paradigm, 14, 15, 105, 110, 128, 155, 169, 229, 237, 238, 317
phonological, 12
phonological rule, 12
  ablaut, 267, 268, 269
  assibilation, 174, 293, 294, 296, 297, 298
  assimilation, 132–134, 136, 148, 149, 161, 162, 164, 181–186, 189, 196, 199, 203, 224, 232, 253, 254, 268, 271
  cluster simplification, 185, 291
  contraction, 198, 298
  dissimilation, 227, 228, 232, 233, 245
  epenthesis, 226, 289
  lenition, 280, 282, 283, 292
  medial vowel weakening, 211, 212, 217–219, 257
  metathesis, 207, 210, 212, 257, 261, 286, 288, 298
  prothesis, 292
  reduplication, 227
  rhotacism, 220, 221
  shortening, 301
  syncope, 259, 288, 289, 291
  vocalization, 282, 283, 285, 288
  voicing assimilation, 162, 164, 182, 183, 184, 186, 189, 199
  vowel raising, 222
phonological rules, 131
prefix, 115
  locative, 147
prothesis, 257
Proto-Indo-European, 30–32, 64, 139, 228, 280
provide, 172

R

rebus, 74, 78
reduplication, 227
reflex, 31
rhotacism, 219, 221
root, 113
rule, 114
  binary, 107
  derivational, 114
  inflectional rule, 109
  phonological. *See* phonological rule
  unary, 107

S

Sanskrit, 4, 27, 28, 30–32, 38, 48, 49, 211
shortening, 301
silent e, 94, 108
spelling rules, 91
suffix, 113
syllabary, 7, 74, 76, 80
syllable, 316
   closed, 316
   open, 316
syncope, 259, 288, 289, 291

T

taxonomy, 113
   affixes, 113
   morphemes, 113
teenage slang, 23
Thai, 7, 54, 76, 97, 104, 168, 305
thematic stem, 155–159, 164, 167, 172, 175, 177, 236, 237
thematic vowel, 155, 237

U

unary rule, 107

V

velum, 34
vigilant, 49
vocalization, 282, 283, 285, 288
voicing, 34
voicing assimilation, 162, 164, 182–184, 186, 189, 199
vowel length, 92, 93, 95, 163, 316, 319
vowel raising, 222

W

word, 101

Z

zero derivation, 305

Index of Latin Roots

A
acid *sour*, 234
ag *drive*, 160, 172, 175, 194, 195, 198, 241, 242, 243, 246
ag *say*, 195
am *love*, 155, 156, 235
anima *life*, 231
annu *year*, 231, 235
aqua *water*, 234, 240
art *art*, 245
at *spirit*, 211
aud *hear*, 155, 158, 174, 236

B
bene *good*, 215, 284
brev *brief*, 182, 235

C
cād *fall*, 163
calc *chalk*, 244
canon *rule*, 234
cap *have*, 197, 213, 243
capit *head*, 244
cau *be on guard*, 221
cav *hollow*, 235
ced *go*, 192, 197
cell *room*, 245
cīd *cut*, 163, 188, 241, 242
circ *ring*, 244, 245
civ *home*, 234, 246
clam *cry*, 188
class *rank*, 234
claud *close*, 163, 188, 233
col *cultivate*, 222, 234
cond *hide*, 192

cord *heart*, 182, 185
corpus *body*, 219
cr *sift*, 208, 209
cre *create*, 155, 158, 247
cred *believe*, 155, 159, 236
cub *lie*, 203
cur *care*, 240
curr *run*, 174, 245

D
da *give*, 198, 213
deb *owe*, 159
dec *befit*, 211
decor *beauty*, 240
dextr *right*, 198
dic *say*, 160, 180, 192, 241–243
diu *god*, 221
doc *teach*, 155, 156, 160, 246
duc *lead*, 189, 192, 195, 196, 198, 199, 237
dur *last*, 158

E
em *buy*, 188, 194, 226, 227
equ *equal*, 231
err *wander*, 173, 234

F
fa *speak*, 181
fabul *story*, 240
fac *make, do*, 156, 160, 191, 197, 213, 215, 222, 237, 241, 242, 246
fall *deception*, 223, 225
fam *fame*, 240
famili *household*, 232, 233

fer *bear*, 191, 246
fer *carry*, 185, 197, 198
ferv *boil*, 247
fet *bring forth*, 191
fid *cleave*, 243
fid *trust*, 174, 185
fig *attach*, 182, 223
fig *mold*, 160, 191
fili *son*, 181
fin *end*, 155, 158, 181
firm *support*, 181
flect *bend*, 167
flig *strike*, 182
flos *flower*, 233, 247
fluc *flow*, 223, 224
flu *flow*, 175, 182, 191
frag *break*, 160, 162, 185, 203, 217, 243, 246
frig *be cold*, 156
front *forehead*, 182
fūd *bottom*, 197
fūd *pour*, 203
fug *flee*, 159

G

genus *kind*, 219
ges *carry*, 186, 197, 219, 237, 245
giga *huge*, 234
glob *ball*, 233, 245
gluten *glue*, 182
gn *born*, 142, 243, 246
grad *step*, 173, 195, 241, 242
gran *grain*, 245
grav *heavy*, 182, 235
greg *flock*, 158, 182, 189, 196
gust *taste*, 187

H

hab *have*, 159
her *stick*, 175
here *choose*, 234
honus *honour*, 219
hor *bristle*, 193
hum *low*, 246

I

ign *fire*, 240
i *go*, 174, 180, 188, 195, 198

J

jac *throw*, 192, 197, 198, 243, 244
joc *joke*, 245
jug *bind*, 180, 245
jug *join*, 197, 232
jus *law*, 219

L

lact *milk*, 234
lapid *stone*, 186
lat *side*, 234
lav *wash*, 192
leg *read*, 156, 160, 189, 196, 231, 237, 233, 242, 243, 309
lev *light*, 181, 189
liber *free*, 234
line *line*, 233
lique *liquid*, 285
litter *letter*, 234
loc *place*, 181, 233
lūd *play*, 163, 181
lumb *loin*, 233
lumen *light*, 235, 247
lun *moon*, 233
luna *moon*, 234

M

mag *great*, 211, 216, 284
manu *hand*, 215, 231, 284
mater *mother*, 245
merc *trade*, 173
merg *plunge*, 197
merg *sink*, 189
met *fear*, 245
met *measure*, 186, 203, 234
misc *mix*, 195, 223, 224
mit *send*, 163, 180, 187, 195, 197, 199
mod *mode*, 182
mont *hill*, 199
mon *warn*, 155, 159, 181
mut *change*, 199

N

nau *ship*, 221, 240
nav *sailor*, 231
nect *tie*, 167, 182
nihil *nothing*, 182
noc *harm*, 240
noc *injure*, 223

nod *knot*, 245
norm *rule*, 192, 231, 240

O
ol *old*, 222, 247
ol *smell*, 194
onus *burden*, 219
op *choose*, 242
opt *choose*, 181
opus *work*, 219
or *speak*, 181
orn *wear*, 181, 197
os *mouth*, 219

P
pag *strike*, 204, 217
par *arrange*, 196
part *part*, 245
pat *feel*, 173, 174
pat *suffer*, 163
pell *drive*, 222, 223, 225
pell *drive* (away), 185
pend *hang*, 165, 172, 174, 182, 185, 188, 197, 243, 245
pet *feather*, 211
pig *paint*, 160, 162
plan *flat*, 233
plant *plant*, 233
plaud *applaud*, 182
plic *fold*, 173, 182, 197
plus *plus*, 233
popul *people*, 232, 240
port *carry*, 188, 197, 198, 236
pos *place*, 197, 203, 243
pot *be able*, 163, 172, 175
prob *test*, 156, 236
pub *old*, 247
puer *boy*, 246
pug *pierce*, 204, 212, 243
put *reckon*, 156, 158
put *think, reckon*, 185, 187
putr *be rotten*, 247
putre *rotten*, 285

Q
quant *how much*, 216, 285
ques *ask*, 219
qui *rest*, 247

R
radi *root*, 175
ram *branch*, 285
rap *seize*, 156
rare *rare*, 285
reg *rule*, 155, 160, 172, 186, 189, 212, 231, 236, 242, 244, 245, 263
ret *net*, 245
rid *laugh*, 245
rīd *laugh*, 163
rōd *gnaw*, 163
rog *ask*, 173
rup *break*, 160, 192, 237, 243
rus *country*, 219, 234

S
sac *holy*, 204
sal *leap*, 222
salu *health*, 221
san *healthy*, 235
satis *enough*, 215, 284
scand *climb*, 165
schol *school*, 232
sci *know*, 172, 173, 174
scrib *write*, 161, 243
sec *cut*, 162, 211, 223, 224
sed *sit*, 163, 172, 182, 212
semen *seed*, 231
sen *be old*, 246, 247
sent *feel*, 170, 175, 182
sign *sign*, 285
sim *same*, 182, 232, 244
sol *sun*, 232
solu *free*, 175, 193
solu *loosen*, 221
sop *sleep*, 211
spec *see*, 160, 184, 187, 188, 197, 212, 240, 242, 244
spir *breathe*, 158, 184, 188
spond *promise*, 165
sta *stand*, 173, 181, 196, 197, 213
stell *star*, 232
stol *stupid*, 222
strig *compress*, 203
stupe *stun*, 285
suad *sweet*, 163

T

tag *touch*, 203, 213, 217, 223, 224, 240, 242
teg *cover*, 241
ten *hold*, 192, 197
tend *stretch*, 165, 174, 183, 185, 188, 263
tenu *thin*, 183
test *witness*, 183
tex *weave*, 263
trag *drag*, 188, 192, 196
tum *swell*, 247
turb *to disorder*, 158

U

und *wave*, 194, 244
urg *urge*, 175

V

val *be strong*, 198, 247
vari *change*, 240
vegh *way*, 223, 224, 245
vell *pluck*, 223, 225
ven *come*, 170, 173, 181
venus *love*, 219
vert *turn*, 165, 181, 193, 199
vest *dress*, 186
vic *conquer*, 203, 236
vīd *see*, 163, 172, 175
vir *man*, 246
voc *call*, 181
voc *voice*, 158, 231
volu *roll*, 221

Index of Latin Words

A
abbreviate, 182
abdicate, 192
abduct, 192
abhor, 193
abject, 192
ablution, 192
abnormal, 192
abrupt, 192
abscess, 192
abscond, 192
absolve, 193
abstention, 192
abstract, 192
accommodate, 182
accord, 182
acidic, 234
acidity, 234
act, 160, 188, 194, 198, 240, 241, 242
acta, 240
action, 242, 243
active, 243
actor, 241
adage, 195
addict, 180
adduce, 181
adherence, 175
adherent, 175
adit, 180
adjective, 192, 197, 198, 243, 244
adjunct, 180
adjutant, 287
admit, 180
admonition, 181
adolescent, 222, 247

adopt, 181
adoration, 181
adorn, 181
adult, 222, 247
adventure, 181
advertise, 181
advocate, 181
affable, 181
affiliate, 181
affinity, 181
affirmation, 181
affix, 182
afflict, 182
affluent, 182
affront, 182
agency, 175
agent, 160, 172, 175, 177, 188, 194, 195, 198
agglutinate, 182
aggravate, 182
aggregate, 182
aggression, 196, 242
aggressive, 241, 242
aggressor, 241
agile, 160, 172, 246
agility, 246
allegation, 181
alleviate, 181
allocate, 181
allude, 181
amateur, 154, 235
ambidextrous, 198
ambience, 174, 175
ambient, 174, 175
ambiguous, 198, 240
ambition, 198

ambivalent, 198
amity, 235
amorous, 156
anchor, 66
angular, 289
animal, 211, 231
animate, 231
annex, 167, 182
annihilate, 182
annual, 231, 235
annuity, 231, 235
antedeluvian, 297
append, 182
applaud, 182
applicant, 173, 182, 197
aquatic, 234, 240
aqueous, 240
aquifer, 234
arrest, 181
arrogant, 173
art, 245
articulate, 245, 289
ascension, 165
ascribable, 175
ascribe, 175
ascription, 176
aspect, 184
assent, 182
assess, 182
assimilate, 182, 244
assist, 228
assistance, 228
astonish, 47
attend, 183
attenuate, 183
attest, 183
attractant, 238
audible, 158, 236
audience, 174, 175
audit, 158
Aurora, 220
avert, 193

B

barber, 51
benediction, 285
benefaction, 215, 285
blaspheme, 291
breviary, 235
brevity, 182, 235

C

cadence, 163, 282, 295
calcium, 244, 295
calculable, 133
calculate, 244
calefacient, 295
calix, 295
calumny, 295, 298
cambial, 297
camera, 289, 295
campus, 295
canal, 295
candelabra, 66
candle, 66, 295
canine, 47
cannabis, 48
canonic, 234
canonical, 235
canonize, 234
canto, 295
cape, 295
capital, 244, 288, 289, 295
capitulate, 244
capricorn, 280
captive, 197
capture, 213, 243
car, 295
card, 295
case, 295
caste, 295
castigate, 295
castle, 295
causal, 235
causality, 235
caution, 221
cave, 235
caveat, 221
cavity, 235, 297
cell, 245
cellular, 245
century, 47
cessation, 170
circular, 245, 289
circulate, 244, 288
circumcise, 188
circumnavigate, 200
circumscribe, 176
circumscription, 176
circus, 244, 245
civic, 234

civil, 246
civilian, 234
civility, 246
classic, 234
classical, 235
classify, 234
clausal, 233
clause, 163, 298
cognition, 48
collaborate, 134
collapse, 134
collateral, 134
collect, 160, 231, 237
collectibility, 239
collectible, 237, 239
collection, 242
college, 156, 160
colony, 222, 234
commeasurable, 134
commerce, 173
commission, 134
compact, 134
compassion, 134
compatriot, 134
compel, 222, 223
compensation, 170
competent, 133
complete, 133
complex, 235
complexity, 235
component, 203, 204
compose, 204
composition, 203
compress, 134
compulsion, 222, 223
computable, 158
compute, 156
computer, 185
concatenate, 294
conception, 280, 281
concern, 209
conclude, 163
conclusive, 133
concubine, 203
conduct, 134, 181
confabulate, 240
confidence, 174, 175
confident, 174, 175
configure, 134

confluence, 175
confluent, 175
conform, 134
congenial, 134
congregation, 158
conjoin, 134
connect, 167, 182
conscript, 176
conscription, 176
consent, 170
consign, 134
consist, 228
consistent, 228
conspicuous, 240
constant, 228
consternation, 210
constituent, 213
constrict, 134
consultant, 238
consume, 227
consumption, 227
contact, 240, 242
contagion, 242
contagious, 240
contempt, 226
contest, 134
contiguity, 235
contiguous, 213
continent, 197
contingent, 217
continue, 235
convalescent, 247
convene, 170
convenient, 133, 170, 173
convent, 170, 181
converge, 134
conversation, 170
convert, 165
convex, 223, 224
convulse, 223, 225
cook, 66
copulate, 289
cordial, 47, 182, 185, 235
cordiality, 235
cornucopia, 47
corporeal, 219
corpse, 219
correct, 160, 231
correction, 212, 242

correlate, 134
correspond, 134, 165
correspondent, 165
corrigible, 236
corrupt, 237, 243
corruptible, 237
create, 158, 247
credence, 159
credibility, 239
credible, 66, 236, 239
credit, 159
creed, 66
crescent, 247
cult, 222
cultural, 234
cuneal, 287
cure, 240
curious, 240
currency, 174, 175
current, 174, 175, 245
curriculum, 245

D
data, 198, 213
debit, 159, 288
decenal, 283
decent, 211
deception, 280, 281
deceptive, 213
decline, 200
decorate, 240
decorous, 240
deduce, 189, 192
deducibility, 239
deducible, 239
deductible, 237
defect, 213, 241, 242
defection, 242
defector, 241
deficient, 213
deity, 48
delude, 163
delusion, 163
dental, 48
dentist, 47
depend, 188
dependence, 174, 175
dependent, 165, 172, 174, 175
deponent, 204

depose, 204
derision, 163
descend, 165
describe, 176
description, 161, 176, 243
descriptive, 176, 243
descriptively, 176
desultory, 222
detect, 241
detector, 241
dexterity, 198
dictation, 170, 192
diction, 160
dictionary, 180
different, 185
difficult, 222
diffident, 185
diffract, 185
digest, 186, 237
digestant, 238
digestible, 237
dignity, 211
dilapidated, 186
dimension, 186, 203, 206
direct, 186
discern, 209
disciple, 66
discord, 185
disgust, 187
disinfectant, 238
dismember, 187
dismiss, 187
dispel, 185
dispense, 185
dispute, 185
disrepute, 187
disrespect, 187
disrobe, 187
distend, 185
disturb, 158
diurnal, 221
divest, 186
divine, 221
docile, 156, 160, 246
docility, 246
doctor, 160
domestic, 48
dominate, 298
duct, 134, 198

duo, 48
durable, 158
duration, 158

E
edible, 48
educate, 189
effect, 213
effervescent, 247
efficient, 160, 213
egregious, 189
ejaculate, 244
ejection, 243
elect, 189
election, 242
elevate, 189
emerge, 189
enormous, 240
equal, 231
equivalent, 231
erect, 189
erosion, 163
errant, 173
erratic, 234
error, 173, 234
evidence, 175
evident, 163, 172, 175
exact, 188
excision, 188
exclamation, 188
exclude, 188
excrete, 209
excretion, 209
exempt, 188, 226
exit, 180, 188, 198
exonerate, 219
expect, 188
expectant, 238
expend, 188
expire, 188
exponent, 204
export, 188, 198
expose, 204
extend, 165, 188
extract, 188
extraneous, 298

F
fabulous, 240, 289
facile, 160, 246
facility, 246
fact, 51, 160, 213
factory, 197
faculty, 156
fallacy, 223
false, 223, 225
fame, 240
familiar, 232
family, 232
famous, 240
febrile, 66, 281
fertile, 197, 246
fertility, 246
fervent, 247
fever, 66
fiction, 160
fidelity, 185
figment, 51, 160
figure, 134
filial, 181
final, 158
finite, 158
firm, 181
fission, 243
fissure, 243
flagrant, 50
flammable, 147
flection, 146
floral, 50, 233, 247
florescent, 247
florist, 233
fluctuate, 223
fluid, 182
flux, 223, 224
foliage, 287
form, 134
forum, 51
fracture, 160, 203, 243
fragile, 50, 160, 162, 185, 246
fragility, 246
fragment, 162, 243
frangible, 203, 206
fraternity, 50
frigid, 156
frontier, 182
fructose, 285

fugitive, 159
fume, 51
fumigation, 217
fundamental, 50, 197, 203
fusion, 203

G
gaudy, 282, 298
gelatin, 49
general, 289, 290
generate, 219
genial, 134
genius, 146
gens, 296
gentile, 246
gentility, 246
genuflect, 48
genus, 219, 296
gerund, 219
gestation, 186, 197
gesticulate, 245
gesture, 245
gigabyte, 234
gigantic, 234, 283
global, 233
globe, 233, 245
globular, 245
glutinous, 182
grade, 195
gradient, 173
granite, 245
granular, 245, 298
grave, 235
gravity, 182, 235
gregarious, 158, 182, 189
gubernatorial, 281
gustatory, 187

H
habilitate, 159
habit, 52, 159
heresy, 234
heretic, 234
heretical, 235
honest, 219
honorable, 219
horror, 193
horticulture, 52
hospital, 291

host, 52, 169
human, 235
humanity, 235
humility, 246, 290

I
igneous, 240
ignite, 240
ignoble, 140, 141
ignorant, 140
illuminate, 146
illustrious, 146
immature, 132, 136
immeasurable, 132
immobile, 132
immoral, 132
impact, 146, 204
imperturbable, 158
impetuosity, 235
impetuous, 235
impinge, 204, 206, 217
implicate, 182
import, 188
important, 197
impossible, 132
impotent, 132
impractical, 132
imprecise, 132
impregnate, 146
improvisation, 170
inaction, 217
incalculable, 133
inception, 213
incipient, 213, 243
incision, 163, 242
incisive, 241, 242
incisor, 241
include, 188, 233
incompetent, 133
incomplete, 133
inconclusive, 133
inconvenient, 133
incorrigible, 212
incumbent, 203, 206
indescribable, 176
indescribably, 176
indicate, 241, 242
indication, 242
indicator, 241

indiscrete, 209
indiscretion, 209
induce, 195
ineffable, 181
infect, 213
inferior, 51
infinite, 181
infix, 223
inflammable, 147
inflect, 167
inflection, 146
inflict, 182
infringe, 217
ingenious, 146
inhabitant, 238
initial, 198
innocent, 223, 240
innocuous, 240
inscribe, 176
inscription, 176
insidious, 212
insist, 228
insistence, 228
insomnia, 211
inspect, 184
inspection, 212, 242
inspiration, 158
inspire, 158, 184, 188
instant, 173, 228
intact, 223
integral, 213
integrate, 213
interaction, 217
intercede, 197
intoxicate, 146
inundate, 244
invidious, 282
invincible, 203, 206, 236
irradiate, 146
irredeemable, 130
irregardless, 147
irruption, 146

J
January, 90
jaundice, 90
jocosity, 245
jocular, 245
join, 134
jugular, 90, 232, 245
junction, 180, 197, 232, 245, 286
jury, 219
justice, 219
juvenile, 90

L
labial, 48
labor, 134
lactate, 234
lactic, 234
lapidary, 186
lapse, 134
lateral, 134, 234
latitude, 234
lavatory, 192
lecture, 243
legal, 44, 45, 181, 231, 233, 283
legend, 160, 243
legible, 196
legion, 242
legislate, 189, 233
levitate, 181
levity, 189
liberal, 234
liberty, 234
line, 233
linear, 233
liquefaction, 285
liquid, 285
literal, 234
literate, 234
local, 233
location, 181, 233
locus, 283
Lucifer, 50, 185
ludicrous, 163, 181
lumbago, 233
lumbar, 233
luminesent, 247
luminosity, 235
luminous, 146, 235, 247
lunar, 233, 234
lunatic, 233, 234
lupus, 47
lustrous, 146

M

magistrate, 211
magnanimous, 285
magnificent, 216, 285
magnify, 211
malign, 142
malignant, 142
manual, 231, 285
manufacture, 215, 231, 285
manuscript, 176
margin, 48
martyr, 66
masculine, 291
maternal, 47, 245
matriculate, 245
mature, 132
measurable, 132
measure, 134
memory, 287, 290
mental, 269
mercantile, 173, 295
merge, 197
meter, 203, 234
meticulous, 245
metric, 186, 234
metrical, 235
minister, 66, 288
minor, 67
miscellaneous, 195, 223
mission, 134, 197
mix, 223, 224
mobile, 132
moderate, 182
monastery, 66
monitor, 159
monument, 159
muscular, 291

N

native, 282
nature, 243
nausea, 298
nauseous, 240
nautical, 221, 231, 240
naval, 221, 231
navigation, 217
nihilism, 182
noble, 141
node, 245
nodular, 245
nondescript, 176
norm, 143
normal, 231, 240
normative, 192, 231
noxious, 223
numeral, 290
nun, 66

O

obstetric, 213
occasion, 163
olfactory, 194
onus, 219
operate, 219
opinion, 242
option, 181, 242
opus, 219
oral, 219
orate, 181
ornament, 181, 197
osculate, 219

P

pact, 134, 146
particular, 245
partition, 245
passion, 134, 163
paternal, 47
patience, 174, 175
patient, 163, 173, 174, 175
patriot, 134
paucity, 47
pauper, 280, 298
pause, 298
pedal, 48
pedestrian, 47
pen, 47
pend, 165
pendant, 197
pendent, 185
pending, 182
pendulum, 172, 245
pennate, 211
pension, 165, 243
pensive, 243
perception, 281
perfect, 200, 237
perfectible, 237

permission, 163
permit, 163, 180, 187, 195
perpendicular, 245
persist, 228
persistent, 228
persuade, 48, 163, 263
persuasion, 163
picture, 160
pigment, 160, 162
piscine, 47
planar, 233
plane, 233
plant, 233
plantar, 233
plausible, 182
plenty, 47
plural, 233
plus, 233
popular, 232
populate, 240
population, 232
populous, 240, 289
portability, 239
portable, 236, 239
position, 197, 243
positive, 243
possible, 132, 163
posthumous, 200
postscript, 176
potency, 175
potent, 132, 163, 172, 175
potion, 287
practical, 132
precise, 132
prediction, 243
predictive, 243
pre-empt, 226
preemptive, 194
prefix, 182
pregnant, 146, 243
prepare, 196
Presbyterian, 66
prescribe, 175
prescript, 175
prescription, 176
prescriptive, 176
press, 134
presume, 227
presumption, 227

prevent, 200
priest, 66
probabilistic, 157
probability, 157, 239
probable, 157, 236, 239
probate, 157
probation, 157
probationary, 157
probe, 156, 280
proclamation, 188
prodigal, 195
prodigious, 217
prodigy, 195
produce, 195
production, 196
profuse, 198
progress, 195
progression, 196
promiscuous, 195
promise, 195
proponent, 204
propose, 204
proscribe, 176
proscription, 176
provide, 172
puberty, 247
pubescent, 247
puerile, 246
pugilist, 204, 212, 243
pugnacious, 212
pulse, 225
punctual, 204, 206, 286
puncture, 212, 243
putative, 158, 187
putrefaction, 285
putrescent, 247
putrid, 247, 285

Q

quality, 47
quantification, 216, 285
quantity, 285
query, 219
question, 219
quiescent, 247
quiet, 247

R

rabies, 297
radiance, 175
radiant, 175
radiate, 146
radius, 282
ramification, 285
ramose, 285
rapture, 156
rare, 285
rarefaction, 285
reactant, 238
reception, 280, 281
receptive, 213
recipient, 213
recondite, 192
redact, 194
redaction, 217
redemption, 188, 194, 226
redolent, 194
reduce, 196
reduction, 196
redundant, 194
refer, 198
reflex, 167
refuge, 159
regal, 59, 186, 189, 212, 231, 244, 245, 283
regardless, 147
regent, 160, 172
region, 242
regression, 196
regular, 160, 172, 245
regulate, 244, 283
relate, 134
religion, 242
repel, 185
reprehendere, 67
resist, 228
resistant, 228
resolve, 193
respond, 134
restitution, 213
resume, 227
resumption, 227
reticular, 245
retina, 245
revolution, 221
revolve, 90, 221
ridicule, 163, 245
risible, 245
rodent, 163
ruby, 51, 297
rupture, 146, 160, 192, 243
rural, 219, 234
rustic, 219, 234

S

sacerdotal, 204
sagacious, 263
salient, 222
saline, 264
salute, 221
salvation, 221, 263
sanctify, 286
sanction, 204, 206
sane, 235
sanity, 235
sapient, 297
satiate, 285
satisfaction, 215, 285
scale, 292
scholar, 66, 232
scholastic, 232
school, 66
science, 174, 175
scientist, 172, 173, 174, 175
scribble, 161
scribe, 176
script, 176, 292
scriptural, 176
scripture, 176
secant, 162, 211
secede, 192
secrete, 209
secretion, 209
sectarian, 223
section, 162
secure, 283
sedentary, 163, 172
sediment, 163, 172, 182, 212
sedition, 195
seduce, 195, 196
segment, 162
segregate, 196
select, 196
semiliterate, 263
seminal, 231
seminary, 231

senate, 247
senescent, 247
senile, 246
senior, 246
sensation, 170
sense, 170, 182
sentience, 175
sentient, 175
sentiment, 170
separate, 196
September, 263
sericulture, 66
serpent, 263
session, 163, 212
sex, 223, 224
sexagenarian, 263
sign, 134, 211, 285
significant, 216, 285
silk, 66
similar, 182, 232, 263, 290
simulate, 232, 244
singular, 289
sock, 66
solar, 232, 263
solitarius, 67
solitary, 287
solstice, 232
solution, 221
solve, 221
solvency, 175
solvent, 175
soporific, 211, 264
sorority, 220
spatula, 292
special, 292
species, 212, 244
specimen, 160
spectacle, 160, 187, 188, 197, 240, 292
speculate, 244
sponsor, 165
spouse, 292
stable, 292
stale, 169
stamen, 292
state, 292
statue, 169, 181, 196, 197, 213
Stella, 232
stellar, 169, 232
stolid, 222

stratum, 169
strict, 134, 203
stringent, 203, 206, 286
study, 292
stultify, 222
stupefaction, 285
stupid, 285
subduct, 196
subject, 197
subjugate, 197
submerge, 189, 197
submit, 197
submittere, 67
subnormal, 263
suborn, 197
subscribe, 176
subscriber, 176
subscript, 176
subscription, 176
subsist, 228
subsistence, 197
subsistent, 228
substance, 228
substantial, 196
subtract, 196
success, 197
suffer, 197
sufficient, 197
suffuse, 197
suggest, 197, 219
suicide, 163
super, 281
superficial, 200
superman, 263
superscription, 176
supplicate, 197
support, 197
suppose, 197
susceptible, 197
suspect, 197
suspend, 197
suspicion, 212, 242
suspicious, 240
sustenance, 197

T
tabular, 289
tact, 213
tactile, 203

tangent, 203, 206
tax, 223, 224
tenant, 192
tendency, 165, 174, 175
tense, 185, 188
tension, 165, 183
tenuous, 183, 290
tertiary, 47
test, 134
testify, 183
thyra, 266
toxic, 146
tractor, 188, 192, 196
tradition, 198, 213
traduce, 198, 199
tramontane, 199
transaction, 198, 217
transcribe, 176
transcript, 176
transcription, 176
transduce, 199
transfer, 198
transfusion, 198
transition, 188, 198
translate, 199
transmit, 199
transmute, 199
transport, 198
transverse, 199
traverse, 199
tremulous, 290
tumescent, 47, 247
tumor, 247

U
unction, 286
undulate, 194, 244
universe, 181
urgency, 175
urgent, 175

V
valor, 247
value, 90, 198
various, 240
vary, 240
vegetable, 90
vehicle, 52, 223, 224
vehicular, 245

vellicate, 223
venereal, 219
Venus, 219
verge, 134
verse, 193
version, 165
vestment, 186
vex, 245
vibrate, 48, 90
victory, 203
virile, 246
virtue, 246
vision, 163
vital, 282
vivacious, 280
vocable, 158
vocal, 158, 181, 231
vocation, 158, 231

Index of Greek Roots

A
aethr *sky, burn*, 261
ag *do*, 2520
all *other*, 257
amoeb *change*, 259
andro *man*, 273
angel *messenger*, 262, 273
anth *flower*, 261
anthropo *human*, 273
arch *rule*, 264
arch *ruler*, 259
astero *star*, 266, 269, 273
aut *self*, 273

B
ball *throw*, 252, 255, 256, 257, 262, 269
bapt *dip*, 255
bar *pressure*, 262
bio *life*, 252, 258, 273

C
calypt *cover*, 259, 262
canth *corner of eye*, 258
centr *centre*, 264, 265
chondr *cartilage*, 261
chron *time*, 252, 255, 256, 273
cop *cut*, 259
cosmo *universe*, 273
cranio *skull*, 267
cyclo *circle*, 149
cysto *cyst*, 267

D
daemon *god*, 262, 273
dec *ten*, 272
delta *triangle*, 266
dem *people*, 258, 273
demos *people*, 149
derm *skin*, 258, 259, 261, 265
di *two*, 272
dot *give*, 258
dox *opinion*, 257
drom *run*, 254
dyn *power*, 273

E
embryo *fetus*, 267
ennea *nine*, 272
enter *bowels*, 265
eor *air*, 257
er *love*, 273
erg *work*, 149, 252, 259, 269
estr *frenzy*, 257
ethno *race*, 273
eury *broad*, 255

G
gam *marriage*, 273
gam *marry*, 259, 263, 265
gen *kind*, 273
gen *seed, birth, kind*, 262, 269
geo *earth*, 273
glott *tongue*, 273
gno *know*, 255, 274
gram *letter*, 255
gyn *woman*, 273

H
heg *lead*, 264
heina *send*, 149

INDEX OF GREEK ROOTS

heli *sun*, 259, 260, 273
hem *blood*, 262
hemo *blood*, 266
hepta *seven*, 272
her *take*, 256, 259, 260
hexa *six*, 272
hod *way*, 255, 257, 260, 264
homo *same*, 274
hydro *water*, 273
hypno *sleep*, 266

I
i *go*, 255, 256

K
kilo *one thousand*, 272
kin *motion*, 263

L
lab *hold*, 252
laryngo *larynx*, 267
leip *leave*, 149, 264
lobo *lobe*, 267
log *word*, 252, 255, 256, 259, 262, 264, 265, 269, 274
lys *loose*, 254, 256
lys *loosen*, 255

M
masto *breast*, 267
mega *one million*, 272
metr *measure*, 252, 255, 257
metro *mother*, 273
miso *hate*, 273
mn *mind*, 263, 269
mono *one*, 272
morph *shape*, 259, 265

N
necr *dead*, 273
necro *dead*, 267
neuro *nerve*, 267

O
octa *eight*, 272
od *song*, 257
onym *name*, 252, 257, 258
opt *eye*, 256

P
paed/ped *child*, 273
paedia *teach*, 149
path *feel*, 252, 258
penta *five*, 272
pep *cook*, 265
phag *eat*, 259, 265
phan *appear*, 255, 258, 269
pha *speak*, 269, 273
phem *voice*, 262
pher *carry*, 269
philo *love*, 273
phon *sound*, 252, 262, 265
phor *carry*, 255, 256, 257, 262, 265
phys *nature*, 257
plasm *fluid*, 265
plasm *form*, 259
pleg *stroke*, 257
pne *breathe*, 263, 265
pneumo *breathe*, 267
pod *foot*, 258
poly *many*, 272
proto *first*, 272
pseudo *false*, 274
pt *fall/feather*, 252
pyre *fire*, 149

R
rhe *flow*, 266
rhea *flow*, 256
rhythm *rhythm*, 262

S
sarc *flesh*, 253
schizo *cut*, 266
sit *food*, 256
soph *wise*, 274
sphere *sphere*, 265
st *stand*, 252
stel *order*, 253, 269
stroph *turn*, 256, 259

T
tauto *same*, 274
tax *arrange*, 252
ten *stretch*, 261
tetra *four*, 272
than *death*, 262
the *place*, 252, 257, 258, 259, 261

therm *warm*, 265
thyra *door*, 266
tom *cut*, 255, 256
top *place*, 264, 265
tracheo *windpipe*, 267
tri *three*, 272
troph *nutrition*, 265

U
ur *urine*, 265, 265

X
xeno *stranger*, 273

Z
zem *boil*, 264
zyg *yoke*, 253

Index of Greek Words

A

aerobic, 136
agnostic, 137, 143, 255, 274
allomorph, 257
amethyst, 51, 71
amnesia, 263, 269
amoeba, 259
Anabaptist, 255
anabolic, 255, 256
anachronism, 255
anadromous, 254
anaerobic, 136
anagram, 255
analogue, 269
analogy, 255
analysis, 254
anaphor, 255, 256, 257, 262, 269
anarchy, 136
anatomy, 255, 256
android, 273
aneurism, 255
Anglophile, 273
anion, 255, 256
anisometric, 136
anisotropic, 136
anode, 255, 257, 260, 261
anoxic, 136
anthology, 261
anthropology, 273
antibiotic, 258
antidote, 258
antipathy, 258
antipode, 258
antithesis, 258
antonym, 258
anuria, 136
apathetic, 137
aphelion, 259, 260, 261
apheresis, 259, 260, 261
aphonic, 137
apnea, 265
apocalypse, 259
apocope, 259
apology, 259
apostrophe, 259
appendectomy, 255
arhythmic, 137
astatic, 137
asteroid, 266, 269
astrolabe, 252
astrology, 266, 269, 273
astronomy, 269
atheist, 137
atrophy, 265
autistic, 273
automatic, 273

B

ballistic, 269
baptism, 255
bigamy, 259, 263, 265, 273
biology, 252, 258, 273, 274
boustrophodon, 256

C

cannabis, 47
cardiac, 47
catabolic, 256
catalyst, 255, 256
catastrophe, 256, 259

cathedral, 295
cation, 255, 256
catoptric, 256
cellophane, 269
central, 265
centre, 264
chlorine, 52
chlorophyll, 50
chondroma, 261
Christopher, 269
chronometer, 252, 255, 256, 273
cosmology, 273
craniotomy, 267
cranium, 267
cystectomy, 267
cystoid, 267

D

decathlon, 272
delta, 266
deltoid, 266
demagogue, 252
democracy, 258, 273
demonic, 273
dermatitis, 261, 265
diabolic, 256
diachronic, 256
diagnosis, 48, 255
dialect, 256, 269
dialogue, 255, 259, 269, 274
dialysis, 254, 255, 256
diameter, 255
diaphanous, 255, 269
diarrhea, 256
diatom, 256
dieresis, 256
dilemma, 48
diopter, 256
diploid, 272
diploma, 272
dipolar, 272
dipterous, 44
diuresis, 256
dynamic, 273
dysentery, 265
dyslectic, 265
dyspeptic, 265
dysphagia, 265
dysphasia, 269, 273

dysphonia, 265
dysphoria, 265
dyspnea, 265
dystopia, 265
dystrophy, 265
dysuria, 265

E

eccentric, 264
eclectic, 264
eclipse, 264
ectoderm, 265
ectomorph, 265
ectopic, 264
ectoplasm, 265
eczema, 264
emblem, 269
embolism, 252
embryectomy, 267
embryological, 267
encyclopedia, 273
endameba, 259
endemic, 273
endergonic, 259
endoderm, 259
endogamy, 259
endomorph, 259
endophagic, 259
endoplasm, 259
energy, 252, 269
ennead, 272
enteritis, 265
eparch, 259
epenthesis, 259
epicanthic, 258
epidemic, 258
epidermis, 258
epiphany, 258, 269
eponym, 258
erg, 49
erogenous, 273
erotic, 273
erythocyte, 51
estrogen, 257
ether, 261
ethnic, 273
ethnocentric, 273
eucalyptus, 259
eurythmics, 255

evangelist, 273
exarch, 264
exegesis, 264
exocentric, 265
exodus, 86, 264
exogamous, 273
exogamy, 265
exosphere, 265
exothermic, 265

G
gene, 269
genesis, 269
genetics, 273
genocide, 269, 273
geology, 273
gigantic, 283
glossary, 273
glossolalia, 273
glottal, 273
gnostic, 137
Gnosticism, 274
gonad, 269
grammar, 255
graphic, 50
gynecology, 49, 273

H
halogen, 264
hedonism, 48, 263
hegemony, 263, 264
helicopter, 252
heliocentric, 263, 273
heliotropic, 259, 260
hemisphere, 263, 265
hemoglobin, 266
hemorrhoid, 266
heptameter, 263
heptathlon, 272
heresy, 256, 259, 260
herpes, 263
hexadecimal, 272
hexagon, 263
hippodrome, 254
histamine, 253
holocaust, 263
homogenous, 263, 274
homology, 274
homonym, 252, 257

hydrology, 273
hypaethral, 261
hypanthial, 261
hypercorrect, 263
hypercorrection, 263
hypergamy, 263
hyperkinetic, 263
hypermnesia, 263
hyperpneic, 263
hypertension, 263
hypertext, 263
hypnoid, 266
hypnosis, 266
hypnotic, 264
hypochondria, 261
hypodermic, 258, 259, 261, 263
hypotenuse, 261
hypothesis, 261

I
ichthyophagous, 259, 265
isometric, 136
isotropic, 136

K
kilobyte, 272
kilometer, 272
kinesiology, 263

L
laryngectomy, 267
larynx, 267
lobectomy, 267
lobed, 267
lobotomy, 267
logic, 252, 255, 256, 264, 265, 274
logorrhea, 256, 266

M
mastectomy, 267
mastitis, 267
mastodon, 48
mastotomy, 267
matriarchy, 136
megabyte, 272
megalomania, 272
megatheatre, 272
metabolic, 257
metaphor, 257

metaphysics, 257
metathesis, 257, 261
meteor, 257
metestrus, 257
method, 257, 260, 261
metonymy, 257
metric, 252, 255, 257
metropolis, 47, 273
misanthrope, 273
misogynist, 273
misoneism, 273
monarch, 259
monarchy, 264, 272
monogamy, 273
monorail, 272
monotone, 272
morpheme, 259
morphology, 265

N
necrophilia, 267, 273
necropolis, 273
necrosis, 273
necrotomy, 267
neuron, 267
neurotomy, 267

O
octopus, 272
ode, 257
odometer, 57, 255, 260, 264
optic, 256
optical, 256
organ, 269
orthodontics, 47
orthodox, 257
oxygen, 136

P
parabolic, 256
paradox, 257
parallel, 257
paralysis, 256
parameter, 257
paraphernalia, 256, 269
paraplegic, 257
parasite, 256
parhelion, 260, 261
parody, 257

paronym, 257
pathetic, 137, 252
patriarch, 47
pediatrician, 273
Pentagon, 272
Pentecost, 272
pepsin, 265
periphery, 269
phantasy, 269
phantom, 258
phenomenon, 255, 269
Philadelphia, 273
philander, 273
philanthropy, 273
philosophy, 273, 274
phlegm, 50
phonic, 137
phonology, 265
phosphorescence, 265, 269
phosphorous, 50
phosphorus, 255
physics, 257
plasma, 259, 265
plethora, 47
pneumectomy, 267
pneumonia, 263, 267
podiatrist, 258
podiatry, 47
polygamy, 272, 273
polyglot, 272
polygon, 48
pretend, 263
prophecy, 269
prophet, 269, 273
prothesis, 257
protohuman, 272
proton, 272
pseudonym, 274
pterodactyl, 47
pyre, 47

Q
quadriplegic, 257

R
regular, 263
rhinoceros, 47
rhythmic, 137

S

sarcasm, 253
schizoid, 266
schizophrenia, 266
semaphore, 269
sophisticate, 274
static, 137
stentorian, 47
sycophant, 269
syllable, 252
syllogism, 252
symbiosis, 273
symbiotic, 252
symbol, 252, 256, 257, 269
symbolic, 255
symmetry, 252
sympathy, 252, 258
symphony, 252
symptom, 252
synagogue, 252
synchronize, 252
syncope, 259
synergy, 252, 259
synonym, 252, 258
synonymy, 257
syntax, 252
synthesis, 259
synthetic, 252
syssarcosis, 253
systaltic, 253, 269
system, 253
systolic, 253, 269
syzygy, 253

T

tautology, 274
taxi, 252
telephone, 252
tenotomy, 261
tetrahedron, 272
textile, 263
thanatophobia, 51
theist, 137
thermometer, 265
thesis, 51, 252, 258
thyroid, 51, 266
topic, 265
topology, 264
trachea, 267
tracheotomy, 267
tricycle, 272
tripod, 47, 48

U

urea, 256
urethra, 265
urine, 136

X

xenophobia, 86, 273
xylophone, 86

Z

zygote, 49, 253

Index of French Words

A
adroit, 285
aid, 287
angle, 289
art, 68
article, 289

B
beef, 278
biscuit, 285
blame, 68, 291

C
cage, 297
cape, 68
captain, 288
chafe, 295
chain, 294
chair, 295
chalice, 295
chalk, 295
challenge, 295, 298
chamber, 289, 295
champagne, 295
champion, 295
chance, 282, 295
chandelier, 295
chandler, 295
change, 297
channel, 295
chant, 295
chanteuse, 295
chape, 295
chapeau, 295
chapel, 295
chaperone, 295
chapter, 68, 289, 294
chariot, 295
chart, 295
chase, 295
chassis, 295
chaste, 295
chasten, 295
chattel, 295
chauffeur, 295
chevron, 280
ch‰teau, 295
circle, 288, 289
close, 298
coin, 287
conceive, 280, 281
conduit, 285
couple, 289

D
danger, 298
debt, 288
deceive, 280, 281
deluge, 297
dignity, 68
doyen, 283
doyenne, 283

E
echelon, 292
envy, 282
epaulet, 292
escalator, 292
escritoire, 292
especial, 292

espionage, 292
espouse, 292
establish, 292
estate, 292
estrange, 298
etamine, 292
etui, 292

F
fable, 289
fever, 281
foil, 287
fruit, 285

G
gendarme, 296
gender, 290, 296
genre, 289, 296
gentle, 296
giant, 283
governor, 281
grange, 298

H
hotel, 291
human, 40
humane, 40
humble, 290

J
joint, 286
joy, 282, 298

L
letter, 68
lieu, 283
lieutenant, 283
loyal, 283

M
main, 285
male, 291
medicine, 68
memoir, 287
merchant, 295
minstrel, 288
minute, 40
minute (noun), 40
mutton, 278

N
naive, 282
noise, 298
number, 290

O
ointment, 286

P
people, 289
perceive, 281
personal, 40
personnel, 40
point, 286
poison, 287
pork, 278
pose, 298
poultry, 278
poverty, 280, 298
prove, 280

R
rage, 297
ray, 282
receive, 280, 281
remember, 290
resemble, 290
rouge, 297
royal, 87, 283
rule, 283

S
sage, 297
saint, 286
second, 40
sergeant, 68
single, 289
solitaire, 287
sovereign, 281
strain, 286
strangle, 289
surcharge, 282
sure, 283
surmount, 282
surname, 282
surpass, 282
surplus, 282
surprise, 282
surreal, 282

surrender, 282
surround, 282
surtax, 282
surveillance, 282
survey, 282
survive, 282

T
table, 289
tender, 290
trait, 285
traitor, 68
tremble, 290
trinity, 68

U
urban, 40
urbane, 40

V
veal, 278
venison, 278
viable, 282

This book's text is set in Warnock, a contemporary typeface grounded in the classic proportions of oldstyle Roman type. The headings, tables, and sidebars are set in Cronos, which derives its appearance from the calligraphically inspired type of the Italian Renaissance. Both typefaces were designed by Robert Slimbach.

This book was printed by Hignell Book Printing on Envirographic 100 paper, which is 100 percent post-consumer recycled. This acid-free paper is processed chlorine free, and is Forest Stewardship Council certified.